The Implementation Game

MIT Studies in American Politics and Public Policy

Jeffrey Pressman and Martha Weinberg, general editors

The Implementation Game:
What Happens After a Bill Becomes a Law

Eugene Bardach

The MIT Press
Cambridge, Massachusetts, and London, England

309.212
B23i
120639
Mar. 1982

Third printing, 1980
Second printing, 1979
First MIT Press paperback edition, 1978
Copyright © 1977 by the Massachusetts Institute of Technology

This book was set in IBM Composer Theme by Technical Composition, and printed and bound by Halliday Lithograph in the United States of America.

Library of Congress Cataloging in Publication Data

Bardach, Eugene.
  The implementation game.

  (MIT studies in American politics and public policy; 1)
  Includes index.
  1. Policy sciences. 2. Mental health laws—California. I. Title. II. Series.
H61.B25   309.2'12   76-52922
ISBN 0-262-02125-0 (hard)
ISBN 0-262-52049-4 (paper)

To Rebecca and Naomi

Contents

Editors' Foreword

Social scientists have increasingly directed their attention toward defining and understanding the field of public policy. Until recently public policy was considered to be a product of the actions of public institutions and as such was treated as the end point in analysis of the governmental process. But in recent years it has become clear that the public-policy-making process is infinitely more complex than much of the literature of social science would imply. Government institutions do not act in isolation from each other, nor is their behavior independent of the substance of the policies with which they deal. Furthermore, arenas of public policy do not remain static; they respond to changes in their political, organizational, and technical environments. As a result, the process of making public policy can best be understood as one that involves a complicated interaction between government institutions, actors, and the particular characteristics of substantive policy areas.

The MIT Press series, *American Politics and Public Policy*, is made up of books that combine concerns for the substance of public policies with insights into the working of American political institutions. The series aims at broadening and enriching the literature on specific institutions and policy areas. But rather than focusing on either institutions or policies in isolation, the series features those studies that help describe and explain the environment in which policies are set. It includes books that examine policies at all stages of their development—formulation, execution, and implementation. In addition, the series features studies of public actors—executives, legislatures, courts, bureaucracies, professionals, and the media—that emphasize the political and organizational constraints under which they operate. Finally, the series includes books that treat public policy-making as a process and help explain how policy unfolds over time.

Eugene Bardach's book, the first in our series, combines a concern for important questions of public management with a sensitivity to organizational and political realities. Drawing on both his own research and a wide range of recent studies of program implementation, Bardach devises an analytical framework for examining implementation issues. In addition to examining the administrative and political obstacles to achievement of programs' specified goals, Bardach speculates about the critical points in the implementation process. In doing so, he provides not only a significant analysis of programs that have already been launched but also a series of signposts that can help guide public managers in formulating strategies for implementation of new programs.

Professor Bardach teaches at the Graduate School of Public Policy of the University of California at Berkeley.

Jeffrey Pressman
Martha Weinberg

Acknowledgments

Friends, colleagues, and students have generously read portions of the manuscript over the past several years and have offered many valuable criticisms. May they continue to be so generous even after observing how little I may seem to have profited by their suggestions. They are Ernest Alexander, Jerome Bayer, Jack Citrin, Peter de Leon, Erwin Hargrove, David Kirp, Frank Levy, Arnold Meltsner, John Mendeloff, William Niskanen, Jeffrey Pressman, Beryl Radin, Allan Sindler, Jean-Claude Theonig, and Richard White, and Aaron Wildavsky. I am especially grateful to those students who patiently endured my earliest, and largely unsuccessful, attempts to conceptualize and analyze the implementation process.

I received extremely able assistance from Margaret Konefsky, Wendy Pfeffer Stern, and Joan Weinberg, who did the bulk of the field work and interviewing. My old friends Frank and Anne Linda Furstenberg, Jr., were very supportive. Nancy Bardach, my wife, edited the manuscript with abundant good will and intelligence. My cousin Celia Witten deserves special thanks for having helped us keep the household running.

The National Institute of Mental Health supported the project financially. Supplementary assistance was received from the Ford Foundation, by way of an institutional grant to the Graduate School of Public Policy. I am very grateful for the assistance.

Carol Kohli, Laurel Kenner, Theresa Clarkson, and Sue Pettigrew typed and retyped the manuscript with great skill and even more good humor.

Finally, I wish to express my thanks to the many individuals and organizations that, in one way or another, facilitated my research. All errors of fact and interpretations are of course my own responsibility.

Introduction: The Implementation Problem

Item. In 1966, the federal Economic Development Administration (EDA) announced that it would spend over $23 million in Oakland, California, and create 3,000 new jobs for unemployed inner-city residents, but three years later only $4 million had been spent and 63 new jobs created. The two main projects were to be built by the Port of Oakland. One was an airport hangar and support facilities to be leased to World Airways, and the second was a marine terminal and access roads. EDA financing was contingent on the agency's approving minority-hiring plans to be submitted in advance by the prospective employer. The plans were a very long time being approved![1]

Item. In 1967, President Lyndon B. Johnson proclaimed a new program to create model communities on surplus federal land in metropolitan areas. The objectives of the program, which became known as "New Towns In-Town," were to demonstrate the federal government's commitment to help the nation's troubled central cities, to build new housing for the poor, and to show how much could be accomplished with an infusion of political zeal matched by the imaginativeness of urban planners and designers. According to Martha Derthick's thoughtful and well-documented study, the program was an absolute failure.[2] After four years, no new towns had been built and practically none had even been started.

Item. Title III of the Elementary and Secondary Education Act (ESEA) of 1965 provided funds for "the development and establishment of exemplary elementary and secondary school educational programs to serve as models for regular school programs."[3] A school district in a large northeastern city determined to use "Cambire School" as a site for such activities, and the program administrator encouraged the teachers to adopt an innovation dear to his heart. He wanted them to act as "catalytic role models," who would stimulate children to become increasingly self-motivated and responsible for their own learning and education. The teacher was to accomplish this with his or her own skills and talents supplemented by a set of stimulating, self-instructional, and "pedagogically sound" materials. An outside evaluation team found that after some three months practically no classroom in the school had gone even a small distance toward doing so. Overall, only 16 percent of classroom time was devoted to this model as opposed to the traditional model.[4]

Item. Title VI of the 1964 Civil Rights Act prohibited the disbursement of federal funds in grants, loans, or contracts to public or private parties practicing racial discrimination. The most controversial area of Title VI enforcement was that of federal aid to education. The controversy became especially heated after Title I of ESEA raised the prospect of enormous subsidies to local school districts.[5] At least in the first year of attempting to apply Title VI to ESEA Title I, the record was gloomy. The number of black children in integrated schools in the states of the old Confederacy did increase from 6 to 16 percent and the U.S. Office of Education achieved "a major psychological breakthrough," but the verdict of one close observer was that, "In important ways . . . the initial effort was a failure." Many of the school districts' desegregation plans, submitted in compliance with Title VI procedures, were merely for show. "Local officials commonly abused the spirit of the freedom-of-choice plan. By the end of 1965 it was obvious that the original guidelines would never be able to eliminate the dual school system."[6]

Item. In mid-1969, the Lanterman-Petris-Short (L-P-S) Act went into effect in California. This law was intended to protect the civil liberties of persons alleged to be mentally ill and to accelerate the trend toward "community" treatment of the mentally ill as an alternative to hospitalization in remote state institutions. One researcher studied a cohort of state hospital patients returned to San Mateo County, noted for having the state's most progressive community mental health service system, to determine how many received what sort of posthospitalization community services. The answer was that surprisingly few received such services. Of 260 patients discharged between June 1972 and December

1973 from Napa State Hospital to San Mateo County, only a minority, 107, received follow-up mental health services. Another 66 received public assistance ("welfare") but no mental health services.[7]

Item. In 1961, the new administration of President John F. Kennedy canceled research and development activity on a nuclear-powered plane. By the time of Kennedy's decision, however, the U.S. government had already spent over $1 billion, over a ten-year period, on what many scientists and engineers had for long believed was a losing proposition.[8]

This brief list illustrates the three principal perils of latter-day public policy: after a policy mandate is agreed to, authorized, and adopted, there is underachievement of stated objectives (creating jobs for the hard-core unemployed, building new towns, getting teachers to act in a different mode), delay, and excessive financial cost. Although this list refers only to programs and policy mandates of the last decade, it is virtually certain that similar afflictions beset such government activities of earlier periods as well. It is only our consciousness of these problems—skeptical, sophisticated, anti-ideological, and probably postliberal—that has changed.

Some Postliberal Heresies

It is hard enough to design public policies and programs that look good on paper. It is harder still to formulate them in words and slogans that resonate pleasingly in the ears of political leaders and the constituencies to which they are responsive. And it is excruciatingly hard to implement them in a way that pleases anyone at all, including the supposed beneficiaries or clients.

Until 1965 or thereabouts, all wise and world-weary liberals, reformers, and progressives understood that it was difficult to win congressional approval of their favored measures. This difficulty eased considerably after the 1964 election, which returned a large, and relatively liberal, Democratic majority to both houses of Congress and which installed a Democratic president, elected by a large majority, committed to completing the work of Franklin Roosevelt and the New Deal. Social programs multiplied and spread: medical care for the poor and the aged, federal monies for elementary and secondary education, community action programs in the cities, more vigorous civil rights measures and enforcement practices, to name a few. Yet there have been many failures. Worse still, divisions have begun to appear in the ranks of the liberals themselves. Most have clung to the old faith, but some heretics have broken away and acquired a following. One heresy has been skepticism about the intellectual foundations of liberal reform. One year after the passage of the Elementary and Secondary Education Act, for instance, a monumental empirical study by a large team of social scientists (themselves mainly liberals) concluded that schooling per se had little or no ascertainable effect on children's achievement levels.[9] The 1968-1969 report of the Social Science Research Council is quoted approvingly by a leading liberal intellectual heretic of this school, Daniel Patrick Moynihan:

Traditional measures are no longer good enough. . . . Many schemes will fail and the most profitable failures will be those which lead to the clarification of understanding of the problems. Many schemes will simply expose additional problems. . . . Both design and evaluation are needed. . . . The overwhelming complexity of the nation's social problems and their immediacy, however, should not blind us to our ignorance of ways to solve them.[10]

A second heresy has asserted that even when we know what ought to be done, and can get political leaders to agree to mandate it, government is probably ill suited to do the job. At the very least, it is likely that the bureaucratic and regulatory strategies government has traditionally relied upon are ineffective if not mischievous. Economists, both liberal and conservative, have taken the lead here and have argued persuasively that manipulating the marketplace may often be a better strategy than trying to abolish it or inventing a substitute for it. Nowhere is this argument more cogently asserted than in the area of pollution control, for example, where it appears that standard setting and the invocation of sanctions for noncompliance are usually quite inferior to effluent charges and other forms of pollution taxes.[11]

A third heresy is built upon the first two. It asserts that even if we know what to do, can get political leaders to agree to it, and can devise an appropriate strategy of governmental intervention (that is, only minimally bureaucratic), we may still not be able to ensure that the strategy will be well executed. In the world of the 1970s, governmental strategies are likely to be as complex as the society upon which, and through which, they work. A single governmental strategy may involve the complex and interrelated activities of several levels of governmental bureaus and agencies, private organizations, professional associations, interest groups, and clientele populations. How can this profusion of activities be controlled and directed? This question is at the heart of what has come to be known, among certain heretics, as the "implementation problem."

The most important approach to solving, or at least ameliorating, this problem is to design policies and programs that in their basic conception are able to withstand buffeting by a constantly shifting set of political and social pressures during the implementation phase. Chapters 3 through 9 analyze the stresses and strains that must be taken into account in trying to design implementable policies.

Design can go only partway, however. One important conclusion that emerges from the present work is that the character and degree of many implementation problems are inherently unpredictable. Even the most robust policy—one that is well designed to survive the implementation process—will tend to go awry. The classic symptoms of underperformance, delay, and escalating costs are bound to appear. As they do, someone or some group must be willing and able to set the policy back on course. The following chapter provides a case history of one such attempt to steer and direct a rather difficult and complex implementation process. It describes how Assemblyman Frank Lanterman and his staff continuously, and with some success, struggled to guide the implementation of the Lanterman-Petris-Short (L-P-S) Act in California. In the final chapter of this book, I shall argue that such activity amounts to "fixing the implementation game," that such "fixing" is much to be desired but rarely to be found, and that, unfortunately, powerful structural features of the American political system inhibit the emergence of "fixers." The vigorous activity by Lanterman and his staff following up L-P-S is almost certainly the exception rather than the rule.

One of the implications of this latter argument is that a much heavier burden must therefore fall on designing policies that avoid the difficulties discussed in Chapters 3 through 9 and make fixing less necessary. Unfortunately, designing implementable policies is scarcely less difficult than finding a fixer to repair damage as it is detected. This is not an optimistic book.

Notes

1

Jeffrey L. Pressman and Aaron Wildavsky, *Implementation* (Berkeley: University of California Press, 1973).

2

Martha Derthick, *New Towns In-Town* (Washington, D.C.: The Urban Institute, 1972).

3

Stephen K. Bailey and Edith K. Mosher, *ESEA: The Office of Education Administers a Law* (Syracuse: Syracuse University Press, 1968), p. 246.

4

Neal Gross, Joseph B. Giancquinta, and Marilyn Bernstein, *Implementing Organizational Innovations: A Sociological Analysis of Planned Educational Change* (New York: Basic Books, 1971), pp. 114-115. The authors used fictitious names to describe the school and the relevant personnel.

5

Beryl A. Radin, "Implementing Change in the Federal Bureaucracy: School Desegregation in HEW," Ph.D. dissertation (Department of City and Regional Planning, University of California, Berkeley, 1973); and Gary Orfield, *The Reconstruction of Southern Education: The Schools and the 1964 Civil Rights Act* (New York: Wiley, 1969).

6

Orfield, *Reconstruction*, pp. 149-150.

7

Larry Sosowsky, "Putting State Mental Hospitals Out of Business—The Community Approach to Treating Mental Illness in San Mateo County," Master's thesis (Graduate School of Public Policy, University of California, Berkeley, 1974), pp. 56-59.

8

W. Henry Lambright, *Shooting Down the Nuclear Plane* (Indianapolis and New York: Inter-University Case Program and Bobbs-Merrill), 1967.

9

James S. Coleman, et al., *Equality of Educational Opportunity* (Washington, D.C.: U.S. Government Printing Office, 1966).

10

Daniel Patrick Moynihan, *Coping* (New York: Random House, 1974), p. 267. The essay cited here is one of twenty-two in this collection and is entitled "Liberalism and Knowledge." It was first published in 1970.

11
Allen V. Kneese and Charles L. Schultze, *Pollution, Prices, and Public Policy* (Washington, D.C.: The Brookings Institution, 1975).

1 | Implementing Mental Health Reform in California

At one level the implementation process surrounding any policy mandate can usefully be construed as the playing out of numerous political and bureaucratic "games." Most of this book is taken up with describing and analyzing these games. This chapter, which describes how Assemblyman Frank Lanterman and his staff continuously attempted to repair the damage done by these games, therefore leapfrogs, in one sense, much of what follows. In another sense, however, it serves to introduce the "implementation process" as a process of strategic interaction among numerous special interests all pursuing their own goals, which might or might not be compatible with the goals of the policy mandate. From the point of view of these various interests, a new policy mandate is merely a blip in their field of programmatic vision and purpose. They have their own agendas, and they are interested in seeing how and whether the new policy mandate could, or might have to be, fit in. Chapters 3 through 9 look at the world from the perspective of the plurality of these interests. In this chapter, as in the final one, we adopt the point of view of those who see these interests, in the aggregate, as the objects of their own intervention and manipulation. From this latter point of view, which is that of a believer in the goals of the original policy mandate, the implementation process is terribly frustrating and tedious.[1] It also tends to make for aggressive interventionists a number of political enemies.

The L-P-S Act

The Lanterman-Petris-Short (L-P-S) Act passed in 1967. This law was regarded as the outstanding accomplishment of the California legislature in its 1967 session; and in its ambitiously reformist objectives it has been hailed as a model for all other states to look to. The act, as we have already indicated, pushed mental health reform in two directions. Its principal thrust was to restore the civil liberties of persons alleged to be mentally ill. This has been the objective most nearly achieved. The other reform goal was to accelerate the trend already in motion in California, as it was in many other states as well, to substitute community-based care and treatment of the mentally ill for care and treatment in state mental institutions. Opinions differ on whether or not L-P-S has been very effective in this regard, though my own opinion is that it has considerably improved the service-delivery system over what it was prior to L-P-S. A brief, and necessarily sketchy, personal evaluation of L-P-S is offered in Appendixes A and B.

Inasmuch as I was a close observer of the political process that led up to the passage of the L-P-S Act in 1967, I chose the subsequent history of this reform legislation as a primary source of data for a study of the implementation process.[2] In addition, L-P-S has many of the features that I believe are relevant to the study of the implementation process in many policy areas besides mental health or social services. It has elements of intergovernmental relations, interagency relations, relations between government and private contractors, professional participation as providers and overseers, interprofessional rivalries, regulatory as well as service-delivery activities, intrabureaucratic politicking, important interface problems with other policy areas, and continuing legislative oversight and intervention.

Assemblyman Lanterman Oversees L-P-S

The L-P-S Act was in Lanterman's eyes and in the eyes of many others the crowning glory of his long and distinguished career as a state legislator. He had labored mightily to give birth to the legislation (which he liked to call "the Magna Carta of the mentally ill"), and he was no less zealous in trying to make it work as he had intended it to work. He was nearly seventy years old when the act took effect. A lifelong bachelor, L-P-S would be his principal claim to immortality.

Lanterman had abundant resources that enabled him to function effectively as an overseer of and intervener in the implementation process.

As a legislator, he of course had the power to introduce bills. In the seven years after L-P-S first was signed into law, he introduced nearly forty separate bills following up on the original legislation. Of these, six were major legislative packages intended to clarify, correct, expand, or overhaul the original legislation. The 1967 legislation had passed without adequate technical assistance from the Short-Doyle Conference of Local Mental Health Directors,[3] from the Department of Mental Hygiene (DMH), or from the County Supervisors Association, largely because these interests had either actively or passively opposed the legislation. When they realized that something like L-P-S would actually be imposed on them, they rallied to cooperate in designing something they could live with and even support. Thus, Lanterman's first major legislative follow-up package was passed in 1968 and established the foundations of the L-P-S Act. In 1971, he sponsored legislation requiring more extensive reliance by the county Short-Doyle agencies on services provided in the private sector and incorporated into the Short-Doyle program by contract. In that year he also sponsored AB 2649, which marked a comprehensive reconsideration of the L-P-S Act and its implementation. AB 2649 required a written aftercare plan for each patient being released from a state hospital. It also required that each county Short-Doyle plan contain detailed information about the size of certain target populations (the "general" mentally disordered, children and adolescents, alcoholics, drug abusers, and mentally retarded) and required that each target population be further categorized by age groups.[4] It stipulated that the DMH must allocate funds for "new and expanded" programs according to the following priorities: crisis intervention, outpatient and day care, partial hospitalization, residential care, and inpatient. (These priorities replaced those of the 1968 legislation, which gave highest priority to the screening of involuntary patients and to the screening of voluntary patients admitted to state hospitals. The 1968 legislation was silent on the priority to be accorded to other target populations or to types of services.) The bill sought to discourage the use of inpatient services, including state hospital utilization, not only by ranking it lowest on the priorities list but also by giving the counties financial incentives: "It is ... the intent of the Legislature that to the extent feasible, counties that decrease their expenditures for inpatient treatment in any year below the costs of inpatient treatment in the previous year shall receive the amount of such decrease for new and expanded services requested in the county plan." A special justification "based upon cost-effective criteria" (sic) was required to accompany county requests for funds for inpatient service for those counties above the statewide average in inpatient utilization. Finally, the bill ordered the DMH to undertake cost-effectiveness studies "of the different types of programs and services being provided for each of the target groups." Furthermore, beginning with fiscal 1975, the DMH was to "use the information developed in the evaluation studies for the allocation of funds for target group programs as presented in the county Short-Doyle plans."

If the legislative thrust of the 1971 session was meant to prod DMH and Short-Doyle administrators, the principal mental health bills of 1972 were directed at local government officials. One bill prohibited localities from establishing exclusionary fire and panic safety regulations with respect to board-and-care homes serving the mentally ill and reserved such powers to the state fire marshal. Another bill declared that state-approved residential-care facilities serving six or fewer mentally ill persons were to be considered residential-use properties and were therefore not to be prohibited from single-family residential zones.

In 1973, it was the turn of the board-and-care operators to come under scrutiny. A bill requiring all board-and-care homes to be licensed had passed the legislature in 1971. It had not been drafted or amended by Lanterman or his staff and it did not come close to remedying what they regarded as the largest defects of the licensing system. In 1973, Lanterman's AB 2262 designed such a comprehensive system. It tried to distinguish its own "quality of care and services" approach from "the traditional bricks and mortar approach" to facilities licensing. Its basic feature was a reimbursement structure linked to the level and type of care or service provided. It projected an elaborate certificating system whereby the Department of Health would define various classes of care and service, map facilities into their appropriate class, and set rates of reimbursement appropriate to each class. It also called for evaluations of all such facilities by the department and publication of the results of the evaluation. Guaranteed loans for remodeling and construction might be made available to nonprofit facilities. A twenty-one-person committee was to be set up to advise the department director regarding policies and regulations. All licensing functions pertaining to community-care facilities were to be removed from the twenty different bureaus and agencies that had them and were to be amalgamated into "a single comprehensive licensing authority" under the Department of Health.[5]

Lanterman's Political Resources

Any legislator may introduce bills, but not all of them have the resources to get them passed and signed by the governor. Lanterman had such resources. He was the senior Republican member of the powerful Ways and Means Committee. He had a reputation within the legislature for expertise, intelligence, diligence, shrewdness, and, above all, integrity. He was liked and respected by members of both political parties. He had generally been a strong supporter of Governor Ronald Reagan and could count on considerable reciprocity from that quarter. Even members of the State Senate had to defer to Lanterman, for he had the power, and if necessary the will, to throttle their bills in the lower house. It was well understood in Sacramento that mental health policy was Lanterman's territory and that no significant changes in that area could be made without his consent or, alternatively, without having him exact a price.

Lanterman also had access to significant analytical resources. During the entire period under review here Lanterman controlled either the majority or the minority staff of the Ways and Means Committee, depending upon whether the Republicans or the Democrats controlled the lower house and its committees. There was always the equivalent of at least one, and usually two, full-time professional staff assistants assigned by him to cover mental health policy exclusively. His own staff worked closely with the staff expert on the committee's Democratic side who scrutinized this policy area. In addition to the Ways and Means staff, Lanterman drew upon the resources of Arthur Bolton, who had done the principal staff work designing the L-P-S Act and had been instrumental in shepherding it through the legislature. From 1967 to 1969, Bolton was director of the Assembly Office of Research. In 1969, he left the legislature to establish his own consulting firm in Sacramento, but this firm continued to work closely with Lanterman under contract to the Assembly. Apart from Bolton, Valerie Bradley, who left the Office of Research for Bolton's firm, worked full-time on California mental health policy during the period 1967-1970. It was she who did most of the staff work on the 1968 legislative package. All these staff people in turn drew upon analytical resources in academia, in the Department of Mental Hygiene, in the State Department of Finance, in the Office of the Legislative Analyst, and in the California Citizens Advisory Council for Mental Health.

Lanterman was also able to count on considerable political support from mental health professionals, from the California Association for Mental Health, and from other interested activists outside Sacramento. By the time L-P-S went into effect, even those who had initially opposed it, like the DMH, had embraced it. Their support was diffuse and nonspecific. Any single such interest might break away on any single issue, but their temporary opposition would in no way weaken the solid mass of support that remained. One of the most important resources contributed by these relative outsiders was analytical in nature. Their large numbers, their dispersion across the state, and their penetration of literally hundreds of different organizations involved either in service delivery or in general mental health promotional activity generated invaluable information about the numerous implementation activities going on in the obsure crevices of the state hospitals and the county programs. Much of this information flowed spontaneously to Lanterman without specific solicitation by him or his staff. When particular pieces of information were required, there was ready access to trusted sources who would be in a position to provide it.

Lanterman held a safe Republican seat. His constituency in the Pasadena area had sent him to the Assembly in 1953 and had continued to do so regularly ever since. At age seventy he had remarkable powers of personal as well as political endurance. He traveled around the state extensively making speeches about L-P-S. Every weekend he flew back home to Pasadena, and he thought nothing of flying from Sacramento to Los Angeles and back in one afternoon just to confer with an editorialist of the *Los Angeles Times* about state mental health policy. His principal concession to his advancing age was his disinclination to work past midnight except in times of real emergency.

His oratorical style was grandiloquent to a point just short of bombast, and his audiences loved it. He had great need of his oratorical prowess throughout most of 1968, when it was necessary to explain to a great many surprised, bewildered, and sometimes antagonistic groups or individuals the nature of the revolution taking place in mental health policy. L-P-S passed in 1967 by outweighing and outmaneuvering the opposition. In 1968, however, Lanterman wanted to conciliate his opponents and gain their cooperation in designing a workable new system. The revolution had to co-opt them or it was bound to fail. Lanterman (and his staff associates) stumped the length and breadth of the state, clarifying, exhorting, and also listening. An illustration of such activity is provided by Lanterman's encounter with the Superior Court judge in San Joaquin County, William Dozier, and the county's Board of Supervisors. On February 28, Lanterman and a large entourage traveled to Stockton to meet head to head with Dozier and the county supervisors, who were bristling with rage at what they believed was going on. Accompanying Lanterman were Bolton, Bradley, two other legislative staffers (from Ways and Means and from the Assembly Public Health Committee), the DMH chief of the Bureau of Legal Services, and Dorothy Miller, a sociologist whose consulting firm had done much of the research that led to passage of the legislation. He was also accompanied by Senator Alan Short and Assemblyman Robert Monagan, who represented all or a large part of the county.

He was acting in response to Dozier's emotional criticism of SB 677 (the 1967 version of L-P-S) to the county supervisors three months earlier, which one supervisor had forwarded to Lanterman. Lanterman responded to Dozier's attack point by point. In his speech Lanterman explained the intentions behind SB 677, suggested the vast amount of analysis that had gone into its preparation, and asserted that it had been endorsed by the DMH and by organized psychiatry and psychology—all propositions that Dozier had evidently denied or been unaware of.[6] He also used one of the techniques he had developed during the legislative fight over SB 677 the past summer, namely, pointing out the derelictions of the particular agency, profession, or county whose representatives he was addressing:

As evidence to support his claim that we are not indiscriminately shunting people off to state hospitals the Judge mentions the excellent patient screening record here in San Joaquin County. The Department of Mental Hygiene's figures on hospital admission show that 75 percent of those mentally disordered citizens admitted to state hospitals last year from San Joaquin were placed there *involuntarily* rather than voluntarily. This is almost twice the state's average commitment rate. This situation is further compounded by the fact that *your admission rate to state hospitals is three times greater than the state average.*[7]

Judge Dozier had also alleged that SB 677 would cost San Joaquin County a loss of additional money. So it would, agreed Lanterman. The county, he said, had the highest per capita admission rate to state hospitals for the mentally ill of the twenty-five most populous counties in the state. In effect, it was receiving a subsidy of $18.50 per capita from the state for mental health spending, while the comparable statewide figure was $6.50. "There appears to be something drastically wrong, and I would be surprised if it doesn't have something to do with the fact that a state hospital is located in your midst with care available at little or no cost to local taxpayers."[8]

The Legislator as Administrator

Once L-P-S was in effect, Lanterman and his staff intervened actively and continually in what would normally be considered administrative matters. They intervened at the level of the individual counties, in the Conference of Local Mental Health Directors, in the Department of Mental Hygiene, in the Department of Social Welfare, and in the Human Relations Agency (which embraced both Mental Hygiene and Social Welfare). Much of this activity by Lanterman and his staff was initiated by complaints received from parties attempting to enlist their support for battles they were in danger of losing in their own local arenas. In no way is this sort of activity unusual for a legislator, except in this case perhaps by virtue of its scope and intensity. More unusual was the sort of interventionist activity that Lanterman and his staff themselves initiated. It is hard to describe its scope except to say that it was extensive, or its frequency except to say that it was regular, recurrent, and in some sense continual. I shall try to suggest the diversity of this activity by recording several examples, starting with the self-initiated interventions.

We have already mentioned the numerous follow-up bills Lanterman carried. A number of these, like AB 2648 (requiring maximum use of private facilities) and AB 2649 (requiring, among other things, the development and application of cost-effectiveness techniques), dealt with matters normally left to administrators. By 1971, however, when these bills were introduced, Lanterman and his staff had already begun to feel that such matters could not be left to Mental Hygiene, since the department was apparently following a relatively laissez-faire policy with respect to the direction of county programming. Lanterman also assigned staff to a task force created in mid-1972 to develop a formula for allocating Short-Doyle funds. This staff contribution was particularly noteworthy, since the bulk of the task force came from the executive branch.[9]

A continuing point of disagreement among many mental health professionals—though probably not a majority—and Lanterman was the limitation imposed by the L-P-S Act on their right to treat involuntary patients who "needed help" but refused to seek or accept it. In his last year as DMH director, Dr. James V. Lowry, who was somewhat sympathetic to this point of view, attempted to enlarge the definition of "dangerous" persons, who were subject to time-limited involuntary treatment (see Appendix A), to include many of these needy but unwilling persons. Lowry's strategy was to write administrative regulations broadening the definition. Lanterman defeated it by telling Lowry that he would not stand for the change.

Of course, there were frequent visits, telephone calls, and conferences between Lanterman or his staff and administrative officials. Telephone calls were daily events. Conferences were reserved for the discussion of major issues, like how the department intended to allocate its Short-Doyle budget among the counties or how the department might reorganize itself. The department routinely sent draft copies of proposed regulations to Lanterman's office. And sometimes, when they were tardy or neglectful in doing so, Lanterman would fire off an admonishing letter to the director like this:

I have indicated to you my concern that local mental health programs have too often been inclined to add staff and create facilities at the expense of existing community resources to be used first. At the Department's request, I carried AB 2648.

Now that AB 2648 has been passed and signed by the Governor, please indicate your plan to implement Section 5600.1 which clearly spells out that existing private mental health resources or facilities should be used. I feel it is imperative that the Department develop forthright regulations which will ensure that the dollars flowing out of the state hospital system are not simply pumped into increased staff and beds at the county level. What do you propose to do with those local programs which are recalcitrant to instructions to contract with existing services and facilities?[10]

To the secretary of the Human Relations Agency he wrote a letter urging speed in implementing a plan to consolidate licensing functions, as required by his bill AB 2406 in the 1970 session:

It appears that the reorganization of existing agencies in a new Department of Health will now be postponed until July 1, 1973. I believe that it is unwise to delay consolidation of standard setting, rate setting, and licensing functions until that time:

As I have indicated to you before, we are faced with a most crucial phase in the implementation of the Lanterman-Petris-Short and Mental Retardation Services Acts [also Lanterman's progeny—au.]. I strongly urge you to direct your attention to this matter of consolidation. I would like to know what steps the Agency now proposes to take to effect consolidation of standard setting, licensing, and rate setting.[11]

In the 1970 session a law was enacted (AB 1640) stipulating that the aftercare services of the Community Services Division (CSD) of the State Department of Social Welfare (SDSW) would henceforth be provided in a county only if the county Short-Doyle program contracted for these services and reimbursed the SDSW for 10 percent of the state's financial share (which was only 25 percent of the total, since the federal government paid the rest). Lanterman kept close tabs on the developments that followed. On the one hand, Lanterman wished the counties to develop their aftercare service functions as best they could, whether or not these would be provided by the CSD. On the other hand, Lanterman did not want the CSD to collapse, should many counties desire not to contract with the agency. At any rate, he did not want the collapse to occur all at once. On October 8, 1971, he took the unusual step of sending a stiff letter of warning and reproach to each of the county Short-Doyle directors (and to many other officials and prominent mental health activists as well):

It has come to my attention that some county Short-Doyle programs may decide to provide aftercare services directly during this fiscal year, rather than contracting with the Community Services Division of the State Department of Social Welfare. . . . To the extent that such services have been adequately provided by C.S.D., it was expected that local programs would continue to utilize C.S.D. . . . In no case should such a change be made in the middle of a fiscal year.

I have requested counties that may be contemplating a midyear changeover to delay that decision until July 1, 1972, so that an orderly transition can be accomplished in accordance with the State Budget timetable and in a manner which allows the Community Services Division sufficient planning time to reflect the revised staffing needs.

There is one other issue related to the utilization of C.S.D. workers which I would also like to bring to your attention. We are receiving considerable evidence that Short-Doyle programs have tended to concentrate on developing inpatient and other medical services but have neglected the area of social services.

The need for effective social services—as alternatives to hospitalizations—and following hospital care is especially important since the L-P-S Act tends to reduce the amount of time patients spend inside the hospital.

Not only was Lanterman telling the Short-Doyle directors how to administer their programs, he was also telling them—all physicians, and many of them psychiatrists—how to run their treatment and service programs.

The CSD had always been a source of problems. For most of its history it had been known as the Bureau of Social Work and was located in the DMH. There it was an alien element, watched suspiciously by the dominant professional group in the department, namely, the psychiatrists. In 1966, it was saved from dissolution by a timely transfer to the State Department of Social Welfare. The move turned out to be a leap from frying pan to fire, however; for in 1971, Governor Reagan's new director of the SDSW began a systematic purge of social worker personnel from the top echelons of the department. The SDSW was taken over by efficiency experts and "management types" who were charged, above all, with cutting the welfare rolls. This environment was even more inhospitable to the CSD than had been the DMH.

During the summer of 1971, the CSD was coming under increasing pressure. Alone within the SDSW, it had so far survived the purge. But its external relations with the mental health system, hitherto its lifeline to a secure foundation, were disintegrating. AB 1640 accelerated its dissolution as a viable state agency, a process that was begun by the decentralization of state hospital release procedures to the county Short-Doyle programs, which often chose to ignore or bypass CSD social workers. More than usually aware of the CSD and its activities after AB 1640, Lanterman could not help but learn that it simply was not performing very well in certain locales and in certain ways. In response to his October 8, 1971, letter to the several Short-Doyle directors, Lanterman received a revealing reply from one of them on October 27:

I am at a loss to understand how you have received the impression that we are contemplating such a mid-year changeover. We have actively been attempting to negotiate a contract with CSD for almost one year! Negotiations have been filled with one frustration after another and finally ended with———County submitting a draft contract (dated August 11, 1971). Our contract was in absolute conformance with Assembly Bill 1640 (1970) *and* its legislative intent. Yet, we have heard no word as to its acceptance. Added to this, on September 29, I received a letter from the Department of Social Welfare that contract negotiations had been temporarily discontinued! . . .

On the other hand, what *we* have received has been less than cooperation. This Department has been unable to obtain placement and after-care services from CSD at the local level. Currently, we have 85 patients in Stockton State Hospital awaiting community placement, and 26 of these could be placed immediately. Nothing seems to happen, even though many of these patients' referrals for placement date back to February.

Lanterman assigned one of his staff to investigate the CSD and its relations with the SDSW and with other agencies. The staff member reported that the top-level administrators in the SDSW had been suspicious of the CSD leadership for some time and had had them 'paper-trailed' to make certain all decisions they were involved in were auditable.

He also said that CSD leaders "often independently contacted legislators to push their own programs and to embarrass the appointees." The staff report described more instances of intradepartment tension and analyzed some of the causes. It noted the

dissatisfaction with Community Services' role in making L-P-S more effective. The belief is that the social workers were more interested in infighting and protecting their jobs as "what I was educated for" than in rethinking the role of a statewide force of field workers. What we needed two or more years ago were community organization and education specialists and people experienced in local government who would have been better equipped to speed and to smooth the transition to local programs. We should have had more para-professionals to handle the caretaker aspects of community placements. This would have left the social worker to specialize in social work . . .

The social worker/administrators are being blamed for not having looked at Community Services in program terms, for not having advanced this concept, and for not implementing it. The department director is taking the first step in this direction of restructuring by putting experienced administrators in charge of administration and by borrowing psychiatric technicians from Mental Hygiene to work in the field . . .

As you saw yesterday, this kind of move will be strongly resisted by the social workers . . .

My only question is "who is going to take care of the client while you decide who is going to do what?"

Shortly after the staff member's report, the CSD chief was replaced, presumably with Lanterman's acquiescence.

Lanterman and his staff did not hesitate to intervene in the politics of cities and counties either, if they thought a good purpose would be served. Their most ambitious undertaking was a study, which took nearly a year to complete, of Short-Doyle programming and operations in Los Angeles County. Los Angeles consumed approximately 30 percent of the state's mental health budget, $90 million in fiscal 1973. The county's mental health program had been a source of considerable dissatisfaction for many years. The director was regarded as an "empire builder" by mental health activists within the county, always preferring to expand operations in the public sector rather than contract with private providers, of which there were many in Los Angeles County eager to obtain Short-Doyle financing for their operations. DMH analysts and budget experts were despairing of being able to ascertain how Short-Doyle monies were being used in the county, much less being able to apply some controls to the expenditures. The program was highly centralized; attempts at reorganization of administration had been erratic and plagued by frustration and confusion. The impulse behind AB 2648 came, in large measure, from the growing displeasure with Los Angeles County. One Los Angeles County supervisor wrote to Lanterman congratulating him on the passage of the bill and adding:

Judge Allen Miller has requested that Dr. Brickman [the Short-Doyle director—au.] immediately commence an investigation and study of comparative quality and cost of private mental health resources and facilities versus County operated mental health resources and facilities. At long last we may stop the County's empire building in the mental health field.

A memo from a member of Lanterman's staff reporting on a meeting between Los Angeles County officials and DMH officials in April 1972, just as the Lanterman staff study was getting under way, stated:

Dr. Brickman indicated both in the meeting and to the L.A. *Times* that if L.A. County's $12 million expenditure for state hospitals were shifted to community services, the cost would rise to $21 million. Drs. Stubblebine and Mayer [the director and deputy director of the DMH, respectively—au.] thought Brickman would have come up with an even higher figure. The problem, as they see it, is that L.A. County still thinks in terms of "beds" and "facilities."

The Lanterman staff study was completed in December 1972 and proposed thirty separate recommendations like the following: "Eliminate requirement that Regional Offices be headed by a psychiatrist. ... Critically review workload of Psychiatric Emergency Teams (PET) in relation to the levels of staffing budgeted for this function. ... Establish written policies regarding moonlighting and conflict of interest. ... Enforce statutory requirement that written aftercare plans are developed for all patients leaving state hospitals, county hospitals and contract facilities. ..." Instead of dealing directly with Brickman, Lanterman's office worked mainly through Brickman's administrative superior, L. A. Witherill, who kept the office informed of steps being taken to implement the recommendations. More important, Lanterman's office set up Los Angeles County Supervisor Peter Schabarum to oversee the process. Schabarum had been a friend of Lanterman's when he was an assemblyman. In effect, Lanterman could thereby delegate the burden of overseeing implementation activities locally to a trusted ally, and Schabarum could make use of free staff resources (Lanterman's) to increase his stature as an expert in an important area of county policy and politics.[12]

The foregoing examples of self-initiated interventions in administrative issues by Lanterman's office can only begin to indicate the nature, extensiveness, and frequency of such activities. Turning now to interventions initiated by others, we shall again have to argue by anecdote and example. In general, it may be said that these interventions entailed acting as an "honest broker" or "ombudsman."

A recurrent source of problems was dissatisfaction on the part of one or another county with the DMH's Short-Doyle allocation to that particular county. In Chapter 8 we shall describe at some length Lanterman's mediating role between San Joaquin County and the department, in the fall of 1970, over the use in local programs of funds allegedly saved by reducing the county's state hospital expenditures. San Joaquin County was not unique. Because of last-minute cuts by the legislature in the Short-Doyle budget for fiscal 1971, several counties faced the same problem as San Joaquin. So much protest was heard in Lanterman's office from aggrieved county supervisors, Short-Doyle directors, and state legislators responding to constituent pressures that Lanterman arranged for the Ways and Means Subcommittee on Mental Health Services, of which he was chairman, to hold hearings on the problem. Following the hearings, he insisted that he be kept informed by the DMH of its allocation methods and the results on a routine basis. Lanterman's continued interest in the allocation process was in part responsible for the eventual development of an elaborate allocation formula intended to distribute the funds according to a rather sophisticated measurement of county "needs" (see Chapter 5).

Private provider complaints against a county's contracting policy—or lack of it—also filtered up to Lanterman. Many such complaints came, of course, from Los Angeles. In addition to carrying AB 2648, and prodding the DMH to stand firm in enforcing its provisions, Lanterman sometimes intervened more pointedly. On January 5, 1972, the chairman of the board of the Long Beach Neuropsychiatric Institute wrote Lanterman complaining that Los Angeles County had just approved a $17.7 million Psychiatric and Clinical Science Building while his institute had a 237-bed psychiatric facility "with all treatment modalities available" that was not being utilized. "Please advise," he wrote, "what can be done to curtail the unnecessary spending of the taxpayer's money on this proposed new Los Angeles County Building." Lanterman responded on January 17 that he had discussed the issue with two top county administrators and that they were calling Dr. Brickman in "for conferences concerning your problem." He added, "I am in agreement that we must take steps to effectuate a closer liaison with private enterprise wherever it is possible to do so. It costs too much for empires to be built at the county level when other resources are available."

Board-and-care operators were another source of complaints. The complaints were directed at the licensing agents, the licensing laws, the reimbursement schedule, placement workers, city officials, health inspectors, and so on. It was often not possible for Lanterman to do more than write back a letter of sympathy including a disclaimer of responsibility for the aggravating condition and of any power to correct it. When he felt that something could be done, however, someone in his office took steps to do it, like phoning the DMH and requesting an investigation. Lanterman's office took a similar approach to complaints by patients and their families about inadequate service or poor facilities. An indication of what might happen when Lanterman did choose to act is provided by an intraoffice memorandum:

Lee Helsel [of the DMH] called this morning to report that he sent a medical review team into the———Nursing Home and they reported that the facility is "clean."

Tom Hibbard of Pete Schabarum's office called this afternoon to indicate that in response to Frank's [Lanterman's] call to him regarding the———Nursing Home that he had looked into the matter and will be making some written recommendations to Pete and will send us a copy of those recommendations. He just wanted to let us know he was doing something in order to avoid another phone call from Frank.

Many of these other-initiated interventions resemble in form the constituent service activities familiar to us from numerous studies of legislative behavior. A study of congressmen and their staffs by Saloma permits the inference that congressmen spend roughly one-third of their working time on constituency service, and that over 40 percent of staff time is devoted to this function. Saloma regards his findings as a challenge to the prevalent myth that congressmen spent *most* of their time "running errands" for constituents.[13] Unfortunately, no study has come to my attention that suggests the amount of time and energy devoted by legislators to such service activities on behalf of a functional policy area. As we noted above, Lanterman's activities in this regard were probably quite unusual, and the absence of studies of the phenomenon surely reinforces this inference.

Lanterman as the Great Protector

Somewhat more prevalent, we might suspect, are activities undertaken in general defense of some policy or program by its legislative sponsors whenever it happens to come under attack. One thinks in this connection of Congressman Chet Holifield's spirited defense of atomic energy policy or Senator Edmund Muskie's ongoing defense of his various pieces of environmental protection legislation. Lanterman functioned as the Great Protector of the L-P-S system when it was attacked by forces hostile to it in principle, even while he functioned as the Great Overseer and Critic of its workings in practice.

The harshest critic of L-P-S was the California State Employees' Association (CSEA), many of whose members stood to lose their jobs in the state hospitals as the institutionalized population decreased in size. (Staffing standards were tied to resident population levels.) Probably the most foolish omission in the original legislative design of L-P-S was its failure to cushion the blow that would surely be dealt to the hospital employees. Not until the 1972 legislative session did Lanterman carry a bill to facilitate the transfer of state hospital employees to local mental health programs. By then the gesture was too little and too late. In January 1972, the CSEA published its blistering attack on L-P-S, "Where Have All the Patients Gone?," and in April it filed suit to enjoin the state from closing any state hospitals. Lanterman's reaction to the CSEA document was swift and aggressive. He issued a press release denouncing the CSEA's "series of exaggerated and inflammatory charges," made "through the use of loaded and accusatory statements, unverifiable quotes, gratuitous facts, and isolated incidents. . . ." He concluded:

The real tragedy of the CSEA report is that it does a great disservice to the mentally ill in California by creating fear and distrust in the minds of the public. This is just the latest of a series of obstructionist efforts to protect the continuity of employment for association members regardless of the needs of patients. In many ways, it is a repeat performance of CSEA's self-serving but unsuccessful effort to block the establishment of regional centers for the mentally retarded in 1969 by court action.

Defending the L-P-S system was made more difficult by Governor Reagan's independent decision to pursue a policy of closing down as many of the state hospitals as he could as quickly as possible. This policy was not the same as that embodied in L-P-S, namely, to reduce hospital utilization as much as possible, but it dovetailed with it up to a point. At any rate, it appeared in the public eye to be an integral part of L-P-S. Behind the scenes, Lanterman attempted to persuade the Republican administration to ease up on the hospital closure campaign. He also tried to ward off attacks on L-P-S from his legislative colleagues responding to CSEA pressure. In this latter effort, at any rate, he was reasonably successful. In February 1973, the State Senate adopted a resolution establishing a Select Committee "On Proposed Phaseout of State Hospital Services," to be chaired by Alfred Alquist, who represented a district in which a hospital had been partially shut down. Through quiet persuasion Lanterman and his staff convinced the Alquist committee to back away from its presumed initial intention of lashing out in all directions. Indeed, the Alquist committee's final report, published in March 1974, began by summarizing the L-P-S Act and hailing it as a "landmark of progress" that had "earned wide acclaim and . . . [had] been emulated in other states."[14]

During the course of the Alquist committee's investigations, CSEA kept up a steady drumfire against Lanterman and L-P-S. Lanterman again and again tried to return the fire. One day in mid-August 1973, he took the Assembly floor to denounce CSEA's "snow job campaign" to discredit himself and L-P-S. "I'm being cut to hamburger. . . . I have taken all the beating I am going to take. . . . They have put out a series of accusations, including improper accusations about the release of criminals and dangerous persons. . . . They are trying to creat an atmosphere of fear in the mind of the public that dangerous mentally-ill people are being released on the streets by the Lanterman-Petris-Short Act." He was defended on the floor by his fellow assemblyman John Burton of San Francisco, a liberal Democrat clearly recognizable as the ideological polar opposite of Lanterman on many issues. Burton said, "I find myself defending myself because I won't attack him. All the work this man did to bring this to public attention when I was just a freshman—it's just not fair."[15]

The press was often a willing, if sometimes an unwitting, ally of the CSEA. Atrocity stories make good copy. Prior to L-P-S, the newspapers culled choice atrocities from the state hospitals. After L-P-S, they found their atrocities in the board-and-care homes. The *Long Beach In-*

dependent Press-Telegram, for instance, ran a series of four articles that appeared under headlines like "Mental Health Patients Thrust into Society," "Nursing Homes: Hell for Mental Patients," "Policing the Mentally Ill—Crisis Widens."[16] Lanterman's office went to some lengths to stimulate articles showing the assets of L-P-S as well as the liabilities, and with a fair degree of success. At no time were Lanterman and his staff attempting to deny the existence of atrocities or to discourage critical publicity that would have a constructive impact. They were confident that if only reporters would take a fair and responsible look at the effects of L-P-S, their appraisal would be, on balance, quite favorable.

Their public relations problems were compounded significantly by the seemingly large number of violent crimes linked to persons who had had some record of treatment for mental illness or who, from superficial indications, were psychopathic—regardless of whether or not these latter offenders had been identified at any time by anyone who might have been in a position to detain them as potentially dangerous. The best defense that Lanterman, and other supporters of L-P-S, could come up with was the proposition that "the incidence of violence in released mentally ill patients is less than the general population," that psychiatric experts were simply unable to predict violence with any tolerable degree of reliability, and that therefore "there can be no justification for preventive detention of the mentally ill."[17] Lanterman's AB 4200, providing for "mandatory outpatient treatment" under certain circumstances, introduced in the 1974 session of the legislature, was in large part a reluctant acknowledgment that to save L-P-S as a whole, certain adjustments would have to be made in its parts. (It is probably also true that he and his staff eventually came to believe that these adjustments were defensible on their merits in any case.)[18]

We may also note that Lanterman was the principal defender of augmented budgets for mental health services in general, and for Short-Doyle in particular, in the face of Governor Reagan's "cut, squeeze, and trim" philosophy of public finance. Short-Doyle expenditures soared

dramatically after L-P-S went into effect, even though some of the increases were canceled out by inflationary trends (See Appendix A).
When the legislative conference committee reviewing the budget for fiscal 1971 made a last-minute cut of $3.5 million from the Short-Doyle
budget, Lanterman later saw to it that this money was, in effect, re-
stored in the budget for the 1972 fiscal year. In 1972, the governor
proposed an augmentation of $19.5 million over the prior year's Short-
Doyle budget, at the same time as he proposed a cut of $14.7 million
in state hospital funding. This proposal sparked a hot controversy.
Local program advocates did not object to the cut in state hospital
funds, but they did demand that the savings on the hospital side be
added to the Short-Doyle budget. At the same time, they contended
that the Short-Doyle augmentation was more apparent than real. The
legislative analyst's review of the figures concluded that "virtually all of
this increase represents funds which will support existing programs or
which were formerly budgeted in other agencies. No new funds for the
care and treatment of additional patients resulting from hospital closure
have been included in local program expenditures." In addition, the
local programs had in a sense "earned" the savings on the hospital side,
having responded to the state's existing policy of rebating to the counties $15 per hospital patient-day which was forecasted on the basis of
past trends but was not used. The analyst's report was critical:

It is apparently the intention of the Department of Mental Hygiene to
realize the full $14,673,324 in reduced hospital operations as a General
Fund program saving. If this is done, the proposed state hospital expenditures will not contain sufficient funds to continue the $15 per day
rebate program and thus the incentive for local programs to continue to
underutilize state hospitals will be eliminated. Furthermore, there will
be no incentive to expand local programs beyond existing levels if additional funding is not provided.[19]

A memo to Lanterman by one of his staff supported the analyst's cri-
tique: "Following the concept of 'the dollar follows the patient,' which
is inherent in L-P-S, $10-$15 million General Fund should be transferred to Community Mental Health Programs during 1972-73." Lanter-

man agreed and said so publicly. If there was any "new money" besides the money transferred from other budgets, it was from federal sources, he said to reporters. He added that he expected the governor to approve the Ways and Means Committee's wish to reappropriate money (estimated at $12 million) left over from the current fiscal year.[20] Lanterman's assessment was correct, for the governor, in part due to Lanterman's insistence, agreed to a "real" Short-Doyle augmentation of over $12 million.

Lanterman as Implementer

Clearly, Lanterman was deeply involved in the implementation of L-P-S, whatever we choose to mean by that phrase. But what, indeed, should we mean by it? We have, so far, said of him only that he "oversaw," "intervened," "followed up," "corrected," "expanded," "overhauled," "protected," and so forth. Of the nature of the process in which he participated in all these ways we have, so far, said almost nothing. Yet it is impossible to understand Lanterman's participation without first clarifying our conception of the implementation process and the problems it creates. This exercise in clarification leads us into the numerous conceptual issues we shall address in the following chapter. In Chapters 3 through 6 we shall elaborate the details of the conceptual scheme proposed in Chapter 2 and illustrate it with numerous examples drawn from L-P-S and many other policies and programs. We shall reserve until the final chapter (11) a review of Lanterman's activities in the context of our conceptual scheme for interpreting implementation processes. At that point, we shall interpret his activities as "fixing" various implementation games, and we shall argue that, if possible, the role of fixer should always be incorporated in the basic policy design from the earliest planning stages.

Notes

1

For a more extended discussion of certain methodological aspects of the " 'point of view' problem," see the section of that name in Appendix C.

2

This political process is described and analyzed in considerable detail in Eugene Bardach, *The Skill Factor in Politics: Repealing the Mental Commitment Laws in California* (Berkeley: University of California Press, 1972). An account of some of the methods used in collecting information concerning the implementation of L-P-S may be found in Appendix C.

3

"Short-Doyle" was the name for the largely state-financed but county-run mental health services program begun in 1957-1958. The financing mechanism relied principally on state matching grants to the counties, the ratio for which increased from 50-50 in 1958 to 90-10 under L-P-S.

4

The L-P-S Act required that annual county requests for Short-Doyle funds be accompanied by a written plan. This county plan was intended as a mechanism for the DMH to control the county programs.

5

In 1974, Lanterman sponsored legislation to deal with the thorny problems of the mentally disordered offender. A number of bizarre murders, some of them mass murders, took place in California in the early 1970s, and some of the newspapers and public had linked them to the latitudinarian philosophy behind the L-P-S Act. Lanterman's response, framed after careful study, was to introduce the possibility of "mandatory outpatient treatment" for a number of problematic social types: for the "criminally insane," for persons who "by means of mental defects are predisposed to the commission of sexual offenses to such a degree that they are dangerous to the health and safety of others," and for persons involuntarily detained under the original L-P-S legislation for whom "continued treatment . . . as an outpatient will facilitate his return to community life and is reasonably necessary to prevent him from repeating the behavior which resulted in his involuntary detention or commitment to a state hospital." Lanterman's bill was not well received, however. The issue was still highly controverted at the time of this writing.

6

I say "evidently" because there is no record in Lanterman's files of Dozier's comments themselves. In the prepared text of his remarks Lanterman states his intention to rebut Dozier point by point.

7

Italics in original. In response to Dozier's assertion that San Joaquin County was already protecting the civil rights of persons alleged to be mentally ill, Lanterman read a slightly paraphrased version of the transcript of a San Joaquin County commitment hearing he had obtained. The patient was said by the examining physician to be in "marginal remission" following a severe disturbance precipitated by the death of his three-year-old daughter in an auto accident. He read the Bible constantly and believed he was the son of God. This belief was confirmed by what the patient believed he heard on the television. The patient testified that he did hold such beliefs, and indeed that he did live by what the Bible told him to do. What did he do? the presiding judge asked. He ran farm machinery, tractors mostly; it was tilling time now and he wanted to go back home and take care of his family, get back on the job. His "religious ideation" might make him a danger to others, said the physician. "He needs medical care." The patient responded: "How can you say I would hurt someone? All I find in the Bible is truth and love, not hatred. I'm no danger to anyone. All I want to do is go back to my family and get to work supporting them." The judge ruled for commitment because, as he said, "The profession of psychiatry feels you to be a potential danger."

8

In a letter to Lanterman two weeks after this small drama, Dozier wrote: "Our basic view of course is that the Act in general would not be necessary if all of the judges of the state had been doing their job in re-commitments conscientiously and intelligently. Your Committee hearings, however, apparently produced evidence that this has not been the case and that hence far reaching procedural reforms are necessary." He added a list of seven suggestions that would "greatly decrease the expense and unnecessary spinning of wheels without materially detracting from your libertarian goals."

9

The DMH program specialist from the legislative analyst's office also participated.

10

Lanterman to J. M. Stubblebine, November 19, 1971.

11

Lanterman to James Hall, Secretary, Human Relations Agency, November 23, 1971.

12

In addition, working for Schabarum was a former assembly staff man who was known to, and trusted by, Lanterman's staff people. The net result of all this oversight, it should be noted, was small. In September 1973, Lanterman wrote Schabarum of his disappointment that after nearly a year "few changes have actually been implemented."

13

John S. Saloma III, *Congress and the New Politics* (Boston: Little, Brown, 1969), pp. 183-189.

14

The spirit of accommodation was nurtured by an announcement in mid-1973 that the administration was officially abandoning its earlier stated goal of closing all the hospitals for the mentally ill and retarded by 1982. Indeed, only three hospitals had actually been closed completely since L-P-S went into effect, and all three had been on the verge of being closed by the DMH and the legislature throughout the 1960s. Wards for the mentally ill had, however, been closed at Agnews State Hospital (the one in Alquist's district) in June 1972, though it continued to serve as a facility for the retarded. Admissions of the mentally ill to Patton State Hospital were restricted to Penal Code commitments only. Stockton State Hospital, after August 1, 1973, admitted mentally ill patients from San Joaquin County only.

15

Sacramento Bee, August 14, 1973.

16

January 21-24, 1971.

17

Testimony of Dr. J. M. Stubblebine, Director of the California State Department of Health, before the Alquist committee, October 9, 1973. Contrary to Stubblebine's assertion, a recent study by Larry Sosowsky ("Putting State Mental Hospitals Out of Business—The Community Approach to Treating Mental Illness in San Mateo County," Master's thesis [Graduate School of Public Policy, University of California, Berkeley, 1974]) suggests that the incidence of convictions for assault among "released mental patients" is substantially higher than in the general population. In absolute terms, both rates are low, however: approximately 225 per 100,000 for the "mental patients" and 33 per 100,000 for the state population. Comparable figures for homicide convictions were 55 per 100,000 and 10 per 100,000.

18

It is interesting to note that the old shibboleths of the radical right about the repressive uses of "mental treatment" and mental institutions were on occasion applied indiscriminately to L-P-S as well, since it did, after all, promise improved mental health services. This attack was limited in scope, however, and did not begin to approach the virulence of the earlier right-wing campaign in California against the Short-Doyle Act as a Communist plot. As the reader no doubt understands by now, the main intent of L-P-S was exactly to expand civil liberties, not to constrict them. Indeed, as I reported in *The Skill Factor in Politics*, the decisive vote in the legislative conference committee that cleared SB 677 in 1967 was cast by Senator John Schmitz of Orange County, the only avowed member of the John Birch Society in the legislature. Schmitz favored the bill on libertarian grounds.

19
State of California Joint Legislative Budget Committee, *Report of the Legislative Analyst*, 1972, pp. 668-669.

20
Los Angeles Times, March 31, 1972. Short-Doyle had had trouble spending its appropriated funds, principally because the county fiscal year began three months later than the state fiscal year, thereby leading to lags in starting new programs, and also because of a peculiar feature of the Short-Doyle financing mechanism. The counties got reimbursed by the state for claims provided only that they did not exceed their allotted amounts. Lags in processing the claims led counties to underspend their budgets in the last quarter of the state fiscal year so as not to exceed their allotment. It is instructive to contrast the year-end fiscal conservatism induced by the reimbursement mechanism with the year-end spending spree induced by the more usual appropriations-plus-obligational-authority financing mechanism.

Whatever else it is, a policy- or program-implementation process is an assembly process. It is as if the original mandate, whether legislative or bureaucratic or judicial, that set the policy or program in motion were a blueprint for a large machine that was to turn out rehabilitated psychotics or healthier old people or better-educated children or more effective airplanes or safer streets. This machine must sometimes be assembled from scratch. It can sometimes be created by overhauling and reconstituting an older, or preexisting, machine. Putting the machine together and making it run is, at one level, what we mean by the "implementation process." "Implementation problems," as we said above, are control problems, but they are specific to the assembly activities that constitute some "implementation process."

What sorts of parts go into this policy machine? Of course, the detailed answer to such a question would depend on a specification of what the machine was supposed to do and where it was to be located. A machine to alleviate mental illness is clearly a different machine than one that distributes agricultural subsidies or one that regulates the price of natural gas. A machine that services the nation as a whole is different from a machine that services Ohio alone or a machine that services Tulsa, Oklahoma, alone. Yet, at an intermediate level of abstraction, one can see that all such machines do look rather similar. One would ordinarily expect to find:

—administrative and financial accountability mechanisms

—the willing participation of presumptive beneficiaries or clients

—private providers of goods and services: professional service workers, developers, landholders

—clearances or permits by public regulatory agencies or elected officials

—innovations in the realm of program conception and design

—sources of funds

—troubleshooters who iron out difficulties and assist in coordinating the more routine activities of the assembly process

—political support that sustains and protects the assembly process

Such a list should be taken as suggestive rather than as definitive. It is certainly not exhaustive. Not all elements are involved in every policy or program. There are other ways of describing some of the inputs that would be equally valid, for example, "budgets and reimbursements" instead of "funds." What is important, ultimately, is that the implementation process be understood, in part at least, as a process of assembling numerous and diverse program elements.[1]

But only in part. The other part of our conception of the "implementation process" is grounded in the fact that these elements are in the hands of many different parties, most of whom are in important ways independent of each other. The only way that such parties can induce others to contribute program elements is through the use of persuasion and bargaining. Some might call the resulting process "politics." And so it is. Yet, implementation politics is, I believe, a special kind of politics. It is a form of politics in which the very existence of an already defined policy mandate, legally and legitimately authorized in some prior political process, affects the strategy and tactics of the struggle. The dominant effect is to make the politics of the implementation process highly defensive. A great deal of energy goes into maneuvering to avoid responsibility, scrutiny, and blame.

This overall conception of the "implementation process" does not differ significantly from the conception found in the previous scholarly literature on the subject. It does differ in certain subtle, and sometimes important, ways, however. Although the previous literature is in fact quite meager—the "implementation problem" having been perceived as an interesting social and political problem only in the last seven or eight years—it has been useful. It has helped me recognize the great importance of arriving at a clear conception of the implementation process before trying to specify the problems that result from it and before trying to speculate about what might be done about those problems. It is worth reviewing the highlights of this literature at this point in order to lead the reader toward my own conclusions about a useful way of conceiving the "implementation process." By way of both preparation and warning, I once again acknowledge to the reader that, in the end, I shall propose to integrate the "assembly" and the "politics" parts of the process through the idea of "a system of loosely related implementation games."

Implementation as Pressure Politics

It is widely and correctly realized that the bargaining and maneuvering, the pulling and hauling, of the policy-adoption process carries over into the policy-implementation process. Die-hard opponents of the policy who lost out in the adoption stage seek, and find, means to continue their opposition when, say, administrative regulations and guidelines are being written. Many who supported the original policy proposal did so only because they expected to be able to twist it in the implementation phase to suit purposes never contemplated or desired by others who formed part of the original coalition. They too seek a role in the administrative process. A convenient, albeit somewhat misleading, description of their activities in both stages is "pressure," a description most aptly provided by David Truman's classic work, *The Governmental Process.*[2]

The implementation process as a system of pressures and counterpressures is the view taken by Jerome T. Murphy in his account of the first seven years of ESEA Title I.[3] The reformist impulse in passing ESEA Title I was "to help eliminate poverty." Title I attempted to target billions of dollars to schools with large numbers of children from poor families. The impulse of other key actors in the passing coalition, however, was simply to get more money to the nation's schools. "The educational associations in Washington were . . . primarily interested in general support for ongoing public school activities. They accepted ESEA's poverty focus as a compromise necessary to achieve passage of ESEA, but their emphasis was on breaking the federal aid logjam, on the ground that this would be a major step toward federal general support later."[4] Since the traditional school establishments at the state and local levels, which actually controlled the distribution of funds, saw Title I as general aid too, the result has been a nearly total neglect of the antipoverty objective. In Murphy's view, ". . . it is not even clear to what extent Title I is expended on eligible disadvantaged children in poverty neighborhoods. Even when it reaches them, it is uncertain that the money buys services in addition to the level provided other school children in each district."[5] Why has it worked out this way? Murphy argues that the most important reason has been the absence of "political pressure by poverty groups and their allies, and meaningful participation by such interests in local school district councils or other comparable devices."[6] To the extent that there has been any attention to the antipoverty objective of Title I, it has come about because of adverse publicity, lawsuits, or the threat of legal action, which constituted "countervailing power" and thus "political pressure, and sometimes support" for the U.S. Office of Education (USOE) to "act more affirmatively with the states in Title I's administration."[7]

Murphy may be right about Title I, but it would be misleading to make the notion of "pressure" into a central concept for understanding the implementation process. What are we to make of implementation failures when everyone is agreed on the principal objectives? In such a case the dialectic of pressure and counterpressure would presumably not exist and could therefore not shape outcomes. But minor disagreements between just a few actors can cause delays, as can simple standard operating procedures in bureaucracies. A vicious cycle of delay, fear of ultimate failure or high salvage costs, withdrawal of previous commitments, more delay, increased anxieties, and so forth, can also cause implementation failure, as Pressman and Wildavsky have shown in their EDA study.

A possible response might be that pressure on the "system" must be sufficient to push it along in the right directions. If that is the response, then the conceptual problem becomes that of delineating the system and its particularly vulnerable pressure points. In an earlier version of his 1972 paper, Murphy seems to have taken this tack. Explicitly or implicitly he advocated pressure on the USOE by a coalition of the NAACP and the National Welfare Rights Organization. USOE in turn was to bring pressure to bear on the state education agencies, which in turn were to apply pressure to the local districts. Pressure at the local level, coming up from below, could be joined to pressure at the national level to reinforce the pressure at the state level. To protect the whole Title I program from being sabotaged by a Congress suddenly aroused by jittery local education establishments, the organized poor would have had to bring pressure on Congress as well.[8]

It should be obvious that there is a conceptual problem with such an argument, in that "pressure" or its absence can become a catchall phrase that by describing everything describes nothing well. There is also a practical political danger: a prescription for applying pressure virtually everywhere is tantamount to prescribing the application of very weak pressures. Political resources are, after all, limited, and a useful model of the implementation process should suggest more precisely how they should be concentrated and their effects focused on particular points in the governmental system.[9] It is for these reasons that my own view of the implementation process tries to take account of the particular program elements that are or might be at issue and from there proceeds to the political interactions that would be likely to transpire in the course of assembling them.

Implementation as the Massing of "Assent"

A paper by Douglas R. Bunker, delivered in 1970 at the American Association for the Advancement of Science, is the earliest attempt (that I have found) to conceptualize the "implementation process" as a distinctive social and political phenomenon. In it, Bunker in effect suggests a possible solution to the problem of identifying the system's particularly significant interaction points by arguing that a simple massing of "assent" is all that is required for successful implementation. Bunker states:

Whether policies, plans, decisions or programs are to be implemented, the essential question is: How are ideas translated into effective collective action? For benefits consistent with the concept or design to be realized, those charged with carrying out the policy, and those to be affected by it, must yield some degree of assent. The requirement varies from passive but tolerant acquiescence on the part of some to scrupulous, informed and intense commitment for others who take responsibility for the guidance and execution of the plan.[10]

He then goes on to argue that "all actors potentially involved with the implementation task at issue may be located at some point in a three-dimensional space" defined by vectors of "issue salience," "power resources," and "agreement." Bunker then proposes to assign all such actors interval-level scores on these three dimensions, after which "multiplicative combinations," summed across actors, "might provide some estimate of the required values for a minimum effective coalition to achieve implementation."[11]

There are numerous problems with this theory, at least two of which are instructive for our own efforts. First, it is hard to know which actors ought to be included in the group of those "potentially involved with the implementation task at issue." In the ESEA Title I case, for instance, Bunker would surely have us include the USOE and the state and local education bureaucracies. Probably the classroom teachers ought to be included as well. But would he have us include the NAACP, angry parents, and the National Welfare Rights Organization? Congressmen? Justice Department attorneys involved in the application of non-discrimination statutes to the granting of ESEA funds? The judges who might have been called upon by Murphy's lawyers to force state-level compliance with the statutes? The schoolchildren themselves, who may or may not have wished to, or been able to, take advantage of the extra services that might have been made available to them? The relevant set of actors is so open-ended that our own conception of the implementation process will have to reflect this fact.

Another problem with Bunker's view is that it presumes a type of coalition politics familiar to us from studies of the policy-adoption process. In the latter process, the general level of "assent" can realistically be conceptualized as the crucial variable leading to policy adoption. Nor would it be terribly misleading to call those who favor the proposed policy a "coalition."[12] In the implementation process, however, politics appears primarily *defensive*. Actors seem more concerned with what they in particular might lose than with what all in general might gain. This, at least, is the picture that emerges from studies like Derthick's, Pressman's and Wildavsky's, and my own investigation of L-P-S. Since there is considerable differentiation among actors with respect to how they view their possible losses, coalitions do not readily emerge. Rarely is there a broad communality of interest that would form the basis for coalition-building. Actor A is concerned about the possibility of increased workload, B about the presumed competition of a new service agency with his existing agency, C about the difficulty of applying established accounting procedures to the activities envisioned by the new agency, D about the possibility that the program will not get off the ground in any form at all. All might approve of the new program in principle, but all would want to alter the terms of its implementation just slightly to assuage their own particular fears.

The outcome of defensive politics of this sort is delay, a diversion of energies toward highly particularistic program goals, and, often, a flight from administrative or political responsibility. Bunker's version of the implementation process rising or falling on waves of "assent," however high or low they may be, misses, and indeed distorts, the more important point that it is *conflict over the terms* on which assent is given or withheld that is crucial to the implementation process. Implementation politics is distinguished from policy-adoption politics by the characteristic absence of coalitions and the characteristic presence of fragmented and isolated maneuvers and countermaneuvers.

The primary reason for this sort of defensive politics in the post-adoption period is that all, or at least many, of the important participants act within a context of expectations that *something will happen* that bears at least a passing resemblance to whatever was mandated by the initial policy decision. A second, if related, reason is that participants who favor the policy goals of the mandate use the existence of the mandate as a moral and sometimes legal weapon in the emerging struggle over the terms on which policy is effected.

Implementation as an Administrative Control Process

If there is one set of actors who can be reckoned as surely relevant to almost any implementation process and who very often play a quite masterful defensive game, it is the bureaucrats. Bureaucrats and bureaucracies are thought to be responsible for many of the problems of implementation. The common perception is that lower-level bureaucrats (or elected officials) do not carry out the instructions and orders of higher-level bureaucrats (or officials). Consider, for example, Allison's and Halperin's hypotheses about the implementation problems confronting a president and other "central players" in the area of foreign and defense policy:

1. Presidential decisions will be faithfully implemented when: a President's involvement is unambiguous, his words are unambiguous, his order is widely publicized, the men who receive it have control of everything needed to carry it out, and those men have no apparent doubt of his authority to issue the decision.

2. Major new departures in foreign policy typically stem from some decision by central players. But the specific details of the action taken are determined in large part by standard operating procedure and programs existing in the organizations at the time.

3. Ambassadors and field commanders feel less obliged to faithfully implement decisions because they typically have not been involved in the decision game. They feel they know better what actions one should want from another government and how to get those actions.

4. The larger the number of players who can act independently on an issue, the less the government's action will reflect decisions of the government on that issue.

5. Where a decision leaves leeway for the organization that is implementing it, that organization will act so as to maximize its organizational interest within constraints.[13]

The bureaucracy problem afflicts policy areas other than foreign and defense as well. The U.S. Office of Education was a major bureaucratic obstacle in the implementation of ESEA, as were its state and local counterparts.[14] State and local welfare bureaucracies have been blamed for many of the perceived failures of public-assistance programs, particularly Aid to Families with Dependent Children.[15] The U.S. Army Corps of Engineers and the U.S. Bureau of Reclamation are commonly regarded as uncontrollable juggernauts of environmental destruction.

The problem of control and accountability is only one aspect of the "bureaucracy problem," as James Q. Wilson has commented.[16] It is probably regarded (rightly or wrongly) as the most important aspect, however, and certainly the one most relevant to the implementation process.[17]

Why this problem of accountability and control? Anthony Downs has suggested that the "leakage of authority" occurs because individual officials have varying goals, "and each uses his discretion in translating orders from above into commands going downward, [and] the purposes the superior had in mind will not be the precise ones his subordinate's orders convey to people further down the hierarchy."[18] Downs has further suggested that the dynamics of recruitment and socialization into an organization frequently cause the lower and middle echelons of any public organization, or bureau, to be populated by more temperamentally conservative individuals than are the upper echelons of political appointees or elected officials. In such cases the authority from the top does not merely leak, it hemorrhages. Another reason for the "leakage of authority" is that lower-level participants in organizations often have autonomous power bases. Thomas J. Scheff, for instance, has explained the failure of a state mental hospital to bring about an intended reform by reference to the dependence of the ward physicians, the sponsors of the reform, on the ward attendants. Given their short tenure, lack of interest in administration, and heavy workload, the ward physicians typically delegated great responsibility to the attendants. If the physicians wished to withdraw some of this responsibility (in order to institute a reform), the attendants could make their lives difficult in several ways. They could refuse to act as "a barrier between the physician and a ward full of patients demanding attention and recognition." They could refuse to handle their customary portion of the physician's paper work and they could undermine his capacity for "making a graceful entrance and departure from the ward."[19]

Management failure also contributes to the "leakage" problem. A recent review of the literature on "planned organizational change" making special reference to "the problem of implementing organizational innovations" concluded that, although there is a "paucity of knowledge" on the subject, "the major explanation" for implementation problems of this sort was failure on the part of management or of some "change agent" to overcome the natural resistance of organization members.[20] The authors of this review also concluded that this explanation was inadequate, in that it ignored "obstacles to which members who are not resistant to change may be exposed when they make efforts to implement innovations" and the foolish derelictions of management in permitting, or even inducing, a negative orientation to change during the course of the change process even among members who were initially favorable.[21] Here I have my own principal objection to Murphy's pressure-resistance conception articulated in a slightly more specific context. But this is not the principal objection to focusing on bureaucratic control as the central implementation process. The principal objection is that it is too narrow a focus. Implementation processes are driven at least as much if not more by interorganizational transactions as by intraorganizational transactions. The array of relevant actors in the implementation process is large and diverse, including, in addition to governmental bureaus, their clients, private contractors, professional associations, publicists, and so forth. All of these actors are quite capable of articulating their own special fears and anxieties. It is perhaps this broad focus that distinguishes the study of "implementation," a subject of fairly recent interest, from the more traditional subject matter of public administration.[22]

The Implementation Process as Intergovernmental Bargaining

A particularly important set of interorganizational relations involves agencies of different levels of government joined in an effort to implement programs and policies financed by a grant-in-aid mechanism. In her study of the failure of the New Towns program, Derthick argues that "the single most inclusive and illuminating explanation" is to be found in the "disabilities" of our central (federal) government in the American federal system.[23] Because of the "division of authority among governments in the federal system, the federal government cannot order these governments to do anything. It gets them to carry out its purposes by offering incentives in the form of aid, which they may accept or not, and by attaching conditions to the aid."[24] Because federal officials (especially those in Washington) have limited knowledge of what incentives a community will in fact respond to; because at best "the supply of federal incentives" is quite limited; and because the federal government is unable "to use effectively such incentives as it possesses," the federal government is destined to fare poorly as an instrument of social activism and broad-scale reform.

In the New Towns program, the principal federal incentive was large tracts of land at bargain prices. Clearly, it was not a strong enough incentive to compensate many of the localities for costs other than the price of the land that they would have had to bear. For instance, the federal government could do little or nothing to compensate the prospective neighbors to the New Towns sites, in a good many of the cities, who feared the influx of low-income, and quite probably black, residents. Furthermore, it was not strong enough to induce local politicians and other elites to push ahead and find ways to turn the federal government's offer to good advantage. It is important to note, however, that we cannot say that the incentive of low-cost land was in any *absolute* sense weak or strong. Nor can we say that the federal government alone was unable "to use effectively" this particular incentive. Local officials who happened to want to go ahead with the projects were also unable to use this incentive effectively. Furthermore, they too had limited knowledge of what others in their communities would respond to. In a number of the cities surveyed by Derthick it would seem that at least some local officials were just as surprised at the obstacles to implementation as were the federal officials. In view of these facts, why does Derthick argue that the fundamental explanation for the program's failure lies in the disabilities of the federal government? More important, what bearing has her interpretation on our own efforts to conceptualize the implementation process?

In a revealing footnote Derthick concedes that there were other causes for failure as well: the relative inability of the poor to organize and assert their interests; the relative strength of local opponents of the program; and "the great difficulty of organizing cooperative activity on a large scale" (including the activities of developers, lending institutions, school boards, and myriad federal agencies with at least some control over the surplus land and its disposition).[25] Derthick suggests that these, and a few others, were not irrelevant explanations of the problems of program implementation, but for reasons she does not state she nevertheless opts for an explanation that emphasizes the nature of the federal system and in particular "the limits of centralization."

To a degree, of course, choices among theoretical perspectives are governed by taste and nothing else. In an earlier work entitled *The Influence of Federal Grants: Public Assistance in Massachusetts*, Derthick explored the possibilities and the limits of federal grants-in-aid on shaping state and local welfare policy and administrative organization. Its basic question was the same as that of the study of *New Towns In-Town:* How can the federal government influence policy in jurisdictions (state and local governments) over which it has no formal authority or power? Federalism has evidently been very much on her mind, and since it has informed the way she has posed her questions it is not surprising that it has also shaped the answers.[26]

Morton Grodzins banished the "layer cake" image of the American federal structure that had sprung from the nineteenth-century judicial theory of "dual federalism."[27] In its stead he offered the "marble cake" metaphor of "cooperative federalism," of different jurisdictions sharing functions. Derthick has taken this analysis a step further, postulating a creative dialectic between federal and local governments. She has alleged that federal policy planners characteristically think of themselves as innovators with a mission to mount "demonstration" projects, "the intangible benefits of . . . [which] can be distributed universally: everyone can share in the symbolic returns from a showing of what the public good requires."[28] Local governments, on the other hand, are "better organized collectively to execute programs," and so "help the federal government with administration."[29] The concluding two paragraphs of *New Towns In-Town*, while intended to be no more than suggestive, are worth quoting in full:

In shared programs, both the federal government and local governments have a political function: both play a part in defining the objectives of public action and in responding to differences of value, interest, and opinion. The federal government, being removed from particular and parochial conflicts, is better able to express idealistic and progressive objectives. Local governments, more deeply engaged in these conflicts, are better able to respond to the actual preferences of active political interests.

In this system, the accomplishments of government constantly fall short of the objectives expressed at the federal level, and disillusionment follows among both the public and public officials. Such a system may nevertheless be fairly well adapted to the governing of a very large and diverse society—providing, as it does, for the expression both of abstract ideals and of particular, tangible interests. In the process of governing, the two have to be reconciled. Tension between the federal and local governments in the American system may be one sign that such reconciliation is occurring.[30]

Thus it appears that New Towns may not have been such a failure after all! It did express "abstract ideals" and "progressive objectives," and this expressive function is, in the last analysis, raised to a position of functional parity with "the actual preferences of active political interests."

Given these original and provocative ideas about federalism, it is no wonder that Derthick has focused on "the limits of centralization" as the summary of barriers to program implementation. Her insights have more general applicability, however, than merely to governmental jurisdictions in a federal system. It is unfortunate that she did not try to abstract from these particular institutional features to the more general problem of "organizing cooperative activity on a large scale," as she suggested might be plausible. Local officials tried to manipulate the incentives of federal officials (and of other local officials) in precisely the same way that federal officials tried to manipulate the incentives of the local officials (and of other federal officials). From her case materials it is clear that the manipulation of incentives under conditions of uncertainty about what the other parties might desire or accept is endemic to virtually all relationships among actors in an implementation process.

A second lesson to be learned from Derthick's analysis concerns the danger of taking a "top down" view of the world of implementation activities. We are led to think too much of the "disabilities" of the federal government and too little of the comparable disabilities of local elites. In large part, this perspective arises from her persistent curiosity about the influence value of money or the promise of money. Money—as cash, or as a subsidy for land acquisition in the New Towns case—happens to be the program element and the political resource with which federal officials are most abundantly endowed. Hence, even though she strains not to take a "top down" perspective on the federal system as a whole, she is not entirely successful. While she is quite careful to avoid construing federal-state-local relationships as being in any sense hierarchical, she does see money as a sort of primum mobile, even though frequently a weak one. In the cases she studied, federal innovators with money or subsidies tried to buy the cooperation of local officials with access to political support and with control over procedural clearances. One could as easily imagine, however, local innovators with ideas or talent or even some money trying to buy the cooperation of federal officials and perhaps the joint financial participation of the federal government. This latter scenario would aptly describe a large number of so-called "pork barrel" projects, university-sponsored scientific research, educational pilot programs, and so on. In this latter scenario, it is the local elites who initiate the project design, assemble some of the necessary inputs (sometimes including cash), and then proceed to extract other needed inputs, like money and certain bureaucratic clearances, from the federal government. When failure follows from such a scenario, would it be correct to ascribe it to the disabilities of the *federal* government? Perhaps it would be—but one's judgment would certainly depend on the circumstances of the particular case. We would probably be more inclined to point to the failures of entrepreneurship at the local level, where the innovative ideas were first germinated.

A third lesson to be learned here concerns the great variety of program elements needed to produce a desired program output, or outcome, a point already emphasized at the beginning of this chapter. A second point that has already been made as well is that no one person or group contributes more than a few of these needed elements. The rest are contributed by parties who exercise at least some autonomy in deciding whether or not to make a contribution at all, and if so in what amount and under what conditions. Derthick's emphasis on the particular disabilities of the federal government vis-à-vis local governments helps us to appreciate a very important but quite narrow portion of the entire spectrum of reciprocal and interacting abilities and disabilities. To the extent that any possible party to such a collective enterprise cannot be coerced to contribute, and that substitutes are found only at some cost, every *other* party to the enterprise has some disabilities vis-à-vis those who cannot be coerced. The implementation process is therefore characterized by the maneuvering of a large number of semi-autonomous actors, each of which tries to gain access to program elements not under its own control while at the same time trying to extract better terms from other actors seeking access to elements that it does control.

Implementation and the Complexity of Joint Action

The explanation favored by Pressman and Wildavsky for the EDA's failure in Oakland rests on what they call "the complexity of joint action," another way of describing what Derthick calls "organizing cooperative activity on a large scale." Thus, the explanation that Derthick rejected in a footnote becomes the cornerstone of their explanation.

The EDA made special efforts in Oakland to avoid "obstacles that were known to have hampered other programs" like "institutional fragmentation, multiple and confusing goals, and inadequate funding . . ." The agency sought to follow a course as simple and as straightforward as possible; but even that course, which was on the surface the best of all possible courses, was "really complex and convoluted."[31] According to Pressman and Wildavsky, the "prosaic" problems that give rise to such convolutions are essentially those of "changing actors, diverse perspectives, [and] multiple clearances."[32] They emphasize especially "the geometric growth of interdependencies over time where each negotiation involves a number of participants with decisions to make, whose implications ramify over time."[33] In a provocative (if somewhat misleading) quantitative rendering of these ramifications, they enumerate thirty "decision points" in the course of implementing the EDA's Oakland projects, seventy necessary "agreements" summed over all these decision points, and a .000395 probability of "success" for the program if the probability of each agreement was as high as .95![34]

Pressman and Wildavsky emphasize that this calculation is merely an amusing illustration and not to be taken too seriously. The principal problem in the calculation, however, is not in the numbers but in the words. The number of decision points and agreements that one can count in the negotiations are not nearly as significant as the substantive issues that made the negotiations necessary in the first place. To state these issues simply, the EDA wanted more in the way of minority hiring than World or the port seemed willing to provide; and the port and World wanted more in the way of financial relief from the estimated cost overruns than EDA was willing to provide. And all parties were more willing to bear the costs of delay than to give up without a fight.

Pressman and Wildavsky clearly have a fine eye for detail and a cultivated taste for irony. Their case materials are the best in print from which to get a full appreciation of the implementation process.[35] Their own appreciation of the ironic details, however, diminished their appreciation of the grosser features of the process. In the EDA-Oakland case, they maintain, implementation was not affected by "dramatic elements that are essentially self-explanatory. . . . There was no great conflict. Everyone agreed. There was only minimum publicity. Essential funds were on hand at the right time. The evils that afflicted the EDA program in Oakland were of a prosaic and everyday character."[36] My own interpretation holds, to the contrary, that if there was no "great" conflict there was still sufficient conflict. When millions of dollars are at stake to the private contractors and the reputation of an already politically vulnerable federal agency is jeopardized by the prospect of paying out $20 to $30 million for essentially nothing, there are good grounds for conflict. This underlying conflict was, to be sure, greatly exaggerated by the ingrained tendencies of governmental agencies to avoid what might be construed as gross fiscal irresponsibility, by the inability of any of the parties to deliver a credible promise about its future behavior under conditions envisioned by other parties, and by the anxieties and suspicions that were nurtured by the negotiating process itself. Indeed, it is precisely because Pressman and Wildavsky have identified so many of the numerous features of the process that tend to *aggravate and exaggerate* underlying conflicts that their study is so worthwhile. They lead us to a critical insight about the implementation process: the maneuvers of the several parties both express conflict and create it—and with every maneuver aimed at reducing it there is an associated risk of actually making matters worse. In an important sense, therefore, much of the implementation process moves along "out of control," driven by complex forces not of any party's making.

Pressman and Wildavsky are the only scholars whose work we have discussed thus far who have attempted a dynamic interpretation of the implementation process, that is, an interpretation that takes the passage of time into account.[37] Consider, for instance, their implied proposition that, under certain conditions, the longer players continue their maneuvering the worse the prospects for program success. Consider also their attempt to quantify what they call "the anatomy of delay"[38] by assigning differential clearance times to each separate agreement requirement and summing them. Given seventy clearances and "arbitrarily assigning a value of one week for minimal delay, three weeks for minor delay, and six weeks for moderate delay," they come up with a total of 233-1/3 weeks. "Under these assumptions the delay thus far would come out to approximately four and a half years, which is not far off the mark."[39] Even when they take into account the expeditious tendency to pursue several clearances simultaneously, they still come out with roughly the same delay—because of the offsetting tendency for negotiations that failed in the first round to go through successive rounds, each of which must be counted as a separate clearance problem.[40] The authors remark that not all delays are of the same sort. Implicitly, they classify the delay of protracted and frustrating negotiations as one type, which they appear also to refer to as "unplanned, accidental occurrences."[41] Another major type of delay is "caused intentionally by participants who wanted to stop an undesired action or to step back and reassess the development of the program." These are called "blocking delays." A third type results from "alternative time priorities." It took eleven months, for instance, for the EDA to grant approval to the Port of Oakland's request for a cost overrun on its part of the project because the EDA "had hundreds of public works projects to supervise" and the Port of Oakland project had dropped to a position of low priority for the agency.[42] Implicitly, also, they appear to recognize a fourth type of delay, that which results from delay itself: the more delay that has already occurred "the more time for intensity [of commitment to seeing the program through to completion] to decay."[43]

This last type of delay is especially interesting because it arises in part from what might be called the "illogic of collective action," to adapt a phrase of Mancur Olson, Jr.[44] The classic case of such illogic is in organizing a labor union or trade association: it is strictly irrational for any particular worker or businessman to join provided all others do it and thereby produce the benefits from which he too will derive advantage; but if everybody feels that way, no organization will come into being, and the benefits will be lost to all. In the case of program implementation the calculus is similar though it starts from slightly more defensive premises: it is strictly irrational not to renege on the terms one has already agreed to provided one is confident that others will meet the new terms demanded; but if others too begin to renege, the resulting turmoil and delay will convince the rest that they ought to cut their losses and pull out altogether. Hence, delay can be taken as an augury of possible collapse, which will induce actors to renege, thereby guaranteeing more delay and substantially increasing the probability of actual collapse. This scenario was played out in the EDA-Oakland case until the federal agency decided finally that it had invested too much to pull out altogether. In the end, the EDA trimmed its objectives, agreed to pick up a number of cost overruns, and heaved a sigh of relief at being able to disengage.

Here again Pressman and Wildavsky have provided us with a critical insight into the nature of the implementation process: it is shot through with gamesmanship. This important conclusion completes our examination of the highlights in the existing literature and puts us in a position to elaborate our own conception of the implementation process as the playing out of a number of interrelated games.

The Implementation Process as a System of Games

The main problem with the Pressman-Wildavsky approach is that it does not go far enough. It suggests that typologies might be important, for example, their three or four types of delay processes, but stops short of suggesting a conceptual basis for such typologies. It is also limited, when it does discuss typologies, to one specialized topic, delay. It does not explicitly identify and analyze implementation processes that result in the perversion or subversion of policy goals or the processes that lead to excessive financial costs. Nor does it attempt to characterize in a moderately abstract and systematic way the interactions that routinely link the different kinds of institutions or roles normally involved in a process of program assembly.

It is a felt need for a usable typology that has led me to the metaphor of "games." Games can be classified according to the nature of their stakes. As a simple organizing device, if nothing else, this classification principle is quite effective. This is not the only way one might attempt to classify games, to be sure. Mathematical game theorists have invented, for their own purposes, much more elegant schemes contained in a vast literature that we shall ignore. For our own, basically descriptive, purposes, relying on the idea of stakes appears far more useful. Readers who can think of a better method are encouraged to try their own hands at it. As a description of the basic activities of the implementation process, it is a helpful refinement of the original idea of "control," which we said in the introduction was at the heart of the "implementation problem." We have seen that "control" is exercised through bargaining, persuasion, and maneuvering under conditions of uncertainty. "Control," therefore, resolves into strategies and tactics—hence the appropriateness of "games" as the characterization of the "control" aspects of the process.

The idea of "games," therefore, will serve principally as a master metaphor that directs attention and stimulates insight.[45] It directs us to look at the players, what they regard as the stakes, their strategies and tactics, their resources for playing, the rules of play (which stipulate the conditions for winning), the rules of "fair" play (which stipulate the boundaries beyond which lie fraud or illegitimacy), the nature of the communications (or lack of them) among the players, and the degree of uncertainty surrounding the possible outcomes. The game metaphor also directs our attention to who is not willing to play and for what reasons, and to who insists on changes in some of the game's parameters as a condition for playing.

By "system" I mean simply a collection of structural elements related to one another through ongoing processes. The elements are games, and their interrelationships are so manifold and convoluted that it is impossible to say much about the system as a whole except that the constituent elements, the games, are on the whole only loosely interrelated.[46]

Consider, for instance, the interrelationships depicted in the case study of the EDA project in Oakland. Within the EDA, the Washington office, the Seattle office, and the Oakland office were all involved in a game among themselves, and the continually changing outcomes of that game affected "the agency's" resources and strategies in its games with the Port of Oakland and with World Airways. Games that the agency was playing with the U.S. General Accounting Office, the Congress, and the Nixon Administration (beginning, of course, only in 1969), constrained its choices of strategy in dealing with the port and with World. The port was constrained by its ongoing game with the city of Oakland, as World Airways was constrained by its games with its business competitors, its stockholders, its customers, and so on.

These relations exemplify cases where different games do in fact interact with each other. The outcomes of certain games set the conditions for the play of other games. Resources committed to one game, and the maneuvering within its rules, affect a player's ability to maneuver in other games being played simultaneously. Yet the illustrations above can suggest weak or absent interactions as well, for example, between the General Accounting Office and the competitors of World Airways, or between the Seattle office of EDA and the Nixon White House. As we list, describe, and analyze the following series of different implementation games, we shall attempt to delineate the plausible interrelationships among them. Of all possible two-way interrelationships, only a minority seem to me plausibly connected with any degree of either strength or regularity, however. The political and institutional relationships in an implementation process on any but the smallest scale are simply too numerous and diverse to admit of our asserting lawlike propositions about them. It is the fragmentary and disjunctive nature of the real world that makes "a general theory of the implementation process" (which has been urged upon me by some readers of the draft manuscript) unattainable and, indeed, unrealistic.

To summarize, then, the "implementation process" is: (1) a process of assembling the elements required to produce a particular programmatic outcome, and (2) the playing out of a number of loosely interrelated games whereby these elements are withheld from or delivered to the program assembly process on particular terms. The next four chapters sketch the most common implementation games and their possible adverse effects. These sketches are intended to serve as a warning to would-be policy designers. Every policy worth its salt is vulnerable to at least a few of these games. Such risks cannot be avoided. The object of describing these games—and, where possible, certain mitigating strategies—is to help designers calculate their risks more accurately and to design policies robust enough to survive them.

Notes

1

The term "program elements" has had a certain currency in discussion of Planning-Programming-Budgeting Systems (PPBS). No such connection is intended here. Some readers might also think it desirable at this point to distinguish between program and policy and would ask whether policy implementation differs in any way from program implementation. I think it does not. Although a program does not imply a policy, it is hard to think of a policy that would not also imply a program structure, no matter that a given policy does not logically entail any *particular* program structure. I shall not distinguish henceforth the process of "program implementation" from that of "policy implementation."

2

David Truman, *The Governmental Process* (New York: Knopf, 1951).

3

Jerome T. Murphy, "The Education Bureaucracies Implement Novel Policy: The Politics of Title I of ESEA, 1965-72," in Allan P. Sindler, ed., *Policy and Politics in America* (Boston: Little, Brown, 1973), pp. 160-198. On ESEA generally, see also Joel S. Berke and Michael W. Kirst, eds., *Federal Aid to Education: Who Benefits? Who Governs?* (Lexington, Mass.: D. C. Heath, 1972); and Stephen K. Bailey and Edith K. Mosher, *ESEA: The Office of Education Administers a Law* (Syracuse: Syracuse University Press, 1968).

4

Murphy, "Education Bureaucracies," p. 169.

5

Murphy, "Education Bureaucracies," p. 194.

6

Murphy, "Education Bureaucracies," pp. 196-197.

7

Murphy, "Education Bureaucracies," p. 196. Murphy reports specifically on Massachusetts, but it is clear he believes the pattern is nationwide. A review of seven states in Berke and Kirst, *Federal Aid*, suggests that Massachusetts may be an extreme example of the dilution of antipoverty objectives, but that it is nonetheless highly indicative of the national pattern.

8

Jerome T. Murphy, "Title I of ESEA: The Politics of Implementing Federal Education Reform," *Harvard Educational Review* 41 (February 1971): 35-63.

9

My own interpretation of the problems of Title I gives central place to the formula-grant system of allocating monies to the states and to local districts. Each eligible recipient felt *entitled by law* to receive Title I monies, and the threat to withhold them was correspondingly weak and halfhearted. Given such a massive rent in the federal purse, it would have taken more than "pressure" around the edges to regain control over Title I expenditures. Murphy considers the formula-grant system a serious weakness, too ("Education Bureaucracies," p. 171). See the discussion of Massive Resistance in Chapter 5.

10
Douglas R. Bunker, "Policy Sciences Perspectives on Implementation Processes," *Policy Sciences* 3 (March 1972): 72. Bunker identifies his idea of implementation with Jones's notion of the application of policy, Dror's concept of policy execution, Gross's idea of "the activation of plans," and Gergen's phase of "sanction and control." He also says that his notion of implementation is what "others describe as follow-through or carrying-out of policies" (p. 72). See K. Gergen, "Assessing the Leverage Points in the Process of Policy Formation," in R. A. Bauer and K. H. Gergen, eds., *The Study of Policy Formation* (New York: Free Press, 1968), Chap. 5; C. O. Jones, *An Introduction to the Study of Public Policy* (Belmont, Calif.: Wadsworth, 1970); Y. Dror, *Public Policymaking Reexamined* (San Francisco: Chandler, 1968); and B. Gross, "Activating National Plans," in J. R. Lawrence, ed., *Operational Research and the Social Sciences* (London: Tavistock, 1966). See also, Donald S. Van Meter and Carl E. Van Horn, "The Policy Implementation Process: A Conceptual Framework," *Administration and Society* 6: 4 (February 1975): 445-488. They stress as critical determinants of "the execution of public policy" both "the amount of change involved" and "the extent to which there is goal consensus among the participants in the implementation process" (p. 458).

11
Bunker, "Policy Sciences Perspectives," pp. 76-77.

12
In my own efforts to conceptualize the policy-adoption process, I have found it useful to distinguish the causal force of the level of "support" (or "assent" in Bunker's terms) from the causal force of those political "resources" utilized by an activist coalition. The coalition uses resources to produce support, which in turn produces a legislative decision. See my *The Skill Factor in Politics: Repealing the Mental Commitment Laws in California* (Berkeley: University of California Press, 1972).

13
Graham T. Allison and Morton H. Halperin, "Bureaucratic Politics: A Paradigm and Some Policy Implications," in Raymond Tanter and Richard H. Ullman, eds., *Theory and Policy in International Relations* (Princeton: Princeton University Press, 1972), p. 54. See also the section "Organizational Implementation" in Graham T. Allison, "Conceptual Models and the Cuban Missile Crisis," *American*

Political Science Review 63:3 (September 1969): 706-707; and Morton H. Halperin, *Bureaucratic Politics and Foreign Policy* (Washington, D.C.: The Brookings Institution, 1974), esp. Chaps. 13-15.

14

Murphy, "Education Bureaucracies."

15

For a conservative perspective on these failures, see California State Department of Social Welfare, *Welfare Reform in California . . . Showing the Way* (December 1972). For a view from the opposite end of the political spectrum, see Frances Fox Piven and Richard A. Cloward, *Regulating the Poor* (New York: Random House, 1971).

16

James Q. Wilson, "The Bureaucracy Problem," *The Public Interest* (Winter 1967), pp. 3-9.

17

The identification of implementation with decisions and activities of government organizations is strongly implied by Thomas B. Smith in "The Policy Implementation Process," *Policy Sciences* 4 (1973): 197-209. He writes: "The implementing organization is responsible for the implementation of the policy. In most instances, the organization is a unit of the governmental bureaucracy." The three "key variables" are the organization's structure and personnel, its leadership, and "the general capacity of the organization to meet the objectives of program implementation" (pp. 204-205). We find the same identification of implementation decisions and decisions by government bureaucracies in Antonio Ugalde, "A Decision Model for the Study of Public Bureaucracies," *Policy Sciences* 4 (1973): 75-84. "Implementation decisions . . . are those made in the process of implementing the formal decision. Frequently several different bureaucracies (ministries, decentralized agencies) make implementation decisions in the process of implementing *one* formal decision" (p. 78, italics in original). Consider also the usage in a representative work from the field of operations research in which the question of "implementing" the OR analysis is often more problematic than the question addressed by the OR researchers in their formal analysis. "Given the confusion that exists about the meaning of the term 'implementation,' " writes Jan H. B. M. Huysmans, it "seems prudent to start out with a provisional working definition of OR implementation. We will say that an operations research recommendation is implemented if the manager or managers affected by the recommendation adopt the research results in essence and continue to use them as long as the conditions underlying the research apply." *The Implementation of Operations Research* (New York: Wiley, 1970), p. 1. A recent draft paper by Martin Rein and Francine Rabinowitz, "Implementation: A Theoretical Perspective," also identifies "implementation" with the actions and decisions of administrators in public organizations.

18
Anthony Downs, *Inside Bureaucracy* (Boston: Little Brown, 1967), p. 134.

19
Thomas J. Scheff, "Control over Policy by Attendants in a Mental Hospital," *Journal of Health and Human Behavior* 2 (1961): 93-105. I have relied on the summary of Scheff's paper in David Mechanic, "Sources of Power in Lower Participants in Complex Organizations," *Administrative Science Quarterly* 7 (December 1962): 356-357.

20
Neal Gross, Joseph B. Giacquinta, and Marilyn Bernstein, *Implementing Organizational Innovations: A Sociological Analysis of Planned Educational Change* (New York: Basic Books, 1971), p. 39.

21
Gross, Giacquinta, and Bernstein, *Implementing Organizational Innovations*, p. 39. They also observe that most studies of planned organizational change were seriously flawed methodologically, and that very few studies focused on the implementation period itself. This period is our central object of concern in this book, and my own review of the literature supports the conclusions of these authors. Like them, I too regard the model coming out of the literature on the diffusion and adoption of innovation as of little use, and for the same reason: it takes individuals as the basic units of analysis and has little room for forces arising from organizational structure, like hierarchical domination and subordination (pp. 21-39).

22
Another reason not to identify implementation problems with the "bureaucracy problem," however the latter is construed, is that bureaucracy is often a solution rather than a problem. Imperfect it may be, but the world might be considerably more problematic without a bureaucratic solution than with it. What appears to be conservatism and inflexibility from one perspective may appear, from a different vantage, as wisdom accumulated through experience and as durability against the many vicissitudes of politics and social transformations.

23
Martha Derthick, *New Towns In-Town* (Washington, D.C.: The Urban Institute, 1972), p. 83.

24
Derthick, *New Towns*, p. 84.

25
Derthick, *New Towns*, p. 83, n1.

26
See her recent work *Between State and Nation: Regional Organizations of the United States*, with the assistance of Gary Bombardier (Washington, D.C.: The Brookings Institution, 1974).

27
Morton Grodzins, "The Federal System," in *Goals for Americans* (Englewood Cliffs, N.J.: Prentice-Hall, 1960).

28
Derthick, *New Towns*, p. 95.

29
Derthick, *New Towns*, p. 101.

30
Derthick, *New Towns*, pp. 101-102.

31
Jeffrey L. Pressman and Aaron Wildavsky, *Implementation* (Berkeley: University of California Press, 1973), p. 93.

32
Pressman and Wildavsky, *Implementation*, p. 93.

33
Pressman and Wildavsky, *Implementation*, p. 93.

34
Pressman and Wildavsky, *Implementation*, pp. 106-107.

35
I am sorry to say that this work will not surpass the EDA study in this regard. For that reason among others I am particularly grateful to Pressman's and Wildavsky's account, which I draw upon frequently throughout the rest of this book.

36
Pressman and Wildavsky, *Implementation*, p. xii.

37
Although Bunker writes near the beginning of his paper that "Implementation may be viewed as a set of socio-political processes flowing from and anticipated by early phases of the policy process" ("Policy Sciences Perspectives," p. 72), the conception his final algorithm suggests is altogether static. Inadvertently, Bunker retreats from this initial view of a dynamic "set of socio-political processes" to a very stationary conception of structure, in which the only conceivable element of

action or change is "power resources." What exactly a "power resource" is, however, remains undefined.

38
Pressman and Wildavsky, *Implementation*, p. 113.

39
Pressman and Wildavsky, *Implementation*, p. 118.

40
Pressman and Wildavsky, *Implementation*, pp. 118-119. These assumptions are arbitrary indeed. One wishes the authors had actually taken the pains to estimate the delay for each of their seventy clearance points, a difficult but not impossible task.

41
Pressman and Wildavsky, *Implementation*, p. 122.

42
Pressman and Wildavsky, *Implementation* p. 122.

43
Pressman and Wildavsky, *Implementation*, p. 120.

44
Mancur Olson, Jr., *The Logic of Collective Action* (Cambridge, Mass.: Harvard University Press, 1965).

45
See Allison's comparable usage and his justification, "Conceptual Models," p. 708, esp. fn 79. See also the usage in Norton Long's classic article, "The Local Community as an Ecology of Games," *American Sociological Review* 64 (November 1968): 251-261.

46
As with "game theory," we shall ignore the large body of literature on "systems theory."

I
Implementation Games

3 | The Diversion of Resources

Our concern is only for those implementation games that have adverse effects on the program-assembly process. These adverse effects are of four general types: (1) the diversion of resources, especially money, which ought properly to be used to obtain, or to create, certain program elements, (2) the deflection of policy goals stipulated in the original mandate, (3) resistance to explicit, and usually institutionalized, efforts to control behavior administratively, and (4) the dissipation of personal and political energies in game-playing that might otherwise be channeled into constructive programmatic action. This and the next three chapters group implementation games according to their dominant adverse effects. It should be emphasized, however, that a game may have more than one type of adverse effect. The grouping of games is, ultimately, therefore, somewhat arbitrary.

Easy Money

Governments raise and spend a lot of money. In fiscal 1973, federal, state, and local governments spent $433 billion, about two-thirds of which was raised from taxes.[1] It should not surprise us that most individuals and organizations who receive money from the government, whether they are civil servants, consultants, or contractors, tend to provide less in the way of exchange than many government officials and most taxpayers would like. The same is true, after all, of those who receive money from the corporate sector—the corporate buyers would like a little more from them than they actually get. In their turn, those who buy consumer goods from the corporate sector would like a little more than they get. The world is full of people exchanging goods, services, and money with each other and all being better off for it even though the parties to the exchange normally are not as satisfied as if they had walked off with the total "utility surplus" created by the exchange instead of just a portion of it. It is not necessary to argue that government parts with money more easily, that is, in exchange for less, than do corporations or consumers, though the fact that it *can* and does do so is of special concern to us here. The government purse may or may not be an unusually easy target, but it is unusually rich. The Easy Money game is played by parties in the private sector who wish to make off with a portion of its contents in exchange for program elements of "too little value."[2]

The game is not necessarily illegal. World Airways saw EDA funds as "an aid in increasing their capital facilities, while the EDA Oakland task force was primarily interested in the rapid development of jobs for unemployed minorities."[3] There was of course nothing illegal in their having a different set of priorities. In fact, one would be hard pressed to say their posture was particularly immoral. World's assumption from the start was that the EDA's minority-hiring objectives would not be incongruent with their own profit-making objectives under certain conditions having to do with labor markets and the business cycle. But what if those projected conditions were too optimistic? World did not want to be responsible for fulfilling its side of the bargain if the terms turned out to be too costly. As the attorney for World wrote on February 20, 1969, "World and EDA recognize the extreme complexity of predicting business expansion and recognize the speculative nature of training programs of organizations such as the East Bay Skills Center as to their ability to train the unemployed and the under-employed for entry level jobs in the airline industry."[4] EDA was not paying World to cut its own throat, after all.

Or was it? The nature of the agreement between World, the port, and the EDA was never entirely clear. Nor could it have been. The EDA was willing to pay money in exchange for a guarantee and a certain commitment to find or invent ways to fulfill the guarantee. But World was obviously unwilling to go to great lengths to be inventive were the need to arise. To do so would almost certainly have entailed costs, and the terms of their deal would have been that much less advantageous. These did not get raised at the outset of the negotiations, however. The EDA's bargaining position at the outset was not strong. The EDA could only hope that the business environment would be favorable and that World would act not only in good faith but with an extra measure of creativity and effort should the situation require it.

As the project took form, however, World seems to have been able to maneuver the EDA into a losing position. More and more it represented itself as unable to promise as much as it had intimated at first, and as time passed, the EDA found itself increasingly locked into its position. If it did not go with World it could not go with anyone, and all its investments in the project (both financial and political) would be wiped out. Here is one variant of the Easy Money game. Perhaps if one were to categorize this formally, it would be called a bilateral monopoly game with only one round of play. If the game were to have been played over a period of many years and across a whole range of different issues, World would probably have tried to be more accommodating in this one case.

Another variant of the Easy Money game, which cynics might call Boondoggle, may be found in the dismal history of the San Francisco Bay Area Rapid Transit District (BARTD). In this case the easy money went to the consulting engineers, the joint venture group of Parsons-Brinckerhoff-Tudor-Bechtel (PBTB). They became the BARTD's principal consultants in May 1959, two years after the state legislature created the district. The contract with BARTD has proved quite lucrative, and it was intended to be so.[5] PBTB was to provide all engineering services involved in design and construction management, and it was also to maintain "continuing liaison with all affected and concerned public agencies and political authorities." The engineers were to receive reimbursement for "all net costs, charges, and expenses incurred in the proper performance of services." Under a separate retainer agreement, PBTB was to receive consulting fees based in part on the overall expenses of the project. This arrangement not only provided no incentive to cut down on costs and avoid mistakes, it gave a positive incentive to increase costs and expenses. As of 1972 the original (1962) $47 million estimate for engineering fees had more than doubled.

One rationale for this lucrative arrangement was that the BARTD directors wanted to ensure high-quality consulting services. But there is circumstantial evidence that the BARTD directors and the engineering group were also playing the Easy Money game, though there was nothing strictly illegal about it. In his study of the BARTD, Stephen Zwerling summarizes the "doubts" expressed to him by "many people" about the district's "standards of professional conduct and the integrity of management" this way: "BARTD has been careful not to do anything illegal, but aside from this proviso, anything else is possible."[6] The BARTD directors concluded their retainer agreement with PBTB in 1962 without competitive bidding. None of the district directors at the time knew anything about engineering, a fact clearly established in the course of a taxpayers' suit against the district in 1963. Only one of the district's sixteen employees at the time "had more than a passing acquaintance with engineering matters,"[7] and that employee had been appointed to the staff on the strong recommendation of a senior partner in the joint venture group.[8]

The Easy Money game can still be played as it was in the days of Lincoln Steffens, complete with graft, kickbacks, bribes, and the like. These games are more often played at the state and local level than at the federal level, but they are probably a lot less prevalent at all levels of government than they were in Steffens's time or even twenty years ago. They are, of course, illegal, and they are so well known that there is little point in commenting on them beyond noting that they exist. They provide an interesting contrast, however, with some of the newer Easy Money games that we have seen exposed in the last decade. The newer games also involve unscrupulous abuses of public trust and public money. Typically, however, they stay within the limits of the law—but only because the players have been very ingenious. Their impact is on governmental *programs* rather than on the institution of government, which was the target of the older style of corruption. The complexity of programs rather than the venality of officials is at the root of the new corruption. One hears, for example, of businessmen attracted by the lure of federal subsidies for training the unemployed in the JOBS program firing and then rehiring their own "unemployed" workers. Physicians caring for Medicare and Medicaid patients have in some cases managed to develop a sort of vertically integrated monopoly, treating patients on a fee-for-service basis, then placing them in nursing homes in which they themselves owned a substantial interest, and then procuring kickbacks from pharmacists to whom they promised the home's business (if they did not purchase the drugs from a pharmacy they themselves owned). Nursing homes are also convenient sites to mass-produce a number of "patient visits," reimbursable under Medicare or Medicaid. A U.S. General Accounting Office investigation in Ohio turned up the case of one doctor who billed for 487 patient visits in a sixteen-day period, including 90 on one day and 86 on another, while handling his usual load of non-Medicaid patients. These and many other fascinating abuses are reported by Mary Adelaide Mendelson in her recent book on the nursing home industry, *Tender Loving Greed.*[9] Unfortunately, neither this nor any other exposé of similar abuses suggests what impact they have on overall program performance, especially in the light of the numerous other factors that tend to pull down performance. That Easy Money games do have an impact on cost escalation, as opposed to performance, no one can doubt; but it is hard to say how much of one.

The Budget Game

One reason the players of Easy Money can do so well is that their nominal adversaries are government bureaus. One of the basic facts of bureaucratic life is that bureaucrats cannot legally appropriate for their own private use any savings they can effect on behalf of the government or the bureau.[10] Nor do they pay especially severe penalties for performance failures. Indeed, the opposite is often the case. The less well a bureau performs, the larger the task left to be accomplished, the larger the bureau may be permitted to grow, and the greater the promotion and advancement possibilities for the bureaucrats. Possibly in this connection one may take note of C. Northcote Parkinson's observation that the growth in the British Admiralty and in the British Colonial Office occurred most rapidly when there was the least apparent need for their services.[11] Of course, to the extent that government programs succeed at all much of the success is due to the bureaucratic form of organization, and many bureaucratic games are highly functional. Nevertheless, it should also be recognized that many contribute to delay and increased costs, and others impair overall performance capability even while contributing to certain sponsor-defined objectives.

On the whole, heads of bureaus, and perforce many of their subordinates down the line, are budget maximizers. They, therefore, do what they can to win favor in the eyes of officials in the legislature and at the highest political levels of the administration. They also do what they can to avoid falling from favor. What they do with respect to implementing some policy mandate, therefore, depends in large part on the incentives shaped for them by those who control their budgets. This is the Budget game.

For an agency such as the EDA, these incentives were to "move money."[12] Its relative success or failure in this particular task was tangible and immediately available for assessment. Congressmen did not wish to wait three or four years to appraise the agency's performance with respect to what the EDA's original sponsors would have regarded as its true mission, namely, providing jobs for the hard-core unemployed. The projects proposed by the Port of Oakland, which the EDA embraced quite warmly at first, were not chosen because they were "the best," nor even because they were particularly "good," but because they were the only ones "ready to go." In this case the bureaucratic game of Budget meshed very well with the Easy Money game of a party in the private sector, World Airways.

As part of their Budget game, moving money somehow, somewhere, and fast, even at the price of programmatic objectives, is the characteristic strategy of virtually every governmental agency that channels grants to other levels of government or to nonprofit institutions. This was true for the predecessor agency of the EDA, the Area Redevelopment Administration. It has been true of the Office of Economic Opportunity, the Federal Highway Administration, the Office of Education, the Law Enforcement Assistance Administration, and a host of others. It is no surprise that very often the social objectives of a new money-moving agency are sacrificed to its so-called "maintenance" objectives, that is, the activities it must engage in simply to survive as an agency. It is also no surprise that the sacrifice becomes more complete as time passes and the agency's officials learn that their agency can survive and even prosper by continuing such a course. Hence, one expects to find that the older a money-moving agency grows the less adventurous and ideological it becomes. This tendency is produced by many conditions, to be sure, but it is surely reinforced quite strongly by the political reward structure to which it is continually harnessed.

Grant-giving bureaus are often involved in games with grant-receiving bureaus as well, the latter playing a game similar to Budget that may be called Funding. The object of Funding is to secure not only money but flexibility in regard to its use. The recipient bureau seeks to maximize the size of its grant while minimizing the constraints on how it must spend the monies. It seeks flexibility in transferring the funds among as many of the activities in which it is engaged, or in which it would like to engage, as possible. Typically, it is an intergovernmental game, in which a bureau at a "lower" level of government attempts to secure flexible funds from a grant-giving bureau at a "higher" level, but it is also played by nominally nonprofit organizations (and individuals) seeking government funds. The basic rules are that a donor bureau makes a grant to a receiving bureau or similar entity in exchange for a promise by the recipient to use the funds—in our terms, a "program element"—for a certain purpose desired by the donor.

The strategies available to the principal players are numerous, and there are usually opportunities for using more than one strategy at a time. The first strategy the recipient may use is to inflate the estimated costs of achieving the purposes of the donor bureau. Since it is very expensive to develop high-quality information about such costs, donor bureaus often tolerate at least a little, and sometimes a lot, of padding. This padding can then be used as discretionary funds. Once the recipient has secured an inflated grant from the donor, the donor has little incentive to police the spending of the grant beyond the point of satisfying itself that some acceptable minimum was spent on initially stipulated purposes. To police the expenditures too carefully would create a risk that it would have to withdraw funds and thereby undermine its own strategy in its Budget game. Once the recipient bureau has the money in hand, its principal strategic problem is to avoid such flagrant manipulation of its funds that the donor agency will be obliged to respond to pressure from its own supervisors to step in and police the recipient's expenditure behavior more closely. In a sense, its strategic problem reduces to a number of smaller tactical problems. It is easier to understand these tactics in the Funding game as played by the recipients if we shift our perspective to the limitations on the surveillance and monitoring tactics of the donor bureau.

The donor bureau typically cannot specify its own purposes well or the indicators by which it will judge whether or not these purposes have been achieved. What, after all, is meant by the "rehabilitation" of a mentally disturbed person or "meeting the special educational needs of educationally deprived children"? How can one tell when these purposes have been accomplished? By means of standardized tests? By means of professional "judgment"? By means of expressed client satisfaction? Since many governmental programs have these necessarily vague objectives and indicators of success, there is a strong tendency on the part of both donors and recipients of grant funds to talk about program "outputs" rather than program "outcomes," for example, about the number of "units of service" rendered by an outpatient clinic or the number of children who have viewed a special ethnic studies exhibit, rather than about the improvement in mental health status of individuals served or the increase in feelings of personal efficacy and achievement motivation.[13] These "outputs" have meaning, of course, only if the program "activities" they describe are meaningful. But it is no easy thing to say what are legitimate activities, either before the granting of funds or in the course of a subsequent review. What can one say about a visit to a beautician as an activity bearing on the alleviation or prevention of mental illness? About the rehabilitative effect of mental hospital patients sweeping the hospital corridors of weeding the potato patch on the hospital farm? About the therapeutic effects, for that matter, of telling one's dreams to a silent and shadow-cloaked psychiatrist? It frequently happens, therefore, that the donor bureau provides funds, for, and therefore monitors, not an outcome nor even an output but some programmatic *input*, such as a crisis intervention team or a staff psychiatrist assigned to make the rounds of the county jails. This monitoring strategy is limited, however, by the donor bureau's unwillingness to specify in minute detail what the programmed inputs should be—the donor wants the recipient to have *some* flexibility, after all—and by the great costs of monitoring the activities of personnel to ascertain how much of their energies go into the activities to which they are nominally assigned and how much into other activities the donor has little interest in supporting.

Even when a donor bureau knows exactly what it wants and how much it costs, it may still not know how much it ought to pay. The reason is that most bureaus in any given Funding game are not in one such game but in many. Budget analysts in the California State Department of Mental Hygiene tried unsuccessfully for years to ascertain how much federal grant money was being received by county mental health programs and by private providers under contract to the county programs. Under L-P-S, the state was paying for 90 percent (and the counties, ten percent) of these programs (known in California as "Short-Doyle" programs). There was a strong suspicion that recipient bureaus were in effect being paid twice for providing the same service, with the surplus being siphoned off into other services for which funding was less available.

Finally, there is the problem of monitoring maintenance of effort. Edward Banfield cites the example of OEO withdrawing $35,000 from the support of a legal services program in Seattle just after the Model Cities agency agreed to expand the program with that amount of funding.[14] In one Short-Doyle program, state auditors found that the local Community Chest agency had reduced its support of a certain nonprofit contract provider in exact correspondence with the provider's enhanced access to Short-Doyle funds following the passage of L-P-S. School districts are often very adroit at making "categorical" grant funds into "general aid" by allowing the grant funds simply to displace general purpose funds, which are then used to expand some other portion of the district's program.[15]

One of the reasons that intergovernmental "revenue sharing" has become so popular is that the categorical grant system had allegedly been substantially or even totally decategorized as a result of what we have called the Funding game. If our understanding of how the game is played is correct, however, this extreme view of categorical grants might not be justified. The categorical grant system gives other players in the implementation game the opportunity to demand some minimally acceptable level of expenditures on the purposes for which the grant is nominally given. The players of Funding do not have total flexibility. As Murphy pointed out with respect to Title I of ESEA, certain implementation successes were achieved by legal and political pressure on several bureaucratic levels. The categorical specifications of the donor agency (and Congress) were indispensable for this purpose. That the Funding game can result in the erosion of mandated policy and program objectives is beyond question. The important questions have to do with whether the game can be held within certain limits of minimal acceptability and whether the "excess" financial costs are acceptable.

Easy Life

Most civil servants do not earn particularly handsome salaries and wages, and many feel entitled to take additional compensation by tailoring their work environment to suit themselves as much as possible. They can ordinarily get away with more than workers in private industry, who play the same game, of course, because they are protected by civil service rules and also because the ultimate impact of their Easy Life game is diffused among the public who must deal with the bureau as customers or clients or objects of regulation. Another reason that Easy Life is so often played successfully is that services in the public sector are frequently rationed by queuing, either through lines at service windows or through waiting lists. Easy Life becomes in effect a game played by bureaucrats against a relatively powerless, voiceless, and disorganized public.[16]

Under certain conditions, we should emphasize, even the easiest bureaucratic life that can be devised is not particularly easy, especially when bureaucrats have a sense of professional obligation to perform certain essential services. Physicians working in a county hospital emergency ward (who must be counted as "bureaucrats" in this instance) must run fast only to stay in place. Also, during periods of transition from one program design to another there may be a lot of confusion, the result of which is to force a certain unit to add a new set of services to its repertoire while continuing the old ones as well, until some new unit is sufficiently broken in to handle some or all of the old ones. This latter difficulty afflicted a number of county public guardian offices charged with L-P-S conservatorship investigation functions of persons alleged to be "gravely disabled as a result of mental disorder."

Sophisticated policy designers will know that bureaucrats play Easy Life and may try to counter with their own Management game (see Chapter 5), either to increase narrowly defined cost-efficiency or to ensure that new monies are used to increase the quality of performance. (One may suspect that the former motive is much more prevalent.) Ironically, the result may sometimes be the opposite of that intended. In 1962, Congress authorized vast new expenditures on social casework services to welfare clients. Yet, of 1,974 welfare workers in Massachusetts interviewed by Derthick, 22 percent felt they gave *less* service after 1962 than before. The reason given was that the federal paperwork requirements designed to monitor the quality and quantity of services displaced their established and customary services not credited by federal standards.[17]

Pork Barrel

Scarce financial resources are often diverted and dissipated through the venerable political game of Pork Barrel. This is the elected official's version of Budget or Easy Money. The Pork Barrel aspects of a program often come to define expectations and to legitimize demands. An excess of such demands may undermine the ability of the program managers to focus and concentrate resources up to some supposed threshold point below which any expenditures at all are likely to be ineffective. The case of the Area Redevelopment Administration (ARA) is instructive here.[18] Senator Paul Douglas, when he introduced his first "depressed areas" bill in 1955, envisioned a business loan program reaching into only forty or fifty labor-market areas, mostly urban. As it became increasingly clear that votes would be required from senators and representatives from rural areas, particularly those in the South, Douglas progressively relaxed his eligibility criteria. His first concession, in 1956, was to permit up to 300 counties in rural areas to be deemed eligible—those with the largest number and percentage of low-income farm families. He further limited to 15 the number of such counties that might be designated in any state. By 1960, he was obliged to accept a list of 662 rural counties designated by procedures employed by the House Committee on Banking and Currency. As a further concession to Senator William Proxmire of Wisconsin, who had been an ally of Douglas in his long struggle for depressed areas legislation, language was drafted urging the administrator of the act "to distribute the projects widely among the several States . . . in order that actual experience with this program may be had in as many States and in as many areas and under as many different circumstances as possible."[19] In the legislative stage it was "generally agreed," moreover, "that Indians living on reservations were an economically distressed group and that any program to aid depressed areas should include them."[20]

The administrative history of the act expanded its coverage even further, against the better judgment of the ARA administrators but in response to political pressures of several kinds. The Agriculture Department had lost the battle to control that part of the program that would serve rural areas. Hence, "as a sop to farm lobbies and to placate the Department of Agriculture," the ARA designated as eligible recipients all 230 counties selected by Agriculture for its rural redevelopment program, without reference to the level of income or unemployment in these counties. Fewer than one-third would have qualified had these latter criteria been applied. The ARA also included 24 counties under a procedure known as "rounding out": designating as eligible a cluster of counties not otherwise eligible that happened to be geographically contiguous with an eligible county. The ostensible reason was that such a cluster "constituted a single economic unit," but the real reason was that the ARA needed to accommodate congressmen who had voted for the legislation and who had made certain promises to their constituents about help they might expect. Finally, the ARA used the ingenious device of breaking up the boundaries of labor market areas officially designated as such (by the Bureau of Employment Security) in order to qualify one of the component counties for assistance. This device was used to qualify Passaic County, New Jersey (in the Passaic-Paterson area), and Schenectady County, New York (in the Albany-Troy-Schenectady area).[21]

Politics not only extended the bounds of eligibility, it also kept them extended despite original errors of classification on the part of ARA officials. Forty counties that had been misclassified as eligible in 1961 on the basis of inaccurate unemployment insurance data were found to be ineligible on the basis of 1960 census data made available only in 1962. "Once the original mistake had been committed, however, the agency found it difficult to retrace its steps. There were usually interests in any given area that saw in the designation such possible benefits as lower interest rates on SBA loans or preferential treatment in government procurement."[22] Also, the Kennedy Administration proposed in the spring of 1962 a program of accelerated public works. Counties designated ARA-eligible were automatically favored under that program, and "it became politically unfeasible to terminate the designation of [these] areas," in all but twenty-four cases.

As a result of all these pressures the ARA, after eight months in business, had approved some 900 counties as eligible for assistance. In these supposedly depressed areas lived fully a sixth of the total U.S. population, among whom were to be counted nearly a third of the country's total of unemployed.[23] In his book on the ARA, Sar Levitan remarks: "This raises the crucial question whether a meaningful program can be developed to aid depressed areas with the limited resources allocated by Congress when the program is so thinly spread."[24]

When the EDA was created out of the ashes of the ARA, in 1965, it is not surprising that "Every consultant to EDA recommended that projects be concentrated in a single growth center in each district." The consultants recommended in vain, however, "Because congressmen had to gain support from constituents all over, the resources were spread."[25]

The story with Model Cities is the same. In mid-1964, President Johnson created a Metropolitan and Urban Affairs Task Force, one of the by-products of which was a recommendation made by at least three members independently, but not included in the Task Force's final report, that the federal government "adopt" two or three large cities and also build a whole new one "in order to show what could be accomplished by well-conceived, large-scale, concerted effort."[26] Budget Director Charles L. Schultze suggested that "saturation" spending had a high potential payoff but could be done in no more than five or ten cities. A second task force, admonished by Senator Abraham Ribicoff that Congress would not buy an expensive program with such narrowly distributed benefits, proposed 66 demonstration cities. The original authorizing legislation raised the number to 75; and a year later, following Republican displeasure at the fact that all but nine of the first 63 grants awarded were to cities represented by Democrats, Congress halved the appropriations and doubled the number of cities to 150.

Pork Barrel politics also sapped the resources of local community action programs of the War on Poverty. One of the most egregious examples comes from the history of the Philadelphia Council for Community Advancement. For the first two or three years there was indecisive competition among "establishment" health and welfare agencies, compounded, complicated, and exaggerated after a point by the insurgency of the Philadelphia NAACP chapter led by an articulate and demagogic lawyer, Cecil Moore. Mayor James Tate then intervened to settle the issue in favor of a committee weighted heavily with grassroots poor people, who turned the agency into a patronage distributor—and away from more broadly gauged reform strategies. As two careful students of the subject sum it up: ". . . efforts to organize blacks and other minority groups were minor at best. Representatives of the poor instead concentrated on securing payment for themselves and positions of employment for their family and friends. The Council for Community

Advancement eagerly sought to cooperate with these requests, for it focused energies of the representatives of the poor on patronage concerns rather than policy questions . . ."[27]

Notes

1
Tax Foundation, *Facts and Figures on Government Finance* (New York, 1975), pp. 15, 19. Original data comes from the U.S. Bureau of the Census.

2
How much is "too little" and how valuable is it to whom? To answer such questions would take us down the tortuous and not very well marked path of public choice theory, wherein I have no competency as a guide.

3
Jeffrey L. Pressman and Aaron Wildavsky, *Implementation* (Berkeley: University of California Press, 1973), p. 30.

4
Pressman and Wildavsky, *Implementation*, pp. 56-57.

5
Stephen Zwerling, "The Political Consequences of Technological Choice: Public Transit in the San Francisco Metropolitan Area," Ph.D. dissertation (Department of Political Science, University of California, Berkeley, 1972), p. 69. I have relied on Zwerling's dissertation for the entirety of this account of BARTD. A somewhat revised version has recently been published as *Mass Transit and the Politics of Technology: A Study of BART and the San Francisco Bay Area* (New York: Praeger, 1974).

6
Zwerling, "Political Consequences," p. 108, n14.

7
Zwerling, "Political Consequences," p. 67.

8
Completion of the BART system is more than three years behind schedule, its construction costs have exceeded the original estimates by well over 50 percent, and it has become apparent to every disinterested party that has studied the system in recent years that the system will certainly run up high operating deficits, despite the BARTD's proclaimed intention to "live out of the fare box."

9
Mary Adelaide Mendelson, *Tender Loving Greed* (New York: Knopf, 1974), p. 74. Mendelson clearly wishes to establish her roots in the Steffens tradition, in that she entitles the first chapter "The Shame of Nursing Homes: The Fraud of Tender Loving Care." From an analytical perspective, however, there is probably more difference than similarity between the older sort of abuse and the newer sort. The comparison would make a fascinating study.

10
For the purposes of this book I use "bureau" as a generic term to cover many public organizations and most nonprofit private organizations. This first fact of

bureaucratic life is actually a defining characteristic of bureaus. The second defining characteristic is that "some part of the recurring revenues of the organization derive from other than the sale of output as a per unit rate." William A. Niskanen, Jr., *Bureaucracy and Representative Government* (Chicago: Aldine-Atherton, 1971), p. 15. See also Anthony Downs's four defining characteristics, of which the most important for his theory is that "the major portion of its output is not directly or indirectly evaluated in any markets external to the organization by means of voluntary *quid pro quo* transaction." *Inside Bureaucracy* (Boston: Little, Brown, 1967), p. 25.

11

C. Northcote Parkinson, *Parkinson's Law and Other Studies in Administration* (Boston: Houghton Mifflin, 1962).

12

Pressman and Wildavsky, *Implementation*, pp. 138-139.

13

For further elaboration of the distinction between "outputs" and "outcomes," see Frank Levy, Arnold Meltsner, and Aaron Wildavsky, *Urban Outcomes* (Berkeley: University of California Press, 1974).

14

Edward C. Banfield, "Making a New Federal Program: Model Cities, 1964-68," in Allan P. Sindler, ed., *Policy and Politics in America* (Boston: Little, Brown, 1973), p. 152.

15

See Jerome T. Murphy, *State Education Agencies and Discretionary Funds* (Lexington, Mass.: D. C. Heath, 1974).

16

For an interesting example of how a university library coped with escalating service demands, see Richard L. Meier, "Communications Overload: Proposals from the Study of a University Library," *Administrative Science Quarterly* 9 (1963): 521-544.

17

Martha Derthick, *The Influence of Federal Grants: Public Assistance in Massachusetts* (Cambridge, Mass.: Harvard University Press, 1970), pp. 149-151. Only 36 workers felt they gave more services than before. The other 99 felt there had been no change in the amount of services, but 61 of these mentioned the increase in record-keeping activity.

18

I have relied for this section on the ARA on Sar A. Levitan, *Federal Aid to Depressed Areas: An Evaluation of the Area Redevelopment Administration* (Baltimore: Johns Hopkins University Press, 1964).

19
Levitan, *Federal Aid*, pp. 55-60.

20
Levitan, *Federal Aid*, p. 60.

21
Levitan, *Federal Aid*, pp. 63-64.

22
Levitan, *Federal Aid*, p. 65.

23
Levitan, *Federal Aid*, pp. 64, 80.

24
Levitan, *Federal Aid*, p. 80.

25
Martin Rein and Francine Rabinovitz, "Implementation: A Theoretical Perspective" (draft paper), p. 48.

26
Banfield, "Making a New Federal Program," pp. 128-129.

27
J. David Greenstone and Paul E. Peterson, *Race and Authority in Urban Politics* (New York: Russell Sage Foundation, 1973), pp. 28-29.

4 | The Deflection of Goals

The goals embodied in a policy mandate typically undergo some change during the implementation phase. They might have been ambiguous and therefore might have required, or at least permitted, further definition. Or they might have been based on a very weak consensus, hastily, and perhaps insincerely, contrived during the contest surrounding the adoption of the mandate. Indeed, interests opposed to the goals of the mandate might have stayed quiet during the adoption contest precisely because they counted on subsequent opportunities to achieve more decisive, and less publicized, victories during the struggle over implementation. As we acknowledged above, implementation is the continuation of politics by other means. The politics of renegotiating goals can lead in several directions: trimming them back, distorting or preventing them, and even adding to them in a manner that eventually leads to an unsupportable political burden.

Piling On

Ironically, the initial successes of a new program contain the potential for its longer-run debilitation. As onlookers see the new program begin to move in its intended direction, some see it as a new political resource, an opportunity to throw their own goals and objectives onto the heap. The net effect of a large number of additional objectives added to the heap may topple it. The sponsoring coalition, which had been supporting one load contentedly, may disintegrate under the heavier burden.

One can see these adverse effects of the Piling On game in the collapse of Project Mohole, a government venture in "big science."[1] In the spring of 1957 a small group of scientists conceived the idea of drilling through the ocean bottom to a hypothesized layer just below the earth's crust and above the earth's mantle known as the Mohorovičić discontinuity, or more popularly as the Moho. The scientists successfully sought funding from the National Science Foundation (NSF), but received it only on the condition that supervision of the effort be given to an established scientific body. The scientists were part of a distinguished but esoteric group known as AMSOC, the American Miscellaneous Society, which specialized in the invention of half-frivolous, half-serious scientific ideas (like towing icebergs from the Antarctic to provide Los Angeles with water). AMSOC affiliated with the National Academy of Sciences (NAS), and in the spring of 1958, NSF made a grant of $15,000 to AMSOC through NAS for initial feasibility studies. The studies were successfully completed in 1961, when the *Cuss I* drilled to a depth of 11,700 feet and retrieved a sample of basalt from 560 feet below the ocean bottom. The drilling phase cost NSF another $1.5 million. Everyone was enthusiastic, including the House Appropriations Subcommittee on Oceanography, which encouraged NSF to continue funding.

At this point a fissure began to separate the executive secretary of AMSOC, Willard Bascom, from the rest of the AMSOC group, from the NAS, and also from NSF. Bascom saw the project as having larger possibilities than simply reaching the Moho: it would be of great scientific interest to undertake widespread sampling of the sedimentary layers above the Moho in order to add to our understanding the history of the oceans and of life itself. A turnover in the AMSOC chairmanship, in July 1961, brought Bascom and equally vigorous and articulate ally, Hollis D. Hedberg, professor of geology at Princeton and a vice-president of Gulf Oil Company. Under Hedberg's leadership, AMSOC eventually swung around to support the broad-gauge objective.

After considerable controversy, the Houston engineering firm of Brown and Root was selected as the contractor. Bascom and some other scientists from NAS resigned to form an independent consulting group, Ocean Science Engineering (OSE), which spent May and June of 1962 in Houston informing and advising Brown and Root. Brown and Root thought their charge from NAS was to drill to the Moho, but Bascom and OSE kept insisting that their mission was the broader one of developing the technology to support a more general ocean-drilling program. The concrete issue that drew these two conflicting objectives into clearer focus was whether to build a single drilling platform to permit penetration to the Moho or to build an intermediate ship, an "experimental laboratory drilling vessel of moderate depth capacity," as Hedberg put it. Sides began to form around the option of one ship and the Moho versus the option of two ships and the Moho plus a program of extensive oceanographic study.

In the fall of 1962, Kermit Gordon, the director of the Bureau of the Budget (BOB), expressed concern that the project's total costs had escalated from the initial estimate of $15-20 million to at least $50 million.

The friction between the contractor (Brown and Root) and AMSOC, and between AMSOC and the NAS and NSF, could not be concealed. Nor could the mounting cost projections, which by early 1963 had swelled to nearly $70 million. In June and again in October-November 1963, House committees held two separate hearings on the status of the Moho project. There was open conflict between AMSOC and the other two scientific bodies. On the senate side, Senator Gordon Allott of Colorado wrote a suspension of funding into the Senate Appropriations Committee report that had to be softened in the conference committee to stipulate that NSF work out plans for Project Mohole with BOB.

By 1964, Project Mohole was beginning to receive adverse publicity in scientific journals and in the newspapers. BOB began to turn a more critical and closely surveying eye on the project. In 1965, the bids came in from four shipbuilding firms that proposed to construct the large drilling platform specified by Brown and Root. They were alarmingly high. Project Mohole now could not possibly cost less than $100 million. An NAS advisory committee opined that the gains in scientific knowledge would justify even that large expenditure; and besides, if Project Mohole were dropped, "The blow to our national prestige . . . would be severe." However, the House Appropriations subcommittee overseeing Mohole was not persuaded. The full House went along with the subcommittee. The Senate's affirmative vote to continue appropriations for the project was beaten back in conference and, as Michael Reagan puts it in his account, Mohole became no hole.

The Mohole story is complicated by many factors, to be sure. But one clear inference is that the Bascom-Hedberg attempt to increase the project's scope and complexity was at the heart of its political, and to a degree its technical, problems. Their gambit divided the scientific community, increased the technical problems for the contractor, alienated necessary allies in the established agencies (NSF and NAS), and fueled the political opposition that had opposed the project from the start even in its less ambitious versions. Perhaps it was, from their point of view, a risk well worth taking. Had it worked out, we would no doubt have given them a high place in the pantheon of "big science" scientists, just below the great cyclotron builders like Ernest Lawrence. As it is, their failure is instructive politically. We may not know much more about the Moho discontinuity as a result of their efforts, but the story of their failure adds a great deal to our understanding of a possible discontinuity in implementation politics caused by the Piling On effect.

One lesson, and perhaps the most important one, is that the Piling On game is in part a game of chance. It is not a foregone conclusion that the play of the game will dissipate political support—always a critical program element—and so undermine the original sponsors' objectives. Indeed, the game might enhance them. This is the scenario usually envisioned by liberal reformers who are willing to start a program on a small scale in the hopes that its initial performance will allay conservatives' fears and thus sap their will to resist subsequent attempts to expand the scope of the program. This was the strategy followed throughout the 1950s and early 1960s by the proponents of federal financing of health care services. In his insightful study of the politics of passing Medicare and Medicaid in 1965, Theodore Marmor refers to this as an "incrementalist" strategy.[2] The American Medical Association, which was the chief opponent of a significant federal (or *any* governmental) role in this area from the early part of the century until 1965 or 1966, always argued that any step in this direction was a step toward government control of medical practice if not socialized medicine. Liberals always countered publicly that no such plan was in mind, but from Marmor's account it is clear that the AMA had something real to worry about. The eventual success of the liberal coalition in health care politics suggests another lesson about the play of the Piling On game. It is especially advantageous to play it when one has little to lose. In this respect the liberal coalition was in a very different position from Bascom and Hedberg. By following an "incrementalist strategy" the liberals had everything to gain and nothing to lose but time. Indeed, one may wonder whether it is proper to call it a strategy at all, since it appears from Marmor's account that they followed the only course that was open to them.

The risky nature of Piling On is perhaps best revealed in the recent disarray of the Democratic party and the political left. Many "old-fashioned" liberals nurtured on the hopes and ideals of the New Deal and postwar reformist politics were dismayed, on taking stock in the mid-1970s, at the ideological baggage they suddenly discovered aboard the political platform they had pulled for so long. Not only was there "equality of opportunity," there was "ethnic consciousness" and "affirmative action." The latter addition, moreover, often looked suspiciously like "quotas," always a bane of traditional liberal reform. Liberal reform was pulling not only blacks but nearly a dozen ethnic minorities, from Aleuts to women. And there was reason to believe that the last were not even a genuine ethnic minority, having no telltale skin color and constituting more than 50 percent of the population. Many traditional liberals deserted the coalition. To a certain extent their portion of the load was assumed by new joiners and by the ones who remained working twice as hard, though it cannot be denied that certain adverse effects of Piling On did occur. The liberal coalition in the Democratic party split badly in the 1972 presidential election campaign, and defections (whether expressed in nonvoting or in switching) toppled the party's candidate in the general election.[3]

Up for Grabs

As noted above, it frequently happens that the policy mandate that starts the implementation process in the first place is either ambiguous or halfhearted or both. The policy mandate may have been the result of strong pressures on government to "do something" about what is generally perceived to be an urgent social problem, even though no one quite knows what ought to or could be done. Or it may have been the result of a campaign waged by a powerful minority, to which some sort of appeasing gesture is deemed necessary on the part of the beleaguered majority. Or it may have been the product of a complex logrolling arrangement in which a weak mandate to do something easy and popular is packaged with a stronger mandate to do something hard and unpopular. In any case, the mandate will have provided certain program elements, usually a piece of bureaucracy and a modest budget, without clearly prescribing or even envisioning what other elements might be conjoined with them and to what exact purpose. In this confused situation, the few unambiguously mandated elements are Up for Grabs by a number of different potential clientele groups to be converted into political resources that can then be used to shape the policy or program goals in ways congenial to themselves.

The basic strategies used by clientele groups are oriented toward top agency personnel. Interests either attempt to control the appointment process, so as to place in power individuals of known and reliable sympathies, or they attempt to reeducate the individuals who do assume power.

The United States Small Business Administration is a good example of a subsidy program that has been Up for Grabs. The Eisenhower Administration created the SBA in 1953 as a concession to a certain form of liberal and populist congressional opinion that opposed the administration's desire to abolish the New Deal Reconstruction Finance Corporation (and which opinion also mistakenly held that RFC was a friend of "small business"). The administration made sure that it was kept under the control of the Department of Commerce and administrators with a "big business" point of view. Nevertheless, over the years, the "small business" advocates in Congress have reluctantly embraced the SBA as their own creation and tried to make of it what they could.[4] In the 1960s, the SBA was the locus of efforts to extend business loans to minority businessmen. It was drastically shaken up by Howard Samuels during the last years of the Johnson Administration. It was shaken back to its more conservative pre-Samuels condition by the Nixon Administration.[5]

Another example of how an unexpected clientele group came to influence, if not actually dominate, a service delivery program comes from the history of the Tennessee Valley Authority.[6] As the TVA began to set down roots in its region of operations, it became clear to the chairman of the TVA Board of Directors, David E. Lilienthal, that compromises would have to be reached with certain local barons. Lilienthal arranged for the appointment of Dr. Harcourt A. Morgan to the board and effectively turned over to him and his associates the administration of the authority's fertilizer program. In exchange Lilienthal received Morgan's political support at the national level for the TVA electric power program. Morgan was former president of the University of Tennessee and in effect "represented the relatively conservative institutional forces in the area, as those were expressed in the established agencies of state and local government." His local and conservative connections were quite valuable, in that "the agricultural extension services, organizations ramified through every county in the watershed, represented a formidable factor which might conceivably turn the scale of popular opinion from support or indifference into antagonism."[7] When TVA was in trouble in Congress in 1938, agricultural extension officials came to its aid. This support had a price, however, in diminished program performance, at least by the criteria held by those New Dealers and progressives who had fought for TVA. The Lilienthal-Morgan alignment "eventually spelled the doom of such development programs . . . as were not acceptable to the land-grant college group. These included an emphasis on self-help cooperatives, subsistence homesteads, rural zoning, and broad regional planning."[8]

Regulatory agencies and programs are notoriously Up for Grabs. Consider, for instance, the allegation that federal regulatory commissions have typically been captured by the industries they are supposed to regulate: the Interstate Commerce Commission by the railroads, the Civil Aeronautics Board by the "regular" (as opposed to the non-scheduled or "supplemental") airlines, the Food and Drug Aministration by the drug companies, and so on. To what extent and in what sense this allegation may be true certainly varies among the regulatory commissions, and it also depends on what one means by "captured." The customary meaning is at least that the regulators are "too soft" on the industry. Another meaning is that the industry gets the regulators to do its bidding, in particular that it induces the commission to exclude new entrants into the industry and assist those who are already in to modulate or entirely eliminate interfirm competition. The ICC, which has been captured by the railroads in the second sense, has actually been quite hard on the railroads in the first sense, in that the commission is indirectly responsible for the bankrupt condition of the country's rail lines. As agent for the railroads, the ICC has attempted, with some success, to force prices on barge and truck traffic subject to ICC regulation high enough so as not to encroach too much on the railroads' freight traffic. (The Achilles' heel of the ICC and the railroads is that much barge and truck freight traffic is not under ICC regulation.) It has also assisted railroads in effecting mergers and convening rate-setting conferences. It has in some instances impeded technical innovation by certain lines that would have permitted them to undercut their competitors by significant margins.[9] In a similar fashion, the regular airlines have indeed captured the CAB and have fashioned it into an instrument for enforcing cartellike behavior, such as setting identical fares between cities, that is probably more effective than even the Mafia. As the Professional Services Review Organizations (PSROs) become established in local communities ostensibly, and according to the design of legislative and administrative policy-makers at the national level, to introduce cost and quality controls into the delivery of federally supported medical care, we are likely to see a similar sort of perversion through capture by county medical societies. No doubt the process by which this occurs will be somewhat different in each locality, but the history of other governmental efforts at regulation strongly suggests that, one way or another, it will occur.

Keeping the Peace

A not insignificant number of policies and programs originate in the desire to extirpate real or imagined evil. Such policies create implementation opportunities for activists whom many political interests will perceive as "hotheads," "extremists," or "zealots." A counterreformation then sets in. A political coalition emerges to scrutinize, criticize, and in some cases to terrorize the agency charged with assaulting the stipulated evils.

The political leaders in the executive branch are usually in this game, though not always too openly. Their interest is in keeping the lid on, or in keeping matters from getting out of hand, or in calming troubled waters, or, most prosaically, in peace. The interests who were most active in the policy-adoption stage expect to have a say in, if not entirely to capture, the program that is being assembled. In the case of a mandate that has emerged from a particularly heated controversy, the interests who fought unsuccessfully to prevent the program from being authorized also expect to have a say and may even expect, or at least hope, to win back in the implementation game—particularly in the writing of regulations and guidelines—what they lost in the policy-adoption game. The bureaucrats who have been placed in charge of the first few program elements are typically compromise candidates minimally acceptable to all the contending forces though probably most responsive to the political executive. The play of the game by all these parties is characteristically unruly and is often accompanied by charges and countercharges of foul play, political cowardice, and irresponsible zealotry. There is ample room here for players and strategies from other games, in particular, Piling On, Easy Money, Pork Barrel, Territory, Tenacity, and Odd Man Out.[10]

This, at any rate, is an ideal-typical sketch of Keeping the Peace. Unfortunately, I have been unable to find much published case material illustrating the game. Moynihan's vivid, and probably somewhat jaundiced, account of community action programs is one source.[11] The history of the Environmental Protection Agency, when it is written, will probably provide another such account. The articulate and activist political constituency that brought it into being has critically supervised the agency since its beginning. An equally alert constituency of aggrieved industrialists (and other polluters) has suspiciously surveyed the agency from the other direction. The Nixon Administration appears to have kept the agency at arm's length, just close enough to keep it collared and just far enough to avoid guilt by association. The succession of agency directors and the more permanent staffers appear to be a weary and hapless crew. What other than physical and mental exhaustion could explain the agency's constant backing and filling, its promulgation of absurd car-pooling edicts one day and their rescission the next?

Federal, state, and local civil rights agencies are natural targets of this game. Officials in the U.S. Office of Education charged with enforcing antidiscrimination provisions of the 1964 Civil Rights Act (Title VI) spent much of their time in 1965 trying to fend off attacks from both the civil rights movement—"a constituency in search of an agency," as Gary Orfield put it—and the segregationists, all the while under pressure from the White House to keep the peace.[12] The White House, of course, was under pressure from Congress.

In his illuminating book on the Massachusetts Commission Against Discrimination, Leon Mayhew summarizes the effects of the shifting balance of political forces on state and local civil rights agencies as follows:

The protection of stability and legitimacy through compromise is an inescapable condition of successful enforcement. . . . All of the commissions established in the late forties and early fifties pursued moderate policies in their early years, but, in recent years, some state commissions have been able to take advantage of their more secure status to respond to the new demands of a larger, more vocal, and better organized Negro community. As the civil rights movement has gained more moral momentum, civil rights agencies have been able to muster countervailing power in the community in support of more militant programs of enforcement.[13]

Keeping the Peace, therefore, is a game in a constant state of change and development.

Notes

1

The account here draws upon Michael D. Reagan, "From Mohole to No Hole" (Syracuse: Inter-University Case Program, 1973).

2

Theodore R. Marmor, "The Congress: Medicare Politics and Policy," in Allan P. Sindler, ed., *American Political Institutions and Public Policy* (Boston: Little, Brown, 1969), pp. 3-66, esp. p. 20.

3

An interesting contrast may be drawn between Pork Barrel and Piling On. The former game risks programmatic impact for the sake of political support, whereas the latter game risks political support for the sake of programmatic impact.

4

Harmon Zeigler, *The Politics of Small Business* (Washington, D.C.: Public Affairs Press, 1961).

5

See Arthur I. Blaustein and Geoffrey Faux, *The Star-Spangled Hustle* (Garden City, New York: Doubleday, 1972).

6

See Philip A. Selznick, *TVA and the Grass Roots* (New York: Harper & Row, 1966).

7

Selznick, *TVA*, p. 92.

8

Selznick, *TVA*, p. 93. Selznick's interpretation of the dynamics behind this arrangement emphasizes the role of Lilienthal's and others' "grass roots" doctrine of administration, an older form of "community control" and "power to the people." In Selznick's view, the TVA progressives admitted—or "co-opted," in Selznick's famous phrase—Harcourt Morgan and the conservative agriculturalist faction almost as a Trojan horse. Not only did they compromise the authority's policy, they compromised the structure of the institution itself. (Chap. I and Preface to the 1966 edition, pp. xii-xiii). The relatively great significance attributed by Selznick to political ideology as opposed to pragmatic politics may be somewhat discounted, however, on the basis of evidence supplied by Selznick himself. Harcourt Morgan's fateful appointment to the board was made by President Roosevelt, not by Lilienthal or by the other exponents of the grass roots ideology. "The President required that one of the directors be a Southern agriculturist" and the representatives of the Department of Agriculture Extension Service nominated Harcourt Morgan as their man (p. 91).

9
See Merton J. Peck, "Competitive Policy for Transportation?" in Paul W. Mac-Avoy, ed., *The Crisis of the Regulatory Commissions* (New York: Norton, 1970) pp. 72-92; and Louis M. Kohlmeier, Jr., *The Regulators* (New York: Harper & Row, 1969), Chaps. 6-11. See also Roger Noll, ed., *Reforming Regulation* (Washington, D.C.: The Brookings Institution, 1971); and G. J. Stigler, "The Theory of Economic Regulation," *Bell Journal of Economics and Management Science:* 2:1 (Spring 1971): 3-21. The pathologies and perversions of the regulatory process are easy to document but hard to explain. Analyzing how they all come about would require a work far more ambitious than this book.

10
For these last three games, see Chapter 6.

11
Daniel P. Moynihan, *Maximum Feasible Misunderstanding* (New York: Free Press, 1969).

12
Gary Orfield, *The Reconstruction of Southern Education: The Schools and the 1964 Civil Rights Act* (New York: Wiley, 1969), pp. 122-135.

13
Leon Mayhew, *Law and Equal Opportunity* (Cambridge, Mass.: Harvard University Press, 1968), p. 271.

5 | The Dilemmas of Administration

Many of the program elements at issue in an implementation process are assembled under the central direction of an administrative agency. More precisely, administrators attempt to assemble program elements but, for various reasons, they often succeed only partially. Tokenism and Massive Resistance are the principal games that bring grief to administrators. Social entropy is a constellation of troubles that a heterogeneous and changeable society is bound to present to rule-ridden and politically accountable administrators who are obliged to cope by playing—and often overplaying—a Management game.

Tokenism

Tokenism involves an attempt to appear to be contributing a program element publicly while privately conceding only a small ("token") contribution. Other variations of Tokenism are procrastinating in making any such contribution or substituting a contribution of inferior quality. Since Tokenism often requires persistence and ingenuity, interests committed to a strategy of escaping from the implementation process as much as possible will not bother with it at all if they are in a secure enough position to do so by more direct assertions of refusal or defiance.

Although Tokenism has been most highly developed in the area of compliance, and noncompliance, with court-ordered school desegregation and with civil rights laws more generally, it commonly turns up in many other policy and program areas as well. Federal officials have made only token efforts to enforce federal fair campaign practices legislation. The Berkeley Police Department makes only token efforts to enforce the laws against marijuana use. In many counties the Short-Doyle programs have provided only token services for the chronically mentally ill. Nearly all the universities that promised in "memoranda of understanding" to use funds under a certain NASA program "to make the scientific community, as well as the industrial and business communities, aware of new opportunities for application of specific developments or processes stemming from the space program" made only the merest gestures toward fulfilling their promise.[1]

Tokenism would be of little concern if the critical elements withheld thereby could be obtained from a variety of sources. Often they cannot be, however. In the private sector, these elements must often be supplied by firms or by individuals, notably professionals, that exercise a monopolistic or quasi-monopolistic power. This power is usually reinforced by political protection. Not infrequently, the most critical program elements are quite directly controlled by agencies of government. The staff and the boards of local school districts, for example, normally have statutory authority over such matters as faculty and student assignments among schools, budgets, and curriculum planning. It would have been difficult if not impossible to implement ESEA Title I or to enforce Title VI of the 1964 Civil Rights Act in the field of education without working through each of the many thousands of the country's school districts. In the New Towns case, the U.S. General Services Administration controlled critical clearances over which it proved unwilling to compromise. Someone wanting to implement a change in a state's juvenile training schools would eventually have to take account of the relevant state department and the department personnel that run them. If a school district or a fire marshal's office or a General Services Administration or a Department of Juvenile Institutions wanted to obstruct the implementation of a given program by means of Tokenism, it would be in a good position to do so.

Monopolies that survive as such in the private-enterprise economy or in the public sector often do so because they are protected politically. Conversely, the political strength of these monopolistic suppliers also leads to increased political protection. The two sources of power are mutually reinforcing. As Grant McConnell has shown, for instance, the political strength of the American Farm Bureau Federation permitted it to dominate the U.S. Department of Agriculture's Extension Service;

the "county agents" in agriculture have in turn strengthened the AFBF; and the combined forces of the two, as expressed through and applied by powerful congressional committees, have functioned to exclude competing government agencies and other farm organizations from areas under their control. New farm programs, and particularly programs with a liberal or reformist thrust, have been absorbed by the Extension Service or killed off soon after birth.[2] In California, the Conference of Local Mental Health Directors (the heads of the several county Short-Doyle programs) was assisted in its 1967-1968 campaign to retain monopolistic control over county mental health services under L-P-S by organized psychiatry and by the California Medical Association. In this case it was the legislative power of a supplier group, rather than a clientele group like the AFBF, that helped create a protective shell around a monopolistically inclined governmental agency.

It should be emphasized, however, that while private-interest group activity can be quite valuable to a public agency seeking to create or maintain a monopoly position, it is not absolutely essential. There is a strong, if unconscious, ideological consensus among legislators and top political executives concerning the evils of "fragmentation," "overlapping jurisdictions," and "duplication of effort." This consensus has made it literally inconceivable that a state might run two explicitly competitive Departments of Juvenile Institutions, say, or that a locality might set up two competitive public school systems in the same geographical area, even though there might be great benefits from doing so.[3] Consider, for instance, the plight of a new, reform-minded director of the Massachusetts Department of Youth Services when confronted by the consolidated obstructionist power of lower-level DYS staff reinforced by legislative protection.

Following the ouster in 1969 of Dr. John D. Coughlin as director, a post he had held for seventeen years, Dr. Jerome Miller succeeded to the directorship. Miller was selected after a lengthy, nationwide search for a reform-minded professional. Coughlin had presided over a basically authoritarian and custodial system of juvenile training schools and had been a vigorous and articulate advocate of the training school philosophy. His resignation was precipitated by his having lost a much-publicized confrontation with the assistant superintendent of the Bridgewater Institution for Juvenile Guidance, the system's most inhumane and degrading maximum-security facility. In the four years prior to Coughlin's resignation, the DYS had been the subject of six major critical studies, including one by The Children's Bureau of the U.S. Department of Health, Education, and Welfare and another by a blue-ribbon panel of state experts, spearheaded by representatives of the Massachusetts Committee on Children and Youth.[4] The professionals were joined by the press and by the politicians in their cries for reform. The *Boston Globe* attacked the institutions as "a mess," "antiquated," "old," and "dreary," in a story headed "There's No Lobby for the Outcasts."[5] Governor Francis Sargent took office in January 1969 and expressed strong support for reform legislation. The legislature, in September 1969, passed a bill drastically reorganizing the DYS. It removed the DYS from the nominal supervision of the Department of Education and elevated the DYS director to the status of commissioner. The commissioner would be entitled to hire four assistant commissioners of his own choosing. Clearly, when Miller assumed his new post on October 28, 1969, he was the chosen instrument of the forces of progress and reform.

Miller has since then acquired some notoriety as a revolutionary, having closed virtually all the Massachusetts training schools with one sudden and unexpected stroke in 1972. According to the account by Ohlin and associates, it was precisely because Miller failed as a reformer that he was obliged to turn to revolution. As a reformer, Miller was simply unable to exert control over the vast array of activities that were nominally under his authority. At best, he received token cooperation, at worst, hostile resistance.

First, it took nearly a year to obtain the appropriations to hire the assistant commissioners promised in the reorganization bill. Miller could not redirect monies in the existing line-item budget because of "a very cumbersome and lengthy process that wound its way through the state Administration and Finance Office and the legislative appropriations committee."[6] Second, the state civil service system "made it virtually impossible to transfer personnel between institutions and services except on a voluntary basis."[7] Nor could they be fired—which apparently would have been the simplest of solutions. The great majority of DYS staff had been thoroughly steeped in the custodial and authoritarian ideology in which the whole DYS had been immersed for years. Staff workers "raised a storm of protest and cries of permissiveness" when Miller issued orders like these: permit institutionalized youth to regulate their own hair length; allow youths to wear their own street clothes rather than institutuional clothing; discontinue the practice of marching youth in silent formation from one activity to another; discontinue the practice of rationing cigarettes as a method of reward and punishment. Miller also issued orders forbidding staff to strike or physically abuse youth and discouraging "the stultifying routines of enforced idleness and silence in the punishment units and the use of strip cells and other measures of extreme isolation." In addition to issuing orders, Miller's staff tried to monitor compliance by means of unannounced inspection visits. But all to little avail. "All of these administrative actions led to strong protests by line staff members to institution superintendents and friends in the legislature. For a time resistant staff members or their friends appeared regularly when Miller gave speeches to community groups to raise questions about the loss of control and the threat of mass runaways to local communities."[8]

Miller's attempts to retrain the staff—change attitudes, in effect—were also strongly resisted. Miller brought Dr. Maxwell Jones, a leading British theoretician of the "therapeutic community" whose writings had greatly impressed Miller, to give a three-day training seminar for staff and youth at the Shirley Industrial School for Boys. Some cottages at the school changed over to the "therapeutic community" model but most did not. In addition, the training seminar signaled to the traditionally minded staff the genuinely subversive agenda that Miller had in mind. In his case study, Yitzhak Bakal observes: "Introducing these concepts in the Shirley structure brought immediate polarization, created staff tensions, and resulted in mass escapes. The older staff, who were by and large unskilled, found these new concepts a threat, and a challenge to their authority. The new staff had difficulty integrating these concepts into the daily operations of the institution without further training and support."[9] The older staff had ample means to fight back, too:

Most of them had long periods of service in the DYS, relatives or friends in the legislature, and influential associations in the small towns in which they resided close to the institutions. They also had long-established working relationships with many judges, probation officers, and public officials who shared their views about the function and operation of training schools. Stories about policies and case decisions that documented the permissive and chaotic state of administrative practices were magnified and circulated. Many judges, probation officers, and police officials, even those initially sympathetic to the idea of reform, began to oppose the new administration. And by the fall of 1971, two legislative investigations of the DYS were underway.[10]

Design Strategies for Dealing with Monopoly Power

Up to a point, the problems of obstruction by individuals or organizations possessed of monopoly power may be foreseen in the design phase of policy and program development. Although the character and extent of their resistance may not become fully apparent until the implementation stage, the potential for, and likelihood of, significant obstruction may be anticipated early. Antimonopoly preventive measures may therefore be incorporated in the program design.

1. Do without. This strategy presumes a willingness to design the program in such a way that whatever elements might be supplied by the

monopoly are irrelevant to its success. Jerome Miller's decision to abolish the juvenile institutions and do without both these physical resources and the associated DYS staff resources reflects a strategy of this kind. Clearly, this is a very high-risk, if not necessarily high-cost, strategy.

2. Create a substitute monopoly you can control. This strategy is reflected in the common practice of creating new bureaus to undertake new programs rather than assigning them to existing bureaus. NASA and OEO are examples. The chief problem with this solution is that a new bureau is likely to have to expand a lot of political resources initially simply in order to survive. It will also not have many of the resources already available to established bureaus.

3. Foster competition. Ordinarily, this means turning to competitors in the private sector rather than attempting to create competing agencies. Voucher schemes for the purchase of many different kinds of services are in deservedly high standing these days as a way of circumventing public agencies with monopoly powers. Medicaid is in effect a voucher arrangement that has liberated the poor from dependence on the county hospital for inpatient care. Education vouchers would give parents and children an alternative to public schools. Rent vouchers would supposedly be an alternative to government-owned and operated public housing, a program long plagued with administrative and political problems.

4. Buy it off. A newly mandated policy might bundle into one package features that the monopolist likes very much along with features that the monopolist dislikes but are desired by the sponsor. A recent study of Title III of the federal Water Resources Planning Act of 1965 demonstrates how monies appropriated under this title were perceived as a "sweetener" to state governments in exchange for their cooperation in implementing Title II. Title II established regional river basin commissions that were "clearly the most controversial section" of the act.[11] Title III provided state water-planning agencies with money to aid in the preparation of state plans, promote state training of personnel,

and develop additional planning capability. According to Helen Ingram's study, there is a correlation, albeit a weak one, between a state's use of Title III monies and its willingness to participate in Title II activities.[12]

5. Co-opt it early. One frequently reads the injunction to policy planners to "bring in" to the planning activity those persons whose cooperation will be necessary to make subsequent implementation successful. Participation, it is said, will give them a sense of commitment to the program, a pride of sponsorship. Baseless anxieties will be allayed. Defensive maneuvers will be cut short, before they have had a chance to do damage to the program.

These are prudent and useful maxims, which like all maxims should be applied wherever relevant and not contradicted by other maxims. The relevant opposing maxims are: "A wise man keeps his own counsel" and "Too many cooks spoil the broth." More prosaically, the strategy of early co-optation creates the risks of stalling the entire program should it fail. The monopolists in question may inadvertently be given too much power to shape, or misshape, the program should they be "brought in" early and not at the same time be converted into friends and supporters.

6. Build and maintain institutions exercising countervailing power. Three separate approaches are available here at least in principle: (a) clientele or consumer organization, (b) organization by providers of program inputs, especially professionals, and (c) other watchdog groups.

(a) Better-organized parent groups would almost certainly have improved the implementation of ESEA Title I, especially if they had been given signoff powers over district-level plans to spend the Title I monies. The implementation of Title VI of the 1964 Civil Rights Act in the education field was greatly assisted by a school desegregation task force that monitored compliance in two hundred southern school districts. The task force was sponsored jointly by the American Friends Service Committee and the NAACP Legal Defense Educational Fund.

The task force not only monitored compliance in most of these districts, it also embarked on a public education campaign. It disseminated three thousand school desegregation kits and over eighty-five thousand copies of a brochure entitled "Message to Parents about Desegregating Schools." The task force released a fifty-nine page report on its findings in November 1965, on the opening day of the planning sessions for the White House Conference on Civil Rights. The report, according to one participant, "scared the pants off the administration."[13] This sort of countervailing power from consumer or clientele populations is, of course, difficult to organize and sustain, even when it is called for by the policy mandate itself (as in Title I of ESEA). The success of this approach also depends in large measure on the grass-roots effort being complemented by political and administrative pressures directed at the monopoly in question from governing elites.

(b) Many government-sponsored social programs involve the delivery of services by professionals, like doctors or social workers or lawyers. It is conceivable that these professionals, moved by the voice of conscience, would exert a moral force upon service-delivery organizations, whether public or private, to implement policy changes beneficial to their program's clientele. No doubt such exertions are made and are often effective. Like other people, however, professionals tend to get caught up in the many implementation games that are adverse to program performance in the interests of program clientele. Even idealistic young legal services lawyers have not been immune to such temptations.[14] Almost certainly, it would require rather unusual circumstances for a cadre of dedicated professionals within a monopolistic government agency or private firm to keep the organization on an idealistic course for very long. Policy designers should probably contemplate that in two or three years at the most idealism will have decayed and its place will have been taken by more ordinary inspirations, whether through turnover in personnel or through a conservatizing of those idealists recruited initially.

(c) The watchdog function can be institutionalized in many different forms, only a few of which can be discussed here. At the level of operations, as opposed to planning and policy-making, it is largely identical with what is popularly thought of as an ombudsman role. This function was incorporated in the L-P-S design in the provision of public defender services for alleged mentally ill persons detained involuntarily and in the conservatorship provisions applying to the "gravely disabled." While the experience with these mechanisms has not been wholly successful, their basic design seems sound. As we shall argue below, the current movement to establish "patient advocates" in an all-purpose ombudsman role for the chronically mentally ill living in the community is almost surely destined to be disappointed. A multipurpose patient advocate would do no harm, but because of his very high information requirements, he would function less effectively than the more narrowly focused advocates like the conservator or the public defender.

At the level of planning and policy-making, the original L-P-S draft legislation envisioned a powerful Citizens' Advisory Council to oversee the Department of Mental Hygiene and in many respects actually to assume administrative powers and responsibilities. (The CAC emerged in the final legislation with advisory powers only.) At the county level there had long been mental health advisory boards under the Short-Doyle law, and L-P-S continued these with an expanded membership. These local citizen advisory boards have had mixed success in influencing the local Short-Doyle programs. A few have been extremely powerful, though informed observers would probably say that these have been the exceptions rather than the rule. The Citizens Advisory Council has been a disappointment, on the whole, but it has served some important information-gathering functions, particularly in relation to the independent game-fixing activities of Assemblyman Lanterman.[15] Watchdog agencies with real power are vulnerable to being captured in an Up for Grabs game, while those without much power are probably most useful as information-gatherers or as counterweights in the political process. The latter role has been played moderately effectively by the California Association for Mental Health.

Massive Resistance

Massive Resistance is a second means of obstructing program implementation by withholding critical program elements. It is a means of evading the responsibility specified in the policy mandate to provide these elements by overwhelming the capacity of an administrative agency to enforce sanctions for noncompliance. Since most administrative control systems supposed to regulate organizational and individual behavior are designed on the premise that compliance will be the norm and noncompliance the exception, Massive Resistance, whether the product of self-conscious coordination or of numerous uncoordinated and independent derelictions, can often cause the control system to collapse entirely. Civil rights and antiwar demonstrators both in the streets and on college campuses showed very clearly, for a time, the great potential of large-scale noncompliance. Police forces could jail, and deans could expel, only so many people at a time. Their control systems were simply not equipped to handle massive numbers of violations simultaneously. The USOE found itself similarly handicapped in its attempts to administer Title VI of the 1964 Civil Rights Act when confronted by Massive Resistance. By late September 1965, the compliance unit of the USOE Equal Educational Opportunities Program (EEOP) had only fourteen staff. During the first six weeks of the school year, they were able to make only one field investigation. By the end of the calendar year 1965, 517 complaints had been received alleging violations in over 150 district desegregation plans, but only 15 significant reviews had been conducted. "In the great bulk of the cases the Office was able to do nothing more than make phone calls or write letters, generally only to local school officials."[16] Many districts refused even to submit plans, and there were of course many more violations than those in the 150 districts about which explicit complaints were received. Initially, the rash of noncompliance was spontaneous and unorganized; but as publicity about USOE's problems with compliance enforcement revealed the full extent of the phenomenon, it appears that a sort of implicit coordination emerged. Local school officials recognized that, failing a general withdrawal of funds across the board, their particular district ran a relatively low risk of being one of the few singled out for intensive investigation and punishment. They did not need to proclaim the doctrine of Massive Resistance aloud, as southerners had done in the mid-1950s, in order to set it to work and, for a time at least, reap its benefits.

Design Strategies for Countering Massive Resistance

Massive Resistance is a reflection of the age-old question in political philosophy of how the few can control the many. Plato suggested the Noble Lie; Hobbes, the Leviathan state; and Machiavelli, the demonstration of princely power through the judicious but uninhibited use of punishments. In a sense, one important contemporary answer to this old question is "organization." The very few at the very top are—to some degree—able to control vast numbers at the very bottom by means of several intervening hierarchical levels each of which controls the level below itself and is in turn controlled by the level immediately above itself. This ingenious social device ameliorates the problem of individual resource constraints without quite solving it, however. Any individual in a hierarchical organization who exercises any control functions at all almost inevitably controls more than just one person. Typically, there is a "span of control" over four to twenty other persons, say. The few/many problem is therefore translated in the individual case into: how shall the one control the several? This problem holds between organizations as it does between inidviduals. In the L-P-S case, for instance, the State Department of Mental Hygiene had to devise a means whereby it could (partially) control the Short-Doyle organizations in more than fifty counties.

In general, the most common answers to the question of how the one may control the several are: prescription, enabling, incentives, and deterrence. The common design feature underlying each of these is that *in the main, each of the several objects of control is "self-controlling."* If the principal burden of control were not shifted from the controller to the controlled, the resource problems of the former would simply preclude any effective control whatsoever. We shall be concerned with these four instruments largely in the context of program implementation, though of course they have wider applicability.

To say that most control is principally self-control does not, of course, imply that no one has done anything to bias the exercise of self-control toward one or another outcome. Indeed, it is precisely by this biasing of the conditions under which self-control takes place that control "from the outside" is exercised. We may also emphasize here that prescription, enabling, and the others are highly imperfect as biasing instruments. They bias too little, or they bias too much, or they bias the wrong things, or they create perverse and undesired outcomes. Let us turn now to examining their utility and their limitations.

1. Prescription. Sometimes people behave as they are told to simply because they believe it is right, proper, fitting, appropriate, or morally obligatory that they should do so. We need not trouble to explicate very carefully the exact psychological nature of this feeling of "oughtness" or to explicate the philosophical basis, if any, on which it rests. The phenomenon is intuitively understandable and sufficiently prevalent that a precise definition is not necessary. Much of what passes between nominal superiors and nominal subordinates in formal organizations are "orders" that are obeyed because the latter take them to be proper prescriptions. Government bureaucracies do much of what legislatures or presidents (or governors or mayors) tell them because their leaders believe in the propriety of doing so. As Chester Barnard has pointed

out with respect to organizational subordinates, "there exists a 'zone of indifference' in each individual within which orders are acceptable without conscious questioning of their authority." There is characteristically "a certain stability" to this zone owing to the collective "interests of the persons who contribute to an organization as a group."[17] By the same logic, bureaucracies obey legislatures or governors because much of what the latter prescribe falls within the formers' "zone of indifference." Barnard also observes that the zone of indifference is "wider or narrower depending upon the degree to which the inducements exceed the burdens and sacrifices which determine the individual's adhesion to the organization. It follows that the range of orders that will be accepted will be very limited among those who are barely induced to contribute to the system."[18] Thus, the zone of indifference to integrationist rulings by the Supreme Court on the part of segregationist southerners (or northerners) is relatively narrow, though these same people might have a much broader zone of indifference for other sorts of Supreme Court rulings. In the case of L-P-S, the most successful reliance on prescription could be observed in regard to protecting the civil liberties of persons alleged to be mentally ill. (See Appendix A, especially Table 1.) It was prescribed that hospital staff were to release such persons after no more than seventy-two hours unless they could persuade the patient to stay voluntarily or they could certify that the patient was dangerous to himself or others or "gravely disabled." Judges were mandated to grant habeas corpus hearings at the request of an involuntarily detained patient within two judicial days after the petition was filed. It was also prescribed that judges not permit further detention unless the petitioner was found "as a result of mental disorder or impairment by chronic alcoholism, a danger to others, or to himself, or gravely disabled."

From the point of view of controllers, prescription is a most desirable policy instrument, since it is virtually costless. Speak and be obeyed—

what could be more attractive? Even if it does not work very well, since it is so cheap, and since it rarely excludes employing other instruments as well, it tends to be used as much as possible. Of course, in the long run issuing too many prescriptions might have a narrowing effect on the zone of indifference. In addition, issuing prescriptions that are not obeyed will have the same effect. The main problem with prescription, however, is its relatively weak effect on actors who are not linked by diffuse norms of loyalty and commitment to some collectivity like an organization. One of the most fascinating analyses of a control system based largely on prescription is Herbert Kaufman's study of the U.S. Forest Service.[19] Part of its fascination lies precisely in the rare, almost exotic, nature of the organization under study. The significant degree of control through prescription has not been achieved in the Forest Service, moreover, without considerable managerial skill or without a common loyalty throughout the organization to quasi-professional ideals. Many significant control relationships in program implementation do not connect individuals in the same organization (or profession) or organizations in the same level of government. It is one thing to tell subordinates to obey their superiors, or agency heads to obey the legislature—but it is quite another for one agency head to command obedience from another agency head of "equal" rank, or for federal officials to give orders to state officials, or for state officials to give orders to county officials.

Prescription is more effective the less controversial the actions prescribed. Since most interesting public policy changes generate controversy, and since one can almost certainly count on opposition among some of the policy implementers, prescription is almost never used alone. It is characteristically backed up by deterrence or incentives.

2. Enabling. One party can in a sense "control" another by giving that party the resources that it needs, but lacks, to undertake activities both parties mutually desired in the first place. This appears to be the control strategy embodied in most government grant-in-aid programs. The federal

government decides to "assist" local law enforcement agencies through the Law Enforcement Assistance Administration, for instance, to do the things that both federal and local agencies have always wanted the latter to do but which federal funds for the first time make possible. Or, as in the case of L-P-S, the state channels more resources into local (county) mental health programs to achieve program goals like "better mental health for more people," presumably desired by the state and counties mutually.

One of the attractions of enabling as a control instrument is that it hardly seems like control at all. Within organizations that are very cohesive, in which the participants have a high consensus on goals, and in which this consensus is buttressed by a common professional identity or commitment, hierarchies built on prescription tend to flatten out into almost collegial work groups. Instead of relying on a "zone of indifference" that "accepts" control, enabling presumes a wellspring of creative energy and desire that positively seeks this kind of control, since in this context "control" is actually equivalent to more "freedom."

Unlike prescription, when enabling fails the costs to the controller are high. If it should turn out, as it often does, that the goals of the controller and the controlled are not quite as congruent as was at first thought, the resources utilized in "enabling" the latter's activities are to that degree wasted, at least from the point of view of the controller. It would be absurd, of course, for anyone to imagine a perfect congruence of goals between any two individuals or organizations, professionalism notwithstanding. Hence, an enabling strategy employed as a solution to the few/many or the one/several problem generates all the problems associated with the Funding game, in which recipients attempt to maximize flexibility subject only to some minimum performance constraint that will satisfy the donor. How much more than the minimum the recipients will provide—and, indeed, whether they even provide the minimum—is ordinarily determined by the effectiveness of backup strategies like deterrence or incentives.

3. Incentives. Sophisticated students of public policy these days favor no instrument of control more than "incentives." While none would say that "incentives" are alchemical reagents that will transmute the base materials of sluggish bureaucracies and self-serving individuals into effective implementers of Public Purposes, enthusiam for the notion is strong and growing stronger. In his preface to *Public Planning*, Robert A. Levine, an economist turned policy analyst, now at RAND and a veteran of OEO and the Defense Department in 1960s writes:

> My contention, then, is that in order to advance policy objectives through public programs effectively, the attempt should be made to use individual and organizational incentives to interpret policies down to operating levels, using rules much less than is done now. The market system is one example of the use of incentives instead of rules in order to move in a socially desirable direction—the profit incentive to move toward greater production in the case of the private market. Within public bureaucracies, bureaucratic incentives might be used, although less is known about bureaucratic motivations than either market or political incentives.[20]

One of Levine's favorite examples is the antipoverty program set up in 1968 called Job Opportunities in the Business Sector (JOBS), which paid firms a subsidy for training the "hard-core poor" hired by the firm.[21] Levine regards the program as having "worked rather well [though] not completely up to expectations . . . until the 1970 recession came close to killing it for reasons having nothing to do with the effectiveness of the program."[22] But it could have worked better, argues Levine, had the government been paying the subsidy "for a final product—a trained and employed previously poor worker—rather than for an effort on the part of business to do the training. In normal markets, after all, those who purchase from business purchase finished products, not good tries."[23] As for bureaucracy, Levine favors "the creative use of bureaucratic rivalry as an incentive . . . [for bureaus] to move in desired directions."[24] Using the example of the military, he also adds a proviso about constraining this rivalry from (1) "making . . . explicit or implicit deals among the services to cut up the pies of appropriations and of roles and missions," and (2) competing in terms of "inputs—soldiers and ships and airplanes" rather than in terms of "the right currency," the output of defense processes—military capability . . ."[25]

It is no surprise, of course, that economists, who have been steeped in their discipline's respect for the allocative efficiency of competitive markets driven by individual incentives to maximize utility, should wish to imbue programs with the virtues of markets.[26] But the appeal of incentive manipulation as a means of control obviously has roots in other disciplines as well. Experimental psychologists train rats and pigeons to perform in quite marvelous ways by offering them rewards like pellets of food or punishments like electric shocks. Political scientists have long relied on incentive-based theories to explain why certain blocks vote for certain candidates or parties, and why organizations, political and otherwise, function as they do.[27] In their analysis of the failures of the EDA in Oakland, Pressman and Wildavsky, both political scientists, speak as respectfully of "incentives" as the economists. They argue that the EDA's subsidy to capital was of little interest to large corporations like General Motors, which derived the bulk of their financing from retained earnings and depreciation allowances against taxes. "A subsidy on wages, however, may well be an incentive to them precisely because they do employ so many men and in jobs that typically require short training periods." This of course was the policy that, with hindsight, they believe the government (whether or not the EDA) should have followed. Implicitly, moreover, they seem to believe that control through incentives is of more general applicability than merely to manpower programs:

"Payment on performance" is a useful premise on which to base employment policy in distressed areas. One of the advantages of an employment subsidy is that money is paid out only on performance, that is, the hiring of a worker and if no workers are hired, then no money is spent—an appealing attribute for the taxpayer. If policy analysts carry bumper stickers, they should read, "Be Simple! Be Direct!" or "PAYMENT ON PERFORMANCE."[28]

While the general notion behind "incentives" is clear enough, the concept needs more precise definition than most writers have given it. I would define an incentive as the promise of a reward contingent on demonstration of certain performance, with the amount of the reward proportionate to the degree of performance. This definition admits of a negative "reward," or punishment as well. Since economists and others who follow them in advocating the use of incentive systems for some reason do not like the concept of punishment, they sometimes use the special term "disincentives" to refer to such negative rewards. But the most common usage, I believe, incorporates the notion of possible punishment or deprivation into the definition of the more general term "incentives."

How, then, is a system of control based on incentives different from a deterrence system? There are indeed as many similarities as differences. Both rely on expectations of the future and presumably involve what Jeremy Bentham, the nineteenth-century father of utilitarianism, called the "felicific calculus." In both systems, too, the bestowal of the fruits of action—whether pain or pleasure—follows in time the action itself.[29] But here the similarity ends. In deterrence systems the amount of punishment is typically disproportionate to the degree of performance: tote that barge and lift that bale or get ten lashes. In deterrence systems also, the objects of control typically wish to evade scrutiny by the controllers, whereas in incentive systems they seek out such scrutiny. After all, if they cannot bring their good works to the attention of the controllers, they will not receive their just deserts.

Thus, one of the significant advantages of incentive systems as opposed to deterrence systems is that they do not impose as high surveillance and detection costs on the controllers. We noted above that all control systems whereby the few control the many are at bottom based on *self-control*, with the direction of behavior "biased" by conditions imposed by the controller. It is obvious that incentive systems are extremely appealing because they shift the burden of proof of satisfactory performance from the controller to the controlled. To Pressman and Wildavsky's bumper sticker "payment on performance" should be added "Prove It."

Unfortunately, the limitations of incentive systems are in proving it. Typically, what is to be proved and the method of proof are designed by the controller, and both are codified in rules, contracts, standard operating procedures, and the like. Periodically, the objects of control submit their proofs, they are inspected and verified by the controllers, and rewards are dispensed accordingly. This rather abstract formulation covers a variety of concrete systems, for instance:

—daily or monthly sales totals, recorded by a cash register, on which sales department supervisors compute salesman commissions

—burglary division "clearance rates," on the basis of which management-level police officials judge whether or not to augment the division's budget or size

—voucher stickers for medical services, which physicians receive from Medicaid clients and submit for reimbursement

—class scores on standardized tests, which become part of the basis for judging teachers' classroom performance and subsequent promotion

—number of job placements made per month by interviewers in a state employment agency, which becomes a partial basis for supervisors' ratings[30]

—number of investigations completed and violations detected per month by a federal law enforcement agency, also a partial basis for supervisors' ratings[31]

—provision of goods and services specified by a contract, for which payment is awarded after the goods and services have been provided

The most serious problem afflicting the design of workable incentive systems is almost certainly the difficulty of devising suitable measures of output (or, better yet, "outcomes") especially when the output is the effect of some service rather than a physical, tangible thing. The typical accommodation to this problem is to use inputs as proxies for outputs, as in the case above in which physicians are reimbursed for their services rather than for improvement in the health status of their patients. As Levine pointed out in a passage cited above, reimbursing firms for putting a person through a training program is not the same as reimbursing them for the desired output of training, "a trained and employed previously poor worker." Under certain federal programs, farmers are subsidized for acreage allegedly withdrawn from production; but they may substitute for this particular input of land other inputs like fertilizer or machinery and end up producing as much as or more than if they had used the fallow acreage. Here, again, the control is exercised over inputs rather than outputs.

In many cases it is simply very difficult to imagine how output might reliably and validly be measured, or even to know what one wants to measure. Should police department effectiveness be measured in terms of the number of crimes prevented? The number of criminals apprehended? The number of criminals apprehended and convicted? Is a classroom teacher supposed to teach skills, creativity, facts, good behavior, or what? How is success to be measured—relative to the students' performance or relative to some target established by outside experts or top administrators? Should standardized tests be used or more subjective evaluations? And which tests and whose subjective evaluations?

Another difficulty is in knowing how to assess the impact of a given activity on output when it is combined with many other activities and prior conditions and circumstances. Should we penalize a firm for training a poor, unemployed person and placing him on a job but then firing him two weeks later after he has been apprehended in a bank robbery? Should we reward a firm for "training" an unemployed person whom the same firm fired last week in order to "hire" him this week and so qualify for the federal subsidy? It can confidently be asserted that all performance measurement procedures are imperfect, that a good many are vulnerable to deliberate abuse, and that therefore the controlling agency must invest resources in monitoring the quality of its reports.

Did a doctor really perform the services he alleged? Did the burglary division really clear a hitherto unsolved crime or did it merely extort a "confession" from someone apprehended in connection with another crime in return for a reduction of charges? Once these monitoring problems are taken seriously, the cost of operating a system of control by incentives mounts and might even begin to approximate that of operating the surveillance and detection components of a deterrence system![32]

4. Deterrence. As we argued above, a deterrence system differs from an incentive system primarily in that punishment is less certain, due to high surveillance and detection costs to the controller, and in that the punishment is disproportionately severe relative to the offensiveness of the undesired conduct.[33] These two features are not unrelated, of course; the severe penalty structure is an attempt to compensate for the imperfect surveillance and detection structure.

As an instrument for the few to control the many, incentive systems have rarely been used in public programs in other than intraorganizational contexts or in the context of contracts between the government, as buyer, and private firms, as sellers, in order to induce the latter to increase performance and/or hold down costs. Deterrence, on the other hand, is quite prevalent, although to be sure there are enormous variations both in the vigorousness of enforcement efforts and in their degree of success. Regulatory agencies of all kinds are almost wholly dependent on deterrence strategies. Grant-giving agencies rely on prescription and enabling in the first instance, but retain as a critical backup system the (deterrent) threat of withholding or cutting off funds.

Deterrence is undeservedly in disrepute as a technique of control, principally because of its presumed failures in curbing criminal behavior and because of its occasional harshness when penalties are indeed invoked. Whether it has failed as grossly as its critics allege in regard to curbing criminal behavior is uncertain, principally because we do not know what crime rates would have been had police and prisons not been functioning.[34] That penalties are unnecessarily harsh is almost surely true, in the sense that lesser penalties could probably achieve the same level of effective deterrence; but this is a complaint directed at the structure of penalties in particular rather than at the concept of deterrence in general. As a tool of management, deterrence is easy to confuse with "authoritarian supervision," which has been studied extensively and seems to have a deservedly poor reputation.[35]

One of the problems with using deterrence in program implementation is that it presumes conditions that do not coexist with the conditions that would make other control methods workable, particularly enabling. Enabling presupposes a relationship of trust and mutuality of goals between the controlled and the controller. Deterrence, in contrast, presupposes suspicion and an incongruity of goals. In reality, deterrence and enabling do coexist very frequently, but not without tension and not without the precarious possibility that the balance will be tipped at any moment too far in one or the other direction. This was one of the problems with exercising control over many of those who worked in the L-P-S system. Whether or not they held professional degrees, or were explicitly trained in some recognized profession, the nature of their work induced many of them to adopt the deterrence-resistant attitudes of the traditional "free professional." They desired, and usually got, the freer conditions of an enabling system.

A more general problem with deterrence is its paradoxically self-contradictory character: once control by means of threat has been seen to fail there may then be little or no point in executing the threat. Indeed, executing the threat may actually be counterproductive for future behavior. In the world of the nuclear balance of terror, which balance rests on the fulcrum of deterrence, once country A has eliminated most of country B's nuclear weapons in a surprise attack, let us say, what is the point of B's fulfilling its long-standing threat to wipe out A's cities by way of retaliation? Killing and maiming of civilians for the sake of revenge alone could be thought immoral by some standards; and, worse yet, A might then choose to retaliate on B's civilian populations!

In the world of domestic programs and policies, of public bureaucracies and interagency contracts, analogous problems are encountered.
Normally, the most severe sanction that can be imposed on an individual in such a context is to remove him from his job; for an organization, it is to have resources withdrawn, particularly money, that it
had been counting on to continue its routine operations. However, an
individual removed from his position is no longer capable of performing either better or worse in that position than he did in the past—he is
simply out of the job. And an organization severely penalized by budget cuts (without on that account being forced out of existence) may
find itself less able or willing to comply with controllers' objectives. If
the Department of Mental Hygiene had decided to penalize certain
counties for poor performance in one year by cutting their Short-Doyle
budget allocations for the following year, how could those counties
have improved their performance on less money? Such, at least, would
have been their argument. In such a case, the inflicting of penalties is
not only pointless, it is harmful to the professed interests of the controller as well as those of the controlled. Who in the USOE or in the
civil rights movement would have desired a wholesale withdrawal of
ESEA Title I funds from poor children as the penalty for noncompliance with Title VI of the 1964 Civil Rights Act? No one, of course.
For this reason, it is generally recognized that the actual application of
sanctions in a deterrence system functions primarily as a *warning* intended (1) to discourage others from the unwanted behavior, and (2) to
discourage the same individual or organization from the unwanted behavior over some future stream of comparable activities. For the first
purpose, warning others (individuals or organizations) not to behave in
some way, severe deprivations applied to offenders might be quite effective: the controller should not hesitate to fire and demote individuals
or to annihilate organizations, so that those who are still around when
the smoke has cleared will have learned a lesson. This method of deterrence is of course not compatible with the second purpose, and the essential trade-off between the two purposes must be recognized. Another

disadvantage to this more Draconian method is that it is difficult to apply politically and sometimes legally. Political forces can often be marshaled to blunt the edge of severe administrative sanctions that are applied discretionarily. Furthermore, the requirement of administrative due process typically escalates the demands for documentation of wrongdoing in proportion to the severity of the penalties to be applied.

One of the reasons that licensing has been such a blunt instrument of control over private facilities for the residential care of the mentally ill has been the difficulty of revoking licenses. One person who had worked in facilities licensing for some ten years told me that he had only once succeeded in having a license revoked and that the process was so cumbersome and time-consuming—the revoking agency having to comply with the provisions of the Administrative Code on such matters—that licensing agents were deterred from attempting to use this technique of control. The *threat* to revoke a license may have been useful under certain circumstances, but not in those cases where the facility operator was sophisticated enough to understand the disincentives facing licensing workers actually trying to initiate revocation procedures.

Another problem for an agency that depends on Draconian deterrence is that it will be unable to draw people or other agencies into its field of control who are particularly averse to becoming as vulnerable as this model of deterrence requires of them. That is, the reputation for Draconian toughness may deter too much if it "succeeds": it will deter undesired behavior from those already locked into the field of control, but it will also hinder recruitment of those who can avoid becoming involved. Any county mental health agency that withdrew contracts or cut off substantial reimbursements from private service providers, like a halfway house or a suicide-prevention group, for anything but major and obvious performance failures would soon find that private agencies were unwilling to enter into, or to renew, contracts.[36]

The nature of the sanctions in a deterrence system designed to warn individuals and organizations about their future conduct is likely to be not some deprivation relative to an *existing* condition but a diminution in the stream of "normal" rewards that might have been expected in the future. That is, for individuals, promotions and raises will be slower in coming; for organizations, new contracts and budget augmentations will be fewer, lower, and less frequent. If the first type of deterrence is "Draconian" this type might be called deterrence by "disfavor." The threat of being cast into such a disfavored status is probably the most widely used method in public programs for the few to exert control over the many. It does not require an elaborate semi-judicialized punishment apparatus. It is so subtle that it is practically invisible, operating quite frequently on the basis of cues and signals outsiders may readily fail to understand. A county that fell into disfavor with the DMH, for instance, might learn of its fall by being asked to submit unusually detailed program evaluations or by having to suffer an unusual number of audits or site visits. While these appear on the surface to be directed at specific actions already completed, their latent, and more significant, function is to send a warning signal about the future.

The subtlety of the deterrence-by-disfavor system is both its strength and its weakness. It might have the appearance of pure and simple bias to insiders as well as to outsiders. Or it might not appear to exist at all. Both weaknesses affected the certification program of the Community Service Division (CSD), whereby it supervised and regulated a large number of board-and-care facilities. When the local CSD office thought ill of a facility it removed its certification, in effect, by ceasing to refer clients there and removing some or all of the facility's current residents. Operators could, and often did, claim bias (sometimes, I am sure, with just cause). When legislators became exercised, in 1971, about what they took to be the low quality of board-and-care homes, they mistakenly believed that these homes were unsupervised and unregulated because they were not "licensed."[37] The legislature thereupon passed a licensing law, which replaced a moderately effective deterrence-by-disfavor system with a wholly ineffective system of Draconian deterrence.[38]

A third type of deterrence is systematic harassment, which is actually a hybrid of incentives and deterrence-by-disfavor techniques. Inspection, audits, demands for reports and records—when these can be ordered selectively, that is, at the discretion of an administrator, they can be used to harass. This sort of administrative harassment appears to have many advantages as a method of control. It does not require the specificity of standards and of measurement expected of incentive systems, and it does not depend on the costly and elaborate surveillance methods required by deterrence. Nor does it rely on the application of fines or highly encumbered legal penalties such as license revocation.

One can only speculate about the prevalence of harassment as a control technique. My own suspicion is that it is not nearly as widespread as its (presumptive) effectiveness might suggest. Cultural norms do not favor it and, more important, firms, persons, or agencies that are subject to administrative harassment normally have ready recourse to legislators and even to higher-level administrators; left-wing groups and individuals that have been harassed by the FBI and the IRS, for instance, are the exception that proves the rule. They were abnormally vulnerable to harassment precisely because their ability to invoke political sanctions was slight, especially under the Nixon Administration.

Social Entropy

Both Tokenism and Massive Resistance are games played between relatively identifiable parties, on one side the controllers and on the other the obstructionists or resisters. We cannot leave the problem of control without mentioning some of the impersonal or nonpersonal forces in the social world that also tend to confound systems. These forces are in a sense part of social nature, which, like physical nature, has a tendency to lose energy, to "run down" so to speak or, in other words, to be governed by the laws of entropy. Social entropy throws up three main problems to plague government programs: the problem of incompetence, the problem of variability in the objects of control, and the problem of coordination.

1. Incompetence. There are some people who can be told again and again what they are supposed to do in the new order of things and who are perfectly willing to do it, but try as they will they cannot. Tell a fourth-rate architect that the building he has designed for your university campus is unattractive, and the chances are that after all the fiddling he does in response to your criticism he will still end up with an unattractive building. If the vice-president in charge of sales of Acme Manhole Covers is incompetent, no amount of exhortation will enable him to improve the sales function, even though the success of the research department's new rectangular cover design may depend on it. The pall of incompetence can occur at any organizational level. The man who chooses architects for the university campus may be the critical incompetent in the design process, just as the Acme sales force may be the critical locus of incompetence rather than their chief in the head office. What James Q. Wilson wrote of bureaucracy can be extended to people in any role:

The supply of able, experienced executives is not increasing nearly as fast as the number of problems being addressed by public policy.
This constraint deserves emphasis, for it is rarely recognized as a constraint at all. Anyone who opposed a bold new program on the grounds that there was nobody around able to run it would be accused of being a pettifogger at best and a reactionary do-nothing at worst. Everywhere, except in government, it seems, the scarcity of talent is accepted as a fact of life. . . . The government—at least publicly—seems to act as if the supply of able political executives were infinitely elastic, though people setting up new agencies will often admit privately that they are so frustrated and appalled by the shortage of talent that the only wonder is why disaster is so long in coming. . . . "Talent is Scarcer Than Money" should be the motto of the Budget Bureau.[39]

Incompetence is not, of course, a trait like having brown eyes. It is a description of a relationship between an individual and a particular task or situation: the individual is unable to perform the task or function in the situation up to a given, though ultimately arbitrary, standard of some sort. An individual who is quite competent to do some things will be incompetent to do others. It may not in any meaningful sense be "his fault" that he is incompetent to perform certain tasks—it may well be the fault of the people who assigned him the task in the first place. Wilson's point about bureaucracy is really an argument against inventing tasks that cannot be performed by people who are likely to be assigned them. Whether for good or for evil, the people who are clever enough to design innovative programs are surely quite a bit more clever than the mass of humankind and are probably more clever than a good many (though not all) of the people who will have to implement their ideas. However, the designers are loath to recognize this fact because they typically derive pleasure from the imaginative expression inherent in the design process itself.[40]

Even more so than the poor, the inept will always be with us. In a most provocative analysis, William J. Goode has shown that society places a positive value on the protection of the inept. It is the price we are willing to pay to avert even worse evils: "a Hobbesian jungle, the undermining of group structure, the loss of the usual benefits of organization and cooperation, and the dissolution of group loyalties."[41] Nevertheless, the existence of ineptitude among those who are located on the path of presumed policy impact does tend to diminish the force of the policy. Their incompetence is a definite barrier to the exercise of control over the system. The L-P-S system in its emphasis on community placement of the long-term mentally ill at least implicitly relied on the services of board-and-care home operators, most of whom had no professional training in caring for the mentally ill and many of whom were not very good at it despite their own efforts and desires to improve. While much more could have been done than was done to assist these operators to improve their skills, there was probably a reasonably low upper boundary on how much improvement was possible. (The ward attendants, or "psychiatric technicians" as they came to be called, in the pre-L-P-S mental hospitals also constituted a barrier to the general improvability of the system.) Another class full of incompetents was the licensing workers and social welfare workers who wrote and enforced the regulations for residential-care facilities. Even more than for the board-and-care operators, who were in theory replaceable by new entrants into the field, these lower-level supervisory bureaucrats and professionals were protected in their incompetence by professional cliquishness and, most of all, by civil service rules.[42]

It is inevitable that a new program will attempt to make at least some use of personnel already performing their old tasks ineptly. New programs will also assign new tasks to officials or bureaucrats or professionals who were perfectly able to carry out their old tasks but cannot be counted on to carry out the new ones. The recipients were given the job because of their credentials, official titles, or positions—more precisely, perhaps, because of the existing jurisdiction of their profession or of the bureau in which they happened to hold positions—but they simply cannot do the new tasks as well as they could the old. In many cases this type of incompetence may result from what Thorstein Veblen and later Robert Merton called a "trained incapacity." That is, as a result of the successful learning that an aspiring bureaucrat has undertaken with respect to one set of tasks, he has learned how *not* to do certain things that would be associated with other tasks. Elie Abel provides an almost macabre instance of this phenomenon in the response given by the chief of naval operations to Defense Secretary Robert McNamara's request for a detailed description of how U.S. ships blockading Cuba might encounter a Soviet ship during the 1962 missile crisis. McNamara insisted on knowing who would make the first interception, whether there were Russian-speaking officers aboard, what would be done about Russian submarines. "Picking up the Manual of

Navy Regulations the Navy Chief waved it in McNamara's face and shouted, 'It's all in there.' To which McNamara replied, 'I don't give a damn what John Paul Jones would have done; I want to know what you are going to do, now.' "[43]

A final source of incompetence that deserves mention is the turnover in an organization's personnel, from which it necessarily follows that the competency that comes of experience is lost to the organization as a whole. This turnover may occur because people leave the organization altogether or because they simply move around a lot within the organization. Although it is doubtful that either Short-Doyle administrators or the Department of Mental Hygiene defined turnover as a serious source of problems, it was. That is, it was one factor—even if not the most important one—that prevented the department from controlling implementation of L-P-S at the county level more than it did. The primary contact between the department and any county program during the transmission period was the community program analyst (CPA). It was primarily through the CPA that the department made its desires about county programs known to the county mental health administrator and his staff in the stages of county planning prior to their submission of plans to the department for approval. The CPA was a broker and intermediary in the other direction as well, supporting the county's desires in the councils of the DMH. A good part of the CPA's value was his knowledge of the county program and of the DMH decision-making process. If he did his work well, county plans would run into fewer snags in the review process, and the department's policy intentions (and to the degree these mirrored the legislature's intentions, the latter's as well) would be reflected in county policy. For instance, it was up to the CPA to tell the county mental health director that the department would insist on more services for involuntarily detained patients, or on more emphasis on crisis intervention services, or on better aftercare planning. In the early years of L-P-S these CPAs were potentially crucial links in the chain of control. But their effectiveness was limited at least in part by their lack of experience: so many of them always seemed to be on the job just a few months. Good CPAs were likely to be moved out of that job into a headquarters or regional office job.

Another example may be found in a NASA experience, recounted by Sayles and Chandler.[44] Serious problems emerged during the fabrication of a sophisticated measurement instrument that was the core of the whole experiments package to be placed on one spacecraft. The project manager did not feel the necessity to monitor closely the contractor's production of this piece of equipment because it was identical to the instrument successfully built by the same contractor on two previous occasions. It was subsequently discovered that several of the steps involving cleaning a surface in preparation for the application of an unusually "tricky" bonding agent had been performed under the close and constant scrutiny of a particular supervisor. These "hand operations" had not been recorded and, not being known about, were of course not written into the contract's instrument specification. By the time the same instrument was built for a third time, the particularly knowledgeable supervisor had been transferred elsewhere and the required additional precautions were not taken.

2. Variability. Nearly all control systems operate on the premise that a certain degree of standardization is possible and desirable. The people or activities to be controlled are assumed to have certain recurrent and common characteristics, and the control mechanism is therefore designed to respond in a standard way when certain standard indicators are registered or observed. Control systems can, of course, be designed so as to discriminate rather subtle differences and to provide correspondingly subtle responses. Hence, the sophistication of control systems is a matter of degree. In the physical world, missile guidance systems and thermostats represent opposite extremes in the degree of sophistication. In the world of social policy, we could contrast the federal Internal Revenue Service and a state auto registration agency as representing similarly opposed extremes in the degree of control system sophistication.

No matter how rudimentary or sophisticated the detection and response repertoire of a social program's control system may be, however, the system will always leave some room for discretion on the part of the controllers. They must have freedom to deal with unpredictable novelty in a given situation, for which no standardized response has been programmed, or to eschew a standardized response that on equity grounds is unacceptable to their superiors or to themselves or to the persons who become the objects of control. Discretion is, of course, widely prevalent in our social institutions. Welfare eligibility workers use discretion, as do policemen, district attorneys, draft boards, college admissions officers, and waiters in restaurants.

Although discretion is legitimate as a social principle, the terms on which it is practiced and the variability of program impact that can be attributed to it are frequently the subject of complaint, outrage, and occasionally even lawsuits. Unfortunately, there is no way to gain the virtues of discretion without at the same time suffering its drawbacks as well.

In the administration of the L-P-S system there were numerous discretionary practices. One important area of discretion was judicial, concerning the application of the conservatorship law to the "gravely disabled."[45] Although the law defined the term quite explicitly as "a condition in which a person, as a result of mental disorder, is unable to provide for his basic personal needs for food, clothing, or shelter," judges differed substantially in their construction of this phrase and its applicability to given cases. One notorious judge in Sacramento County instituted conservatorships with as much abandon as he had formally committed people to state hospitals who were, under the old law, "in need of treatment, care, or restraint." A judge in San Joaquin County was said, on the other hand, to have refused to grant conservatorships under almost any conditions. Even within the same county the behavior of judges was quite varied. One judge whose conservatorship hearings I witnessed appeared to make every effort to apply the law fairly and with the intent to balance libertarian and paternalistic values much in the way that the framers of L-P-S intended. The judge who succeeded him in that division of the superior court granted conservatorship for the least cause, wishing thereby to protect himself against post hoc recrimination for turning loose persons who might subsequently commit crimes of violence.[46]

An important source of variability in a program's impact is in the behavior of the clientele. This source of variability is in a sense the opposite, or perhaps the complement, of discretion, which originates in the behavior of program administrators. The operative variables here are usually initiative, in the case of programs distributing benefits, and evasiveness, in the case of programs imposing sanctions or penalties. As we have already discussed evasiveness in the section on deterrence, we shall discuss here only initiative.

Many intergovernmental grant programs require some matching contribution from the recipient level of government, a contribution that some are unwilling to make. Typically, these contributions are measured in dollars or dollar-equivalent contributions in kind, the latter being the type of local contribution often made, for example, by localities seeking to participate in federal urban renewal programs. When the donor government gives money away under a project-grant program for which no dollar or dollar-equivalent contribution is explicitly required, there is still the in-kind contribution involved in the time and energy devoted to applying for the grant. In view of these explicit costs, even when there are no additional conditions attached, the potential recipient's cost-benefit calculations may lead to nonparticipation or to relatively low levels of participation. One outcome of this process is that the rich get richer while the poor just pay taxes.

The Short-Doyle program, in which the counties put up 25 percent of the funds in the years just before L-P-S and 10 percent thereafter, provides some clear illustrations of this process.[47] Marin and San Mateo counties, two of the very richest counties in the state, each received in fiscal 1973 almost double what the DMH's equity-based allocation formula would have given them. Marin received $2.3 million when the formula would have provided $1.3 million; San Mateo received $6.7 million when the formula would have provided $3.7 million.[48]

Some relatively wealthy counties did not choose to participate at high levels for other reasons. Orange County, whose population had a fairly conservative attitude toward the public provision of social services in general and mental health services in particular, did not begin Short-Doyle participation until 1964, six years after the Short-Doyle system came into being. San Diego County did not begin until 1962, probably for similar reasons. Sacramento County joined only in 1964, primarily because the county could rely on a fairly nearby state hospital.

In some cases, skillful or assertive local Short-Doyle directors could mobilize local support and at the same time could bargain effectively for additional funds from Sacramento. Contra Costa County started its Short-Doyle participation in 1958 and by 1973 it enjoyed approximately a 20 percent "surplus" of mental health resources relative to DMH-determined "need." San Joaquin County began in 1958 and by 1973 enjoyed a 90 percent "surplus." Orange County managed to increase its Short-Doyle program from $3.4 million in 1970 to $6.6 million in 1972, even though it was still in 1973 a "deficit" county. All three county programs were led during these periods by politically skillful and vigorous directors. Thus, political leadership, like riches and local popular support, can be an important component of what we have called "initiative." In these three cases, initiative by local forces combined with the discretionary latitude of DMH administrators to produce significant variability of program impact.

3. Coordination. A practically universal complaint about public programs is that there is insufficient coordination. "Better coordination" has a niche in the hierarchy of virtues close by motherhood and apple pie. An especially attractive feature of "better coordination" is that it

ostensibly costs so little. All it would seem to require is common sense, good will, and opportunities for those whose activities are to be coordinated to confer regularly. If coordination is in fact so cheap, why then is there apparently so little of it? The reason, of course, is that it is actually quite costly, perhaps even impossible under certain conditions.

"Coordination" is a slippery term, and we had best say what we mean by it. One possible meaning, and probably the most common one, is bringing together all the parties who have something to say about the different aspects of a problem and its possible solutions and letting them choose a mutually acceptable solution. If this process takes place in the mind of a single all-knowing individual, he is a statesman to those who like his solution and a czar to those who do not. If the process is a multiparty affair with broad participation, it is called planning by those who like the solution and elitism by those who do not. In any case, this decision-making connotation of "coordination" is not what we shall intend by the term. We shall focus on the operations, or activities, that affect relevant program outputs. These operations or activities may or may not be produced by a "coordinating" type of decision-making process. At the level of operations, "coordination" is very much akin to what economists mean by "efficiency" or "cost-effectiveness." If many activities, performed by different people and by the same people acting over time, are involved in the process of producing program outputs, then coordination exists when the productive activities are combined with minimum cost in order to produce a specified output. Alternatively one can say that coordination exists when the combination of activities is such that, whatever their cost, the most highly valued level or quality of output is achieved. The focus here is on the way activities are combined. Ordinarily one would expect that the products of one set of activities would be almost fully utilized, and utilized with only minimal delay, by some other set of activities. If such an efficient matching of people's diverse activities in space and time can be achieved, then the program is internally well coordinated.[49] The signs of poor coordination, then, will be surpluses, shortages, and delays. Let us examine some of the reasons we can expect these problems, particularly shortages and delays, to be endemic in a publicly sponsored service-delivery program, using the California mental health program as an example.

For simplicity, let us say that the program in some localized area combines activities by three groups: clients, treatment service providers, and providers of residential care. Within each group there is considerable individual differentiation. Clients vary greatly in their legal status, their level and type of disability, and their ability to profit from different types of service. Service providers vary with respect to the type of service offered, and within each type there is variation also in quality (some are better than others). Residential facilities differ among each other with respect to a complex bundle of services we shall call "amenities," each bundle containing such diverse items as proximity to public transportation, color television in the living room, and the amicability of the residents.

Even if new providers are free to enter, it is very likely that there will normally be an apparent shortage of services. Each individual provider has a limited capacity to offer service. Since most beneficiaries of the public system receive services free, or else pay some flat rate that is independent of the type and quality of service they use, the limited service capacity of any provider is rationed among the entire clientele population on some basis other than willingness to pay, usually queuing (by being entered on a waiting list). The only way to get the high-quality service without waiting is to be sponsored by someone with "pull." High-quality services charge no more than low-quality services; hence, the former always appear to be in short supply. The apparent shortage is not confined, moreover, to the "highest"-quality service. It appears everywhere. No matter what service one is receiving, there is always something just a little better. But other clients in the same status think so, too. Hence, there is likely to be congestion in front of all doors except the ones that lead to the very lowest-quality services.

Appearances aside, however, there are likely to be shortages of services, and of course delays in obtaining what services there are, even when clients are assigned to providers strictly according to "need." The reason is that there are normally fluctuations in the number of clients who have the need for some service. Even if there is enough capacity to take care of the *average* need for a service during any randomly chosen time interval, approximately half the time there will be more demand for service than the existing capacity can supply. The other half of the time, capacity will be underutilized. The appearance of some "slack" might even convince legislators and county supervisors that there is an *excess* of capacity! At any rate, they are certainly not likely to think that there is a need to create and maintain the capacity to handle anything like the "peak" load. Most public officials have a hard time accepting "slack" in police, fire, and ambulance service, for which peak-load capacity normally is, or at least ought in principle to be, the planning target.[50] How much harder, then, for them to accept "slack" in social service programs!

Even if there were no obvious shortages (whether apparent or real) or delays, there would still be the problem of generating the information needed to effect an appropriate match between a given client and a given treatment or residential service. Because so many mentally ill persons living in community settings seem to "fall between the cracks" of the many service agencies and facilities, many observers of mental health programs have proposed a "patient advocate" system whereby each patient would be monitored to assure that he does not go without appropriate services. Let us begin to consider how such a system would work by imagining what would happen at the time of a patient's reentry into the community from an institution.

The patient advocate would make an assessment of his client's needs. He would then shop about among available residential facilities and available treatment programs to find the best combination. Since there are many such facilities and programs in our hypothetical community, the patient advocate will utilize the services of two experts, probably from a public social work agency, who respectively have specialized knowledge about the qualities of the available treatment programs and the available residential facilities.

So far so good. But what happens once the patient is settled into the best combination of services? He changes. He gets better or worse—or just plain dissatisfied. The services also change. New residents move into his board-and-care home while old ones move out. The treatment personnel (say, the psychiatrists or the recreation therapists or the vocational rehabilitation teachers) redesign their programs; or they quit and are replaced; or the program goes out of business entirely because it did not receive its grant renewal. The match between the client and the services is no longer as good as it was in the beginning. It is time for him to change. Who should arrange for the change?

The residential-care operator sees the client most frequently and knows more than anyone else in the system about his ability to function in the most approximately normal setting that the client experiences. The head of the treatment team or program is a professional trained to make clinical judgments and therefore judgments about the appropriateness of the patient's shift in treatment modalities. But his knowledge is suspect, because he has an interest, ordinarily, in keeping the patient where he is, that is, in ignoring the need for change. Therefore, the patient advocate has to take the leading role in effecting change. But the patient advocate lacks information. Unless the advocate literally lives with the patient twenty-four hours a day, as a sort of guardian angel, the advocate is at a disadvantage in his dealings with either the operator or the treatment professional. If they insist that the patient is well off where he is and the advocate insists otherwise, who should win?

No one should win, of course. The decision should be consensual, or at least as much a product of consensus as possible, with the advocate deciding in the event consensus cannot be reached. But such an arrangement would reduce the advocate's role to less than most proponents of the patient advocate system imagine. The advocate could prevent the patient from falling "between the cracks" at his time of entry into the community, but he would have considerably more trouble in *removing* the patient from the cracks after they have opened up around him.

The problem is magnified if we discard our assumption that there are no real or apparent shortages and delays. Now the availability of alternative services is constantly changing. The brokerage experts from the social work agency who monitor these fluctuations have even more influence on placement decisions, while the other actors have correspondingly less influence. In order to keep the service facilities operating productively, these brokers need to keep them supplied with clients who can benefit from their services. The brokers will either try themselves to keep track of the various members of the available—and ever-changing—patient population or they will demand the services of a person or agency that specializes in keeping track. The patient advocate will thus have even less influence. Indeed, it is probable that his role will be reduced to outwitting other patient advocates, all of whom are competing for the brokerage services of the social work placement agencies.

Such a system might be better than the present one, in which it is certainly true that patients fall "between the cracks" or stay there without anyone caring. It might be, however, that the principal difference would be only the guarantee that *someone* would *care*. There would still be cracks and there would still be patients in between them. The system would be called poorly coordinated.

As we can see, the high costs of assembling the right information about the right things at the right time are likely to act as a significant barrier to coordination.[51] The only single person in the system who could conceivably have enough current information, on a continuing basis, to make decisions about the patient's conditions and treatment is the patient himself. If a chronically mentally ill person were in fact capable of gathering such information and acting on it in this fashion, however, he would very likely not be mentally ill at all and would certainly not remain in this dependent status for very long!

High information costs are not the only deterrent to better coordination. While men and women in responsible positions normally find ways to "do business" with each other, sometimes personality clashes disrupt or destroy working relationships. This problem is quite familiar, though its prevalence may not be so great as its widespread familiarity might indicate. In one county I observed, the placement of mentally ill patients in community facilities suffered because a social worker employed by the state and her counterpart employed by the county did not like to speak to each other. Each especially disliked having to initiate the contact with the other. In another county, a halfway house lost federal funds because the Short-Doyle director automatically vetoed any proposal for funds that came from the Short-Doyle program chief.

A particularly pernicious result of personality clashes goes beyond "poor coordination." Occasionally some group or person will withhold needed program elements from an administrator or manager trying to assemble (that is, "implement") a program. The object is to give the manager (or his organizational unit) a black eye by making him (or the unit) appear inept or foolish. I observed such behavior in the Department of Interior during 1975. Certain officials had committed the department to an accelerated schedule for leasing federally managed oil and gas lands on the United States' outer continental shelf. A bureau within the department that opposed the accelerated schedule once tried to show the inadvisability of the program by omitting certain presumptively important steps in evaluating the resources put up for auction.

Their object was to show that the accelerated schedule imposed such a heavy work load on them that it was "not a feasible program." Such a demonstration, if successful, would have discredited not only the program but the original decision-makers. The demonstration was not successful, however. It backfired, and the offending bureau was brought under even closer scrutiny by the department.

The Management Game

There is a mistaken notion on the part of many people that the problems of social entropy—incompetency, variability in the objects of control, poor coordination, and perhaps others—can be solved by designing better management tools and procedures and by giving more power to institutions specializing in management, like the personnel department or the auditor's office of the comptroller's bureau. The result is a Management game against the entropic forces in social nature played out in the hopes of achieving better control. The players on the "better management" side usually include central budget authorities, government auditors and accountants, fiscal committees in the legislature, and other such efficiency-minded persons. Their demands are for better "information systems," more audits and controls, more detailed instructions from headquarters to field offices, more explicit and formal procedures, and the like. Although such demands need not lead inevitably to a flow of power and authority from the private sector toward the government, or away from the field and toward the central office, or away from the civil service and toward political appointees, such are often the results. These centralizing tendencies are viewed with ambivalence by both political liberals and conservatives. Conservatives applaud the consolidation of power when they believe they can direct how it is used, but deplore it when it seems to be used to further liberal goals and social values. Liberals are inherently more suspicious of centralized power, but they too applaud it when they believe it will serve other social values.

Given that the Management game against social entropy cannot be "won" in any conclusive sense, and given that liberals and conservatives alike have reasons both to embrace and to reject the tendencies toward centralization, it is no surprise that periods of centralization are followed by a rush to decentralize once again and loosen up what are perceived as overly restrictive institutions of control. Hence, the current popularity of revenue sharing following a generation of growing federal government authority; and hence, too, the popularity of community control in opposition to bureaucracy, and market mechanisms in opposition to government planning.

From a certain point of view, such a dialectic is probably healthy and beneficial. To argue that no conclusive victories can be won against social entropy does not imply that temporary and localized victories are impossible or undesirable. Similarly, to argue that overcentralization and overcontrol are always clear and present dangers does not imply that it may not often be worthwhile to risk them and even, as is inevitable, sometimes fall prey to them. Nevertheless, it is difficult to keep the Management game in what might be called an optimal state of inconclusiveness. These difficulties may best be observed at the level of individual administrative behavior. Consider, for instance, Seymour Sarason's poignant natural history of the premature aging of a new public school program:

Practically everyone . . . automatically assumes that becoming principal of a new school is much to be preferred over assuming leadership of an older school. The reasons seem obvious enough: a new school is expected to have better physical facilities; school personnel, children, and parents will take great pride in the new school; the principal will have greater freedom to organize things his way, that is, it will be easier for him to innovate and to depart from past practices; the principal has more of an opportunity to choose teachers who fit in with his plans; he will not have to deal with an entrenched faculty who, because of their loyalty to a previous principal (or other reasons), are not likely to change their accustomed way of doing things.

But: 1. From the time of appointment until the formal opening of the school the new principal spends almost all of his time in what can only be called housekeeping matters. . . . Particularly in the case of the principal new to his role the complexity of housekeeping is more than he imagined and was prepared for. In very quick order the principal sees as his major goal—a goal determined by others but which he fully accepts and in relationship to which he has increasing anxiety—opening the school on time and in good order.

2. Up until the opening of school the bulk of the meetings in which the principal participates are with the administrative personnel not only for the purpose of setting up house but in order for the principal to learn the rules and regulations relevant to whatever decisions he must make and plans that he has. . . .

3. There is nothing the new principal in the new school desires more than an "orderly" opening. . . . Smoothness of operation tends to become an end in itself, and anything and anyone interfering with smoothness are not favorably looked upon.

4. A variety of problems inevitably arises concerning parents, children, teachers, and various assortments of visitors, formal and informal. But of greatest concern to the principal are those with teachers who have changes to suggest, difficult or problem children they wish to discuss and about whom they want the principal to take action, or emerging conflicts with other teachers about procedures and practices. . . .

I can summarize our observations and experiences by saying that by the end of the first year, life in the new school is remarkably similar to that in old ones. . . .[52]

Notes

1
Laurin L. Henry, "The NASA-University Memoranda of Understanding" (Syracuse: Inter-University Case Program, 1969).

2
Grant McConnell, *The Decline of Agrarian Democracy* (New York: Atheneum, 1969). See also Theodore J. Lowi, *The End of Liberalism* (New York: Norton, 1969), pp. 102-115 and references cited therein.

3
See William A. Niskanen, Jr., *Bureaucracy and Representative Government* (Chicago: Aldine-Atherton, 1971), especially Chaps. 11, 15, 18.

4
Lloyd E. Ohlin, Robert B. Coates, and Alden D. Miller, "Radical Correctional Reform: A Case Study of the Massachusetts Youth Correctional System," *Harvard Educational Review* 44: 1 (February 1974): 76-79.

5
Yitzhak Bakal, "Closing Massachusetts' Institutions: A Case Study," in Yitzhak Bakal, ed., *Closing Correctional Institutions* (Lexington, Mass.: D. C. Heath, 1973), p. 157.

6
An interesting maneuver to circumvent the civil service system was to assign authority and responsibility without regard to formal civil service rank. Miller appointed a new administrator to function as superintendent of the Shirley Industrial School for Boys who was listed, and paid, as a maintenance worker. Ohlin, Coates, and Miller, "Radical Correctional Reform," p. 90.

7
Ohlin, Coates, and Miller, "Radical Correctional Reform," p. 90.

8
Ohlin, Coates, and Miller, "Radical Correctional Reform," p. 83.

9
Bakal, "Closing Massachusetts' Institutions," p. 158-159.

10
Ohlin, Coates, and Miller, "Radical Correctional Reform," p. 93.

11
Helen Ingram, "Policy Implementation Through Bargaining: The Impact of Federal Grants-in-Aid" (Department of Government, University of Arizona, 1974), p. 10.

12
Ingram, "Policy Implementation," pp. 21, 25-26. Ingram does not establish, unfortunately, that even the weak correlation she observed is not spurious.

13
Beryl A. Radin, "Implementing Change in the Federal Bureaucracy: School Desegregation in HEW," Ph.D. dissertation (Department of City and Regional Planning, University of California, Berkeley, 1973), pp. 268-269. The leading figure in
this drive was Jean Fairfax of the American Friends Service Committee. See also
Gary Orfield, *The Reconstruction of Southern Education: The Schools and the
1964 Civil Rights Act* (New York: Wiley, 1969), pp. 124-125.

14
See Harry Brill, "The Uses and Abuses of Legal Assistance," *The Public Interest*
(Spring 1973). According to Brill, many of these central office lawyers would
seem to have been playing the Reputation game.

15
See Chapter 11 for a discussion of the "eyes and ears" function of the CAC.

16
Orfield, *Reconstruction,* pp. 114-115.

17
Chester Barnard, *The Functions of the Executive* (Cambridge, Mass.: Harvard
University Press, 1966, orig. 1938), p. 167.

18
Barnard, *Functions,* p. 169.

19
Herbert Kaufman, *The Forest Ranger: A Study in Administrative Behavior* (Baltimore: Johns Hopkins University Press, 1960).

20
Robert A. Levine, *Public Planning* (New York: Basic Books, 1972), pp. v-vi.

21
Robert A. Levine, *The Poor Ye Need Not Have with You* (Cambridge, Mass.:
The MIT Press, 1970), p. 110.

22
Levine, *Public Planning,* p. 173.

23
Levine, *Public Planning,* pp. 173-174.

24
Levine, *Public Planning,* p. 182.

25
Levine, *Public Planning,* p. 182.

26
Generally, this statement is true of both "liberal" and "conservative" economists
in America.

27
See, for instance, Samuel Lubell, *The Future of American Politics*, 2nd ed. (Garden City, New York: Doubleday, 1956); Peter B. Clark and James Q. Wilson, "Incentive Systems: A Theory of Organizations," *Administrative Science Quarterly* 6: 2 (September 1961): 129-166.

28
Jeffrey L. Pressman and Aaron Wildavsky, *Implementation* (Berkeley: University of California Press, 1973), p. 159.

29
Both are variants of an accountability system, therefore. An accountability system biases the choices that actors make during the course of action by specifying what will, or might, happen to them following post hoc appraisal of their actions by other parties. In this respect, both deterrence and incentives differ from both prescription and enabling. We might mention here that control through requiring "prior clearance" is a special case of a deterrence system, even though it appears not to have the features of an accountability system. When prior clearance works perfectly, there are no offenders to be called to account and punished. When it works rather imperfectly, on the other hand, those offenders who are caught having acted without prior clearance are called to account and punished. The latter case makes it plain that prior clearance is actually a form of deterrence system and hence an accountability system.

30
Peter M. Blau, *The Dynamics of Bureaucracy* (Chicago: University of Chicago Press, 1962).

31
Blau, *Dynamics*.

32
It is worth noting also that many of the obstacles to implementing an incentive system are the very same ones that obstruct the implementation of any program, that is, monopoly power, political protection, and massive resistance. See the account of the lamentable experience of the "Chapter 3" program in the Michigan schools by Jerome T. Murphy and David K. Cohen, "Accountability in Education—the Michigan Experience," *The Public Interest* (Summer, 1974): 74-81.

33
Another difference, of course, is that a deterrence system offers only punishment while an incentive system can offer either punishment or reward. Although this will appear in many people's eyes, I am sure, as the most important difference between the two systems, it appears to me minor relative to the other two.

34

Some very interesting, though to me not wholly persuasive, efforts to assess the efficacy of deterrence have been undertaken in recent years with respect to the rate of crime. See Isaac Erlich, "Participation in Illegitimate Activities: A Theoretical and Empirical Investigation," *Journal of Political Economy* 81 (May-June, 1973): 521-565. Also see the brief summary by Gordon Tullock, "Does Punishment Deter Crime?," *The Public Interest* (Summer 1974) pp. 103-111, and Simon Rottenberg, ed., *The Economics of Crime and Punishment* (Washington, D.C.: American Enterprise Institute for Public Policy Research, 1973).

35

Peter M. Blau and W. Richard Scott, *Formal Organizations* (San Francisco: Chandler, 1962), Chap. 6. I have found no studies of deterrence per se.

36

One of several reasons why Draconian deterrence is likely to be more effective in the criminal law than in administrative practices—if, indeed, it is more effective there—is that no one can opt out of the field of control without emigrating from the jurisdiction, which for serious crimes might in effect mean leaving the nation-state itself.

37

The difference between "licensing" and "certification," as I use these terms, is that denial of a license forces a party to cease operations, while denial of certification merely withdraws official recognition that a "certified" level of care is provided.

38

The appropriate remedy would have been to improve the certification system by making the criteria for certification more explicit, increasing the slack on the supply side of the residential-care sector by offering higher rates, and increasing the supervision of placement workers. See Appendix B for a fuller treatment.

39

James Q. Wilson, "The Bureaucracy Problem," *The Public Interest* (Winter 1967): 7, pp. 3-9.

40

See Martha Derthick, *New Towns In-Town* (Washington, D.C.: The Urban Institute, 1972), pp. 101-102.

41

William J. Goode, "The Protection of the Inept," *American Sociological Review* 32: 1 (February 1967): 15.

42
On the existence of incompetent civil servants, see E. S. Savas and Sigmund G. Ginsburg, "The Civil Service—A Meritless System?," *The Public Interest* (Summer 1973): pp. 70-85. There is also the famous Peter Principle as an explanation of the prevalence of incompetence: people rise to their own level of competence and then one level higher, where they stay. This last promotion occurs by mistake, as it were, since they *did* seem competent until they moved to their new job!

43
Quoted in Graham T. Allison, "Conceptual Models and the Cuban Missile Crisis," *American Political Science Review* 63: 3 (September 1969): 707.

44
Leonard E. Sayles and Margaret K. Chandler, *Managing Large Systems* (New York: Harper & Row, 1971) p. 312.

45
ENKI Research Institute, A Study of California's New Mental Health Law (1969-1971) (Chatsworth, Calif., 1972), pp. 179-183.

46
One reason that judges at the superior court level had such discretion was that higher courts in California had established virtually no legal precedents in this area of the law. The lower courts had as much discretion as they did in part because higher courts exercised their own discretion in allowing such freedom to the lower courts.

47
In the early years of the Short-Doyle program, the state-county matching formula was 50-50.

48
See *Equitable Allocation of Short-Doyle Funds* (DMH, 1972). The formula was primarily population based, and extra weights are given to "high-risk" subpopulations deemed especially in need of mental health services, such as the poor or disabled (as measured by the county Aid to the Totally Disabled case load). It also took into account available "funding resources," including federal community mental health center grants, Law Enforcement Assistance funds, and the like. The formula was used only in the allocation of funds for "new and expanded" rather than "existing" Short-Doyle programming, and was first employed in allocating funds for the fiscal year 1973.

49
Again, I remind the reader that the means of achieving this coordination is irrelevant to this definition. The means might range from letting all the activities be priced and exchanged as if in a marketplace to having the job done by a very capable administrator.

50
Of course, the idea of "peak load" cannot be stated as a load level alone. One can always imagine a load of that much plus a little more. Hence, the peak-load capacity is the one that handles some "large" load that is likely, on a statistical basis, to occur once every so-and-so many months or years.

51
On the question of information costs, see the remarkable essay by the economist Ely Devons, "The Problem of Co-ordination in Aircraft Production," in D. N. Chester, ed., *Lessons of the British War Economy* (Cambridge: Cambridge University Press, 1951), pp. 102-121. Devons observes, for instance: "Every official in the central [planning] directorate [the Ministry of Aircraft Production] was continually being faced with this dilemma. He knew that if he was to draw up a realistic programme for the component which he was looking after, he ought to know nearly as much about production possibilities as the production directorate. Yet he also knew that if he spent his time becoming a specialist in that field he would have little or no time to find out what was happening to related components or to the prospects and production plans for the aircraft to which his component was to be fitted" (p. 111).

52
Seymour B. Sarason, *The Culture of the School and the Problem of Change* (Boston: Allyn & Bacon, 1971), pp. 115-118; quoted in Sarason, *The Creation of Settings and the Future Societies* (San Francisco: Jossey-Bass, 1972), pp. 88-90. An interesting hypothesis emerges from an account by I. Ira Goldenberg of the opening of a residential youth center for inner-city youth in New Haven, Connecticut: whatever the level of management control at any time, there will always be a "hawk-dove" conflict over whether there should be more. The center's staff was initially divided along these lines during the first two tumultuous weeks, when the residents habitually acted wildly and destructively. After the center settled down into a period of relative order and social tranquility, it was visited by a representative of the funding agency from "downtown." The latter was shocked at the *disorder* still evident. *Build Me a Mountain: Youth, Poverty, and the Creation of New Settings* (Cambridge, Mass.: MIT Press, 1971), pp. 274-311, esp. 301-310.

6 | The Dissipation of Energies

This chapter describes a grab bag of games that do not fit neatly into any of the categories developed previously. Yet they are often important and it would be remiss not to mention them. Perhaps there is, however, a common theme: individuals, organizations, and groups waste a good deal of energy avoiding responsibility, defending themselves against maneuvers by other game-players, and setting up situations advantageous to their own game-playing strategies. The main outcomes of these games are underperformance with respect to mandated goals and, perhaps most important, delay.

Tenacity

Tenacity is a game for everyone—bureaucrats, legislators, professional associations, interest groups, community organizations. All it takes is the ability and the will to stymie the completion, or even the progress, of a program until one's own particular terms are satisfied. It is not necessarily any party's intention actually to kill the program, or even to delay it by much—indeed, all players may be very eager to get on with it —but death of the program or lengthy delays can be the consequence nevertheless. Consider, for example, the manpower training program planned for Oakland, California.

Three federal agencies were supposed to cooperate on mounting such a program, the EDA, the Department of Labor under provisions of the Manpower Development and Training Act, and the Department of Health, Education, and Welfare. There was no disagreement that there should be a training program, but there was total disagreement on what kind, who should run it, and who should pay for it. HEW wanted the task to be given to the East Bay Skills Center, one of its Oakland clientele agencies. The EDA wanted the funds to go to World Airways, which proposed to assume the job itself (offering to train 510 new aircraft maintenance personnel). The EDA felt that this would hold down the costs per trainee, though at the same time HEW felt it would provide too much easy money for World. At the state level there appear to have been disagreements on specifics between the California Department of Employment and the Department of Education. The whole training program also had to progress through a lengthy sequence of clearances called for in the routine administration of the Manpower Act. The result was first delay and then the utter collapse of the training component.[1]

For another example of Tenacity, let us turn again to the history of community action in Philadelphia.[2] In 1960, the Ford Foundation sponsored the Philadelphia Council for Community Advancement (PCCA) as part of its nationwide program of helping to uplift and renovate the spreading "gray areas" of central cities. The PCCA brought together representatives of city government, the board of education, the Greater Philadelphia Movement, the Citizens' Committee on Public Education, the United Fund, the Health and Welfare Council, a local foundation, the University of Pennsylvania, Temple University, the NAACP, organized labor, and the business community. Led by a cadre of three strong-willed men from the Greater Philadelphia Movement, the Citizens' Committee on Public Education, and Temple University, PCCA took as its guiding light a document entitled "A Programme for North Philadelphians." The document was written by Herman Niebuhr, Jr., the ambitious director of a new Center for Community Studies at Temple, and was characteristic of the left-liberal social scientific ideology of the period: critical of established social service agencies, critical of the insensitivity of the agencies' professional staffs to the lower-class culture of their black and Puerto Rican clientele, and critical of the remoteness of policy-making by these institutions from the clientele they were supposed to be serving. Ironically, PCCA itself was an example of the very conditions criticized in the planning document. Not only were the individual sponsoring groups among those indictable by Niebuhr's criteria, but PCCA itself had altogether excluded any representation from among the black residents of North Philadelphia! Its first executive director was a white district attorney, Samuel Dash, who gained the job as a compromise candidate after a yearlong standoff between the competing candidacies of Niebuhr and Manuel Kaufman, the city's deputy commissioner of welfare, both of whom were white.

On January 12, 1963, Cecil Moore, a black lawyer, used the occasion of his inauguration as president of the local NAACP chapter to attack white liberalism in general and the PCCA in particular. PCCA and its members were denounced as paternalistic, self-serving, bent on undermining the self-image of blacks. Moore demanded an immediate halt to PCCA activities in North Philadelphia and threatened to picket all Ford automobile dealers in the city if the Ford Foundation continued to support the PCCA. Partly in response to such pressures, PCCA backed off from its commitment to comprehensive, detailed, innovative planning and looked for smaller projects with immediate political payoff and good prospects of accomplishing at least a few of the many goals PCCA had in mind.[3]

Another study suggests the effect of the Tenacity game on the flow of federal OEO funds to cities under the Community Action Program. Greenstone and Peterson compared Chicago, Philadelphia, New York, and Los Angeles with respect to the "dispersion of political power" and the "political efficiency in distributing material perquisites." They found that the greater the dispersion the less the efficiency. In effect, political-machine cities were relatively good at getting large chunks of OEO money and "reform" cities were not. Of the four, Chicago did best, of course, hauling in over $200 per poor family (defined as having an income under $3,000) in the first two years of OEO, and Los Angeles did worst, obtaining only $25 per poor family. Greenstone and Peterson are careful to point out that not all this money necessarily reached the poor.[4]

Thus, while the Tenacity game does not always lead to the total collapse of a program as it did in Oakland, it does lead to delay and sometimes, as in the case of PCAA, to withdrawal of financial and political support. These are the risks and costs associated with the possible benefits of altering the balance of program objectives in some way. Whether after the fact one regards these benefits as worth the price depends in large part on one's values as well as on one's conception of long-run political goals and possibilities. Before the fact, however, the cost-benefit calculus must also take into account the possibility that other actors in the Tenacity game may also choose to hold fast rather than give in. If the calculations by all parties are too optimistic, the result will be worse for all concerned, except, of course, for those who prefer no program to any program not run on their terms.

Territory

All bureaucratic organizations play Territory. This game can have very positive results so long as no one really wins, that is, so long as the competitive forces among bureaus with overlapping jurisdictions or similar missions generate information that enables review officials either in the legislature or at higher levels of the bureaucracy to evaluate their performance and choose among their alternative service offerings. Rivalry among the military branches, for instance, has proved very advantageous in this regard.

One serious problem with L-P-S has been that the Short-Doyle programs in each county have won too much. They have been granted a monopoly on planning and administration. The rationale for this has been that it is necessary to prevent "fragmentation and duplication of services." One important result, however, has been the effective blockage or slowing down of nonpsychiatric and rehabilitation oriented services. The Short-Doyle program chiefs have been almost without exceptions psychiatrists. In the years prior to L-P-S many of the larger Short-Doyle programs had built up a substantial bureaucratic commitment to psychiatric services, even if in many instances "community-oriented" psychiatric services. The sheer momentum of these existing services was enough to preclude the allocation of new monies to rehabilitation services, especially in nonmedical settings: when there was so much clamor from existing services for their share of new money, how was it possible to free enough funds to start something really offbeat?

Competition for territory can have quite adverse effects if it interferes with operational responsibilities that ought properly to be coordinated. Following L-P-S, the Community Services Division (CSD) of the State Department of Social Welfare assumed the placement responsibility for patients released from the state hospitals. But the CSD was out of favor with both the Department of Mental Hygiene (DMH) and most of the Short-Doyle directors. The CSD wished to maintain and expand its territory by adding to its placement function a more general supervisory function, becoming in effect the organization with a "patient advocacy" mission. Many other players had it in mind, however, to break up the statewide CSD organization and turn the pieces over to the Short-Doyle programs to do with as they pleased—which in many instances would have meant destroying them. Whatever the best long-run solution might have been, in the short run, while the struggle was being carried on, the patients were allowed to "fall between the cracks." Worse still, in some counties the whole social service function fell into disrepute as a result of the constant haggling over who ought to do it, and no voice was heard on behalf of developing more social and rehabilitative services. When federal funds from the Social and Rehabilitation Service of HEW became available to the DMH for distribution to the counties largely on a project basis, many counties had no interest in, or capacity for, developing proposals.

If the struggle of the CSD with other organizations in its environment is like guerrilla resistance following a revolution or a coup d'etat, the BARTD's struggle with other mass transit systems in the Bay Area was like the Napoleonic wars.[5] BARTD seems to have been intent on capturing the entire territory of public mass transit in the Bay Area. It would have permitted surface bus systems to continue to exist, of course, but it would have forced them to alter their patterns of service and their fares to accommodate the needs of the BART system, no matter what impact these alterations would have had on their other services, their overall fare structure, their financial standing, or their political stature. BARTD's ultimate weapon in the game was its technologically determined inflexibility. BART trains are limited to a rail network, but buses can travel on almost any street. Under such conditions it is clear who has to accommodate to whom with respect to service patterns.

The principal dispute was between BARTD and Alameda-Contra Costa (AC) Transit, the bus system serving the East Bay and the only system, before BART, to carry transbay traffic. In the early 1970s, BARTD insisted that AC give up its transbay route when BART began its own (long-delayed) transbay service. It also insisted that AC redesign its service pattern to provide feeder service to and from all the East Bay BART stations. AC was one of the most successful public transit systems in the country. It had a relatively high ridership, a moderate annual operating deficit, and a high degree of public acceptability. Certainly a large portion of its success was due to the transbay route, which accounted for 25 percent of the system's patronage and was the only route on which AC did not incur a deficit. To give up this route would have been a hard enough blow, but it would have been doubly hard to do that *and* maintain a proposed nineteen-route feeder service to BART stations on which it would have lost approximately $.36/ passenger-mile, more than it lost on any other route. Other issues on which BARTD and AC clashed were joint fares and transfer privileges. BARTD installed a sophisticated automated fare-collection system without consulting AC or any other surface system. This maneuver once again would have forced the surface systems to modify their own fare-collection methods unless they were to increase inconvenience to passengers using both systems. BARTD was willing to share the costs of a free (to the passenger) transfer arrangement but was unwilling to absorb more than half the revenue loss and proposed to absorb as little as 20 percent.

BARTD was consistently high-handed in its negotiating tactics with AC. On June 5, 1970, AC Transit sent BARTD a set of preliminary and tentative proposals concerning routing adjustments it was prepared to make when BART began to operate. BARTD did not respond for two months, and when it did it leaked its response, which charged AC with being competitive rather than cooperative, to the press before conveying it to the relevant AC officials. In January 1971, following further negotiations between the two agencies, a BARTD consultant's report was made public that charged the AC Transit staff with being "negative and unimaginative . . . defeatist . . . laboring under some serious delusions." In August 1971, BARTD decided to provide free parking facilities at its stations, thereby undermining AC's ability to attract patronage on its feeder service and thus decreasing AC's projected revenues on these routes. It made this decision without consultations with AC staff or directors. AC Transit asked BARTD for compensation for AC's prospective revenue losses incurred in shifting its operations to help service BART. BARTD said no and complained that it was obliged by law to "live out of the fare box," a restriction that Stephen Zwerling in his study has convincingly argued was fictional rather than real.[6]

Zwerling has offered two explanations for BARTD's conduct. The first is like my own, namely, that BARTD was playing to win big and that it had the resources, including financial strength and political support outside its service territory, particularly in the federal government, to do so. The second is that BARTD suspected that its system would fail miserably and was maneuvering AC Transit into the role of scapegoat. This latter explanation fits under the rubric of another implementation game, to be discussed below, called Their Fault.

Both mental health and public rapid transit are policy areas in which the principal, if not the only, objective is service delivery. When the bureaucratic Territory game interferes with performance objectives, clients or customers get less than they otherwise would have. The Territory game has more complex effects on programs in which some form of regulation is at issue, that is, in which the identifiable population most directly affected is constrained from engaging in conduct offensive to certain laws. It is frequently alleged, for instance, that law enforcement functions are impaired by the rivalry among local police departments within a certain geographical area or among state, local, and federal enforcement agencies. One can readily understand the source of such frictions, in that the visible signs of agency success, taking an alleged offender into custody and sending him to jail, are very hard to parcel out among different agencies. The higher levels of government are generally able to preempt the lower ones in such matters. Hence, the lower-level law enforcement agencies tend to exclude representatives of the higher-level agencies from their territory as much as possible. The complexity in this sort of Territory game arises from the fact that one of the key technical resources in regulatory operations is information, and the flow of information through tips and informal friendship channels is not always very obedient to policies established at the policy level by agency directors. The information flow can be either larger or smaller than the directors would wish, and the channels of flow are complicated and confusing.

The immediate result of such a process is spotty and erratic enforcement. This proves a source of embarrassment to agency directors. There is pressure either to consolidate and standardize or to separate the territories more cleanly. Sometimes there are attempts to pursue both strategies at the same time. The result may be further political embarrassment, intensified territorial gamesmanship, demoralization of agency employees, and a drift toward a wait-and-see attitude on the part of bureaucrats on the firing line. This appears to have been the general course of events during a troubled period in 1965 and 1966 in USOE and HEW as various bureaus struggled to enforce compliance with Title VI of the 1964 Civil Rights Act.

The original enforcement efforts were lodged in the Equal Educational Opportunities Program (EEOP).[8] This office was isolated both from the educationists in the Washington office of OE and from the regional offices. The office was also very understaffed, given the very large job that had to be done. EEOP staff and their ring of outside consultants were primarily lawyers, who saw their tasks as technical and professional and who had relatively limited understanding of the political and administrative aspects of their work. The office was headed by David Seeley, a Yale Law graduate who had had some training at the Harvard Graduate School of Education and was therefore known to and trusted by OE Commissioner Francis Keppel. Enforcing Title VI was treated as a problem subject to standardization of procedures and basically manageable from Washington.

This view of the problem was vigorously disputed by the Office of Civil Rights (OCR), established in 1967 within the office of the secretary of HEW and first headed by Peter Libassi.[9] Libassi assumed his post after the EEOP and Keppel had drifted into a major political disaster. A combination of poor communications and political ineptitude had led the OE to attempt to cut off Title I funds to Chicago. The OE was quickly repulsed by the political forces of Mayor Richard Daley, acting upon and through President Johnson. Libassi's view of the problem was basically political. He wanted to decentralize civil rights enforcement to the HEW regional offices, to centralize more managerial control in the regional office chiefs over the various technical and program personnel in their offices, and to have the OCR develop somewhat tighter controls over the regional office chiefs. This strategy would, it was hoped, have the effect of bringing more "wholeness" and internal coordination to the department, a policy direction strongly desired by John Gardner, recently appointed as department secretary by Lyndon Johnson. It would also permit Gardner and the department to avoid damaging confrontations like the one in Chicago. As Beryl Radin puts it in her study, "Not only were there substantive interdependencies between the various agencies and bureaus involved with health, education and welfare, but Gardner tended to view the political survival of the Department as a whole piece."[10]

A fierce conflict ensued between the EEOP and the OCR, and between their respective heads, Seeley and Libassi. Despite a blizzard of memoranda from Libassi and his associates, Seeley and his associates persisted in the belief that only the OE, and only OE personnel in Washington, could hope to enforce compliance with Title VI. Seeley's position was perhaps easier to defend for its principles than for its practice, however. In fact, the EEOP offices throughout the first round of compliance review in 1965 were "chaotic, piled with papers, impossible for anyone to work in."[11] Seeley's attempts to improve the situation only made it worse. As the EEOP geared up for the second round of review in 1966, the office was broken into five area desks with a fair degree of autonomy for each area desk director, but with all of the directors based in Washington rather than in the geographical areas they supervised. The area directors were independent on some issues but obliged to defer to Seeley on many others, which were not well specified and sometimes "picayune." "The arrangement was capricious and, as a result, area directors could not predict what demands would be made on them and their staff members."[12] "The animosity between the two programs," moreover, "not only involved differences of roles . . . the personal antagonism between Seeley and Libassi could not even be hidden within the language of official memoranda."[13]

The continuing conflict between the two offices made it extremely difficult for compliance efforts to proceed either from the HEW regional offices or from the EEOP. The HEW regional offices had always occupied an uncertain niche within the department, and their powers had oscillated with the shifting doctrines of administrative control and responsibility emanating from Washington. Even secretaries who believed in decentralization were reluctant to vest much power in the regional offices. Whatever power went to the regional offices diminished the small quantity the secretary had left after one took account of the power already conceded to the many functional offices and programs in the department. Libassi's attempts to withdraw power from the

EEOP, then, did not necessarily entail reallocating it to the regional directors. Even in the one case in which this was a plausible course of action owing to the special talents of the regional director—"Pete" Page in the Atlanta regional office, a tough and civil rights-minded native southerner—Libassi balked. Page won out in the end, but hardly any of the other regional directors got anything like Page's authority out of Washington.[14]

Congressional intervention both before and after the Chicago debacle muddied the waters even further. Powerful congressmen were becoming displeased at the enforcement activities of the OE and demanded that such activities be moved to the secretary's office, where they could be brought under closer congressional scrutiny and control. Secretary Gardner and Libassi agreed, since it was on their minds to shift the EEOP operations to the OCR and the regional offices anyway. Yet Libassi's plans for "decentralization" did not give increased responsibilities to the regional directors. "Already uncertain about their role, their unclear expectations were only compounded by Congress."[15]

One result of these territorial games in HEW was a shift of responsibility for Title VI enforcement in the education field toward the Civil Rights Division in the Department of Justice. This unit was staffed with high-caliber attorneys and headed by John Doar, a man of undisputed vigor, intelligence, and courage. Doar and his staff successfully demanded of HEW a more "lawyerly concern for due process," a concern shared by Libassi. They all believed Seeley's office had proceeded haphazardly and had not made effective use of the court system to develop a body of case law to be used as an instrument for administering Title VI. Doar's strategy was "to begin with the very worst cases and gradually work up the list." Gary Orfield's assessment of this strategy is unfavorable. It implied concentrating on the Deep South and ignoring districts that merely "needed a push to move toward total desegregation . . . . The practical result was that it soon became obvious to many southern schoolmen that they were safe if they ignored the guidelines and simply stayed a few jumps ahead of the worst districts still receiving funds."[16]

Whether Orfield is right or wrong about the merits of this shift in strategy, one can plausibly infer that, within the parameters of the whole Title VI enforcement game defined by the 1964 Civil Rights Act, it was virtually the only alternative. HEW simply lacked the administrative competence to execute a more sophisticated strategy. It was too much encumbered by territorial games that impaired operating efficiency. The flow of responsibility from HEW to Justice represented one of the positive effects of the Territory game to which we have already alluded. Justice was clearly able to do a better job than HEW. It is of special interest that Justice's superiority was recognized in this case by its nominal territorial competitor, OCR, which voluntarily pursued the course set by Doar and his staff. The bureaucratic Territory game does not usually get settled so easily without intervention by a common superior—and even then it may simply be slowed down rather than settled.

Not Our Problem

Another important bureaucratic game is Not Our Problem. Bureaus typically desire augmented budgets and expanded territories, but this desire normally evaporates as soon as the bureau recognizes that the program will impose a heavy work load or that it will take the bureau into realms of controversy or that the required tasks are so difficult that it lacks the capacity to do the job. If the program is that unattractive, a bureau may try to shift certain of the operating responsibilities to a different bureau. If nobody wants the responsibilities, the services or regulatory activities that would flow from them are not performed. Citizens get the runaround as they are directed from one office to another.

One of the most troublesome problems with L-P-S was the displacement of the mentally ill offender from the mental health services system to the criminal justice system. The L-P-S Act was quite explicit about who could or could not be detained for an initial seventy-two-hour "evaluation" and possibly for subsequent fourteen-day "intensive treatment." Many persons who behaved offensively or annoyingly became the object of police attention. Mental health evaluation and screening units would refuse to deal with such a person when brought in by a policeman (or by anyone else) if he would not accept treatment voluntarily. Often the officer would have to take such a person to jail. If there were no grounds for jailing him or if—as was probably more likely—the officer did not wish to book him, the person would return to the setting whence he had come to continue the same behavior. The mental health agency did not like to cope with such persons, especially if they were likely to be difficult or disruptive. The law enforcement agencies did not like to cope with them either, partly because they felt that such people should be "treated" rather than "punished," and partly because bizarre or psychotic behavior could disturb the policemen's and the jailers' established routines. Often enough no agency had to. To anyone who asked they could say, "Not our problem."

This is perhaps more a basic policy design problem than a problem of implementation. A more clear-cut instance of Not Our Problem as an implementation game can be seen in regard to the development of Short-Doyle services for the chronically mentally ill. This was not a population Short-Doyle had ever had much to do with, since it had always been possible to ship such persons off to the state hospitals. After July 1, 1969, the effective date of L-P-S, such methods would no longer be permitted, however, and, indeed, many of the existing chronic cases in the hospitals were to be returned, within a year, to the community.

In retrospect it is possible to see that no one was adequately prepared for this case load. Short-Doyle offered few relevant services. The legislature and the governor were prepared to inundate DMH and Short-Doyle with huge annual budget increases, but no one was at first prepared to require the targeting of such monies specifically to the chronically mentally ill. The county plans called for in the L-P-S Act required an inventory of all public and private mental health resources, but no county plan writer seemed to think of the many existing proprietary "board-and-care" facilities, which had for years been the receiving stations for patients released from the state hospitals, as a mental health resource. Hence, their absence or insufficiency was overlooked for some time. No one had much of a theory for how to increase the supply or upgrade the quality of such facilities. Licensing was the only theory, but its utility is questionable. (See Appendix B.) When the legislature mandated facilities licensing in 1971, all three state licensing agencies—Public Health, Mental Hygiene, and Social Welfare—played Not Our Problem with the unpleasant responsibility for almost a year. The initial policy, which remained in force for the first four years of L-P-S, was that "scarce mental health monies" should not be spent to pay for room and board but for mental health services. Hence, the chronically mentally ill were encouraged to live on welfare stipends (Aid to the Permanently and Totally Disabled).

Even if they had known what to do, top administrators in the DMH would probably have been unwilling to do it. Dr. James Lowry, the director, was planning to resign the directorship. Like his predecessors, he believed in the ideology of local autonomy for the Short-Doyle programs; and the prospects of a relatively short tenure in office gave him little motivation to change the traditional laissez-faire approach. In any case, Lowry had always been more oriented to the administrative problems of the state hospital system than to those of the Short-Doyle system. In the larger budgetary and management picture of top DMH officials, Short-Doyle, with its annual expenditures of state money in amounts of only $20-25 million, occupied but a small corner.

Only a handful of DMH people knew much about what went on in that small corner. Chief among them was Dr. William Beach, a soft-spoken but well-respected administrator with several years of experience as the department's man in charge of the Local Programs Division. The principal burden of designing the post-L-P-S Short-Doyle system fell upon a task force of four or five young but quite capable technical specialists from the middle-management ranks: budget experts, community program analysts promoted from fieldwork to headquarters jobs, audit specialists, and the like. Even had these technical experts in the area of local programs been willing to assign the DMH a larger role in the emerging new system, however, they lacked the strength of numbers. They did not have the leverage internally to get the department to accept such an assignment.[17]

Under such conditions, it is not surprising that the task force construed its job as (1) assuring a smooth transition, and (2) continuing and expanding the traditional DMH role in local programs of assisting counties with no Short-Doyle programs or with only minimal programs to start them or develop them. It scarcely occurred to anyone in the DMH that the department might try to push the counties into one or another *kind* of program, particularly not a program designed to care for the chronically mentally ill in the community. County mental health agencies were thus permitted to drift more or less as they always had. The DMH said, in effect, Not Our Problem. It was not the immobilizing effects of conflict at higher levels that permitted this drift at the lower reaches, as it was in the case of Title VI enforcement, but the ideological commitments to laissez-faire on the part of some in the higher echelons and on the part of others an inability and unwillingness to convince the first group that there were alternatives better than laissez-faire, or at least more appropriate to the department's role in the emerging new order of things.[18]

An aggressive version of Not Our Problem is Their Fault, in which actors seek to deflect any prospective blame for program failure. In its most extreme form, actors might even try to define a particular scapegoat. Even one actor playing Their Fault can cause the ruin of the entire project if that actor controls a critical program element for which no functional substitutes are available. More generally, the more actors who are playing Their Fault, the less likely the program is to be completed, the less likely it is to succeed if it is completed, and the more likely it is that the assembly process will suffer delays.

We have already come across one plausible example of Their Fault in the maneuvering of the BARTD vis-à-vis AC Transit (see above, Territory). This example suggests the particularly corrosive effects of the game. We do not yet know the full extent of BART's potential failure, of course, but we can be sure that it will have been greatly amplified beyond what it might have been if BARTD had been more willing to cooperate with the Bay Area's surface transit systems. Sayles and Chandler report the prevalence of "gold plating" by engineering contractors working on NASA projects, a practice that involved unwarranted time and expense in order to make a particular component more foolproof than anyone, particularly the project manager, wanted. The contractor's objective, of course, was to ensure that if something went wrong with the project, it would not be the fault of that contractor's component(s). Spread across the many contractors' contributions, "gold plating" or other forms of Their Fault (like building only familiar hardware or using only traditional standards) could lead to enormous delays, escalating costs, and perhaps a total spacecraft weight in excess of the allowable maximum.[19]

Odd Man Out

We have described the policy-implementation process as a program-assembly process with control over the required program elements in the hands of relatively autonomous actors. One consideration in the minds of these actors as they weigh the decision whether or not to make some contribution is an estimate of how successful the program is likely to be. If ultimate success depends in part on whether or not *other* actors will make *their* contributions, this condition typically introduces a degree of uncertainty into calculation. The evolution of the assembly process itself either reduces or magnifies this uncertainty. Hence, whatever other implementation games the various actors play, they normally play, at the same time, a game in which they attempt to create or maintain their option to withdraw and cut their losses while they monitor the remaining uncertainty, and in which they at the same time try to maneuver other players into foregoing their own options. This is the Odd Man Out game.

In a sense, the protracted haggling between EDA and the various parties to its Oakland construction projects involved maneuvering in a game of Odd Man Out. Each party began to feel increasingly uncertain about the venture. Eventually the EDA did get struck with the excessive financial costs they apparently feared all along.

If the uncertainties of the Odd Man Out game are sufficiently great, no party will be willing to make enough of the early moves and a program all would like may never even get started. Consider the problems in implementing "the apparently highly promising V/STOL (vertical and short take-off and landing) technology."[20] Designs for both the engines and the airframe had been produced by several manufacturers, but no other actors seemed able or willing to commit the additional functionally requisite program elements. Affirmative production decisions were withheld pending a commitment by the airlines to purchase a sufficient number of units to make production profitable. The airlines could not make such commitments until they knew what would be the operating requirements of the Civil Aeronautics Board and the Federal Aviation Agency. The CAB was wondering what kinds of airports and supporting facilities could be used or would be built in the future to accommodate V/STOL craft—central city or suburban. The FAA's choice of safety controls would depend on the location of the airports and the CAB's route-planning decisions. The context of choice for several of these parties included also the actual or contemplated network of ground transportation. The actions of local planning and zoning boards were of course relevant but highly uncertain, as was the type and degree of governmental support for further research and development—program elements that would not be forthcoming until the airlines, the manufacturers, the CAB, and the FAA could resolve some of *their* uncertainties! Sayles and Chandler conclude, "It is difficult to specify the appropriate sequence of decisions, and Congress is frustrated over 'the industry's' inability to resolve the stalemate."[21]

A similar sort of stalemate has prevented halfway houses for the mentally ill from being started in numbers anywhere close to those truly needed by the L-P-S system.[22] Like the more custodial board-and-care homes, halfway houses were expected to spring forth unassisted from the private sector. Unlike the board-and-care homes, however, halfway houses, by virtue of their self-imposed mission, finance a treatment program, and move residents out and into more independent living arrangements as fast as possible. Thus, their costs are higher than those of a board-and-care home and their revenues less stable (and possibly, as a result of higher vacancy rates caused by turnover, also lower). Largely for these financial reasons, halfway houses have not sprung up except under rather unusual circumstances, like the appearance on the scene of a well-heeled philanthropist. No important decision-makers at either the state or the county level thought it appropriate to spend "scarce mental health monies" on room and board. Hence, halfway houses were to be financed, if at all, principally from residents' room-and-board charges, which in turn were typically levied against the residents' meager welfare allotments. I have not yet heard of a county being willing to supply any of the start-up funds needed for a halfway house. In cases where a county has been willing to pay a portion of the operating costs, the county has been unwilling to pay on other than a per capita basis and has been unwilling to guarantee a minimum occupancy rate. Even in cases where a county has evidenced willingness to pay at all, the county mental health planners would typically say they would do so only after seeing evidence of competent performance. In effect, these counties were playing Their Fault and Odd Man Out from a very strong position.

In the process of starting a halfway house in one county I studied, Odd Man Out games continued almost till the day the house finally opened.[23] In August 1971, the county mental health director approached the director of the Community Service Alliance (CSA), a church-related social service agency, with the proposal that the CSA establish a halfway house for the mentally ill in the county. The CSA had long been considering such a move on its own. One of the members of the CSA board of directors had over a year earlier proposed that the CSA start such a facility in order to provide a training site for local seminarians who were interested in working professionally with the mentally ill. The executive director of the CSA was told by county officials that a halfway house run by the CSA, which had an excellent reputation built on its success in numerous other social service projects, would be virtually assured full occupancy and that federal funds from the federal Social and Rehabilitation Service (SRS) would be available to pay for staffing costs.

On this understanding, the CSA executive director hired Bill Rogers and charged him with overseeing the project. Rogers was to locate a site, supervise the necessary remodeling, and assemble the rest of the staff. Rogers took the job without pay on the understanding that once the house was operating and the funds were flowing he would be paid retroactively (a rather small salary, in any event). Within a very short time a spacious old Victorian home was found that Rogers and the CSA board of directors thought would make an ideal halfway house, and the board voted to approve the purchase. Owing to its excellent reputation in the community, the CSA secured a 100 percent mortgage and a $5,000 remodeling loan. (The bank officers nevertheless told Rogers that they regarded the loans as an act of community service rather than as a good business proposition.)

Remodeling proceeded over the course of the winter. Rogers and the CSA staff negotiated a tortuous series of clearances: a construction permit, fire marshal certification, a zoning variance, a recreation department permit, and a facility license from the county welfare department. Rogers tried but failed to secure a license from a state health or social welfare agency. No agency recognized the classification "halfway house" as being within its jurisdiction, though each was certain that it would be illegal to operate such a facility unless *some* license were obtained. (See above, Not Our Problem.) By spring it was clear that the remodeling would cost $4,000 more than the original estimates and that the federal SRS funds were not coming through as the county mental health director had hoped and promised.

In fact, it turned out that the county had not even applied for the SRS funds to the DMH, which was the state-level conduit for the money. The county mental health director had refrained from pressing the application at the state level because he was sure that his immediate bureaucratic superior, the county public health officer, would disapprove the plan and he saw no way to surmount that hurdle. He had not informed the CSA of this problem because (1) the CSA would have put unwelcome pressure on him to solve it, and (2) CSA had taken all the risks so far and would have to continue to do so. The CSA demanded of the county public health officer that he request the SRS funds from the DMH, but he refused on the grounds that the halfway house had not been approved in the county mental health plan submitted by the county to the DMH many months earlier. Privately, he was pleased to be able to frustrate the mental health director, whom he disliked intensely. Rogers and the CSA appealed to the DMH for help but to no avail. If and when the federal funds came through—they had been delayed for reasons unknown—and if and when the county applied for them properly, the DMH would be glad to help. In the end, four members of the CSA board of directors had to pledge their own assets as collateral for a bank loan for the needed $4,000. Needless to add, Rogers never did get paid retroactively for the initial months he worked without pay: he was the Odd Man Out.

Reputation

All the games we have described so far have featured as the main players either organizations or persons playing out some organizational role. The interpersonal conflict between the county health officer and the mental health director to which we alluded above was the first suggestion of games played by individuals in order to fulfill some personal need or ambition. Yet the world of implementation games is populated by human beings with private as well as public lives. Should we not take these into account?

Anthony Downs in *Inside Bureaucracy* has postulated five ideal-typical varieties of the species "bureaucrat": climbers, conservers, advocates, zealots, and statesmen.[24] He has provided a fairly elaborate list of reasons why certain types of bureaucrats fill certain organizational roles and an equally elaborate set of hypotheses about how these roles are played given the condition that they are occupied by a certain bureaucratic type. It took Downs over thirty pages merely to sketch the connections between five personal types and the play of perhaps half a dozen *intra*bureaucratic games. Clearly, it would require a major effect, virtually a book in itself, were we to undertake an analysis of how even two or three different personality types were connected with the fifteen or more games we have described so far. In the interests of economy, let us postulate that the players of implementation games have only one dimension to their private lives worth talking about, namely ambition, and that the realization of ambition is intimately related to their ability to play these games either well or poorly. Ambition is linked to game-playing through "reputation," which is both a product of and a facilitating condition for playing well (or poorly). Players seek reputation partly as an end in itself but principally as an instrument for achieving other ends, like getting reelected or winning a promotion or having news reporters treat them with deference or being able to bluff effectively in their next round of implementation games.

A reputation for what? That depends on the player and his personal situation. Presidents seek reputations for being sensitive to their power stakes.[25] Senators seek reputations as popular figures with good television images so that they may hope to win their party's nomination for the presidency. Reporters seek reputations for being "in the know" so that officials will choose to cooperate with rather than to outwit them. Advisers seek a reputation for being sound, discreet, and loyal. They may also seek a reputation for having given experience-tested "good" advice, that is, advice that has issued in "success" when it was followed.[26] Administrators seek a reputation for being good at Budget, Territory, Funding, Tenacity, and Up for Grabs. Politicians of all kinds seek the reputation of being good at Pork Barrel and Tenacity. In general, everyone avoids the reputation for excelling at Easy Life, Easy Money, and Not Our Problem. Piling On has an ambiguous status. A particularly destructive Reputation game takes place in bureaucracies in the course of playing Odd Man Out: officials write an endless, and time-consuming, series of memos to one another in order to protect themselves against being held liable should anything eventually go wrong. In short, wherever there are political games or implementation games proceeding at a public (if occasionally covert) level, there are also in progress a multitude of private Reputation games.[27]

Unfortunately, in the few studies I have been able to find that bear at all on the implementation process as I have conceived it, there is little information that sheds light on Reputation games. One reason is that it is quite difficult to acquire such information. It is almost necessary to be a participant in order to capture all the nuances of Reputation gamesmanship. Typically, individuals play not one but many Reputation games simultaneously, each for a different audience and perhaps for different purposes. To understand how any small bit of behavior fits into one of these games at a given moment requires close observation and skillful interpretation. An "outside" researcher conducting interviews months or years after the events would find respondents' memories clouded (partly because people repress consciousness of their own and others' Reputation games even in the present) or their willingness to talk about such unseemly things slight (unless they have been particularly hurt by someone else's game). It is also quite difficult to raise such issues in the interview situation lest the respondent become defensive and be led to withhold other information with which the researcher is actually more concerned.[28] This, at least, has been my experience doing research on L-P-S. A second reason that little is written about Reputation games is that they are, in a sense, not very important in the context of all the other games being played. Though I cannot of course say so with much confidence, I suspect that this is the case. Because reputation is built largely on performance in relevant policy and implementation games themselves, any given player's strategy in his private Reputation game is likely to be coincident with his strategy in the more public game. When this is the case, Reputation has little independent influence on action except perhaps to reinforce it.

When is Reputation likely to be a game with independent significance? This is likely to occur when actors seek out means of persuading an audience that they are doing more or doing better than they really are, and more concretely still, when actors seek a reputation for boldness, toughness, or innovativeness. These are qualities that quite frequently advance one's position in the world of politics and administration provided others recognize them, but which others have a hard time recognizing without some dramatic display of evidence. One thinks here of the rhetoric of a demagogue, of Cecil Moore, perhaps, playing Tenacity and Pork Barrel publicly and Reputation privately. Amory Bradford, who was the first director of the EDA-Oakland projects, seems to have been playing Reputation as well. In 1968, he published an account of his and the EDA's work in Oakland, *Oakland's Not for Burning,* in which he "appeared to suggest that the city had recently been saved from riot and ruin by the infusion of $23 million in federal funds."[29] Since he was obviously playing Reputation in 1968, it seems likely he was making the early moves in that game during 1966 while on the job.

Another instance of the Reputation game is suggested in the account by Gross, Giacquinta, and Bernstein of how the "catalytic role model" ideal of teacher behavior was introduced in "Cambire School."[30] It was presented to the faculty of this inner-city public elementary school, recently converted into an ESEA Title III "laboratory" school, by the newly appointed director of the school district's Bureau of Educational Change, Mark Williams. Williams described his innovative ideas in a document distributed to the teachers in January 1967. Williams stressed the teacher's role in encouraging children to become increasingly self-motivated and responsible for their own learning and education. The teacher was to accomplish this with his or her own skills and talents supplemented by a set of stimulating, self-instructional, and "pedagogically sound" materials. Williams urged immediate implementation. The teachers were more than happy to try. They too were interested in innovation and in helping children learn better. An assessment performed by Gross and his associates in late April and May 1967, however, showed that there had been little change in the way classrooms were actually conducted.

Why not? In large measure there appears to have been a basic design problem. Who really knows how to make students "self-motivated"? But there were genuine implementation problems as well. The largest, it seems, was Williams himself. Williams' document told the teachers about his catalytic role-model ideal in general terms but offered no specific advice about how to attain the ideal. In fact, the teachers themselves doubted that he was capable of offering such advice since, as one teacher put it, "Williams has no classroom experience so he can't think it through; his philosophy is that it's an idea that the teacher has to work out."[31] Williams came to a teachers' meeting but "didn't say anything," claimed one teacher. Another said, "We didn't talk about it very much. This was Williams' philosophy, this is what he believed. I took it [the document] home and read it." A subject specialist at Cambire observed: "He wrote up his description and assumptions for the catalytic role model, but there was no communication after that." As to the "highly motivating self-instructional materials," the teachers did not know what they were, did not know how to create them, and were not given any. Williams tried unsuccessfully to order them but was rebuffed by the district-level purchasing office, which did not find them on the "'approved'" list. Gross and his associates argue, however, that even if Williams had had complete freedom in this respect, "the types of materials teachers needed did not exist. The administration, in effect, was requesting teachers to carry out an innovation that required unique types of instructional materials that were not available."[32] As the spring term wore on, the teachers' enthusiasm turned to resentment, and the likelihood of their implementing the concept of the catalytic role model (then or ever, one suspects) fell to zero. In March and early April it was discovered that Williams was unwilling to commit himself to reassigning the teachers to Cambire in the following year. "This fact and their growing belief that the director was 'using them' in an unprofessional manner to promote 'his' innovation added to their mounting frustrations and feelings of disillusionment."[33] Title III, laboratory schools, Bureau of Educational Change, a new classroom concept brought over from England—add paper and pencil and these are the only materials needed for the Reputation game. It is almost hard to imagine Williams *not* playing!

Notes

1

Jeffrey L. Pressman and Aaron Wildavsky, *Implementation* (Berkeley: University of California Press, 1973), pp. 45-47, 110.

2

I have relied for this account on Peter Marris and Martin Rein, *The Dilemmas of Social Reform* (New York: Atheneum, 1967), pp. 94-119.

3

One of the projects they invested in was the Opportunities Industrialization Center, conceived and managed by Leon Sullivan, an influential Baptist minister in North Philadelphia, who already had assembled buildings, equipment, and staff. They also gave financial support to the North City Congress, a community organization originally started by a North Philadelphia leader with the encouragement of Temple University. Both programs were relatively successful, both politically and with respect to their stated goals, though neither owed very much of its success to the backing of PCCA.

4

J. David Greenstone and Paul E. Peterson, "Reformers, Machines, and the War on Poverty," in James Q. Wilson, ed., *City Politics and Public Policy* (New York: Wiley, 1968), pp. 267-292, esp. pp. 286-287. Although they modified certain other conclusions of this early paper in their 1973 publication, *Race and Authority in Urban Politics* (New York: Russell Sage Foundation), this conclusion remained intact.

A similar finding emerges—albeit not very sharply—from a study by Gilbert and Specht of the Model Cities program. (United States Department of Housing and Urban Development, Office of Community Development Evaluation Division, *The Model Cities Program*, prepared by Neil Gilbert and Harry Specht for Marshall Kaplan, Gans, and Kahn, a San Francisco-based consulting firm.) In this case, the dependent variable was not the amount of funds received but the amount spent. In general, the first year of the program was (not surprisingly) marked by considerable underspending of appropriated funds. Gilbert and Specht examined a number of city characteristics in an attempt to explain intercity variations in ability to spend. Only two of their seven tested independent variables seemed to have a clear and consistent relationship with underspending, namely, city size and the percent of categorical funds included in the Model Cities program's budget. The relationships were not very strong, and their meaning not very clear, however. It is very likely that the underspending problem originated as much at the donor end as at the recipient end, which fact, if true, would explain their relatively low success at explaining underspending by looking solely at the cities. In the context of our present discussion, however, one suggestive finding was that there was a slightly negative correlation between city spending ability and the degree of citi-

zen influence. The gamma coefficient relating citizen influence and the proportion
of funds spent in the first six months was —0.20. Looking at the full twelve-
month period, the coefficient is only —0.06; but a closer look at the data reveals
a curvilinear relationship. A "low spending pattern" was observed in 30 percent
of the cities with "weak" citizen influence, in 29 percent of the cities with
"moderate," and in 44 percent of the cities with "strong" citizen influence. After
the first year (though not after the first six months), a negative relationship of
—0.26 was also observed between spending ability and the number of agencies in
the Model Cities program, another suggestion of the impeding effects of the Tenacity game. (pp. 28-30). The study was based on data from 147 cities. Nowhere do
the authors report what is meant by "low, medium, and high spending patterns."
Their judgment of degree of citizen influence in any city is based completely on
ratings provided by HUD officials, though the authors themselves grouped these
ratings into the "weak/moderate/strong" trichotomy.

5
The account which follows is based on Stephen Zwerling, "The Political Consequences of Technological Choice: Public Transit in the San Francisco Metropolitan
Area," Ph.D. dissertation (Department of Political Science, University of California, Berkeley, 1972), Chap. 4. Zwerling interprets the conflict of BARTD and the
surface systems as a clash between "technological rationality" and "organizational
rationality." My own interpretation would be that all organizations in the game,
including BARTD, manifested "organizational rationality" but that only BARTD
had technologically derived political resources. "Technological rationality" seems
to me to convey little more than "rationality."

6
Zwerling, "Political Consequences," pp. 145-146.

7
Zwerling, "Political Consequences, "pp. 156-157.

8
I have relied for the following account principally on Beryl A. Radin, "Imple-
menting Change in the Federal Bureaucracy: School Desegregation in HEW,"
Ph.D. dissertation (Department of City and Regional Planning, University of Cali-
fornia, 1973); and Gary Orfield, *The Reconstruction of Southern Education: The
Schools and the 1964 Civil Rights Act* (New York: Wiley, 1964).

9
It was also unpopular with Libassi's predecessor in a similar assignment, HEW
Assistant Secretary James Quigley. A former Pennsylvania congressman, Quigley
preferred to treat each school district as a separate problem and to enforce Title
VI as much as possible in each case. For an interesting statement of the limitations
of this seemingly appealing strategy, see Orfield, *Reconstruction*, pp. 87-92.

10
Radin, "Implementing Change," pp. 177-178.

11
Radin, "Implementing Change," p. 181.

12
Radin, "Implementing Change," p. 190.

13
Radin "Implementing Change," p. 197.

14
Radin, "Implementing Change," pp. 149-154, 207.

15
Radin, "Implementing Change," pp. 189-190.

16
Orfield, *Reconstruction*, pp. 335-336.

17
Although abundant expertise was located in the department's several regional offices around the state, whose almost exclusive function had been to oversee Short-Doyle operations, these regional officials also had relatively little leverage in Sacramento.

18
None of this is meant by way of criticism. Beach and his task force may have been quite correct to wish to tread lightly in the transitional period, especially in light of Lowry's relative disengagement from the problem. Lowry's disengagement was itself probably not inappropriate, since he almost surely sensed that he was not the right man to steer the DMH on its new course. It is significant that Lowry's successor in 1971, Dr. J. M. Stubblebine, came from the directorship of one of the state's largest Short-Doyle programs, that of San Francisco.

19
Leonard E. Sayles and Margaret K. Chandler, *Managing Large Systems* (New York: Harper & Row, 1971), p. 210.

20
Sayles and Chandler, *Managing*, p. 139.

21
Sayles and Chandler, *Managing*, p. 140. In the light of CAB performance over the last thirty years, one might suspect that the stalemate could be resolved if the CAB were to refrain from playing the role of superplanner for nearly all of the country's civil aviation. See Richard E. Caves, "Performance, Structure, and the Goals of Civil Aeronautics Board Regulation," in Paul W. MacAvoy, *The Crisis of the Regulatory Commissions* (New York: Norton, 1970), pp. 131-151.

22
Whether or not these are valuable treatment modalities is of course arguable. Al-
though I am no expert on the subject, I believe they have great therapeutic poten-
tial and are probably more cost-effective than most of the treatment modalities
funded through L-P-S. See Charles Richmond, "Therapeutic Housing," in H.
Richard Lamb, and others, *Rehabilitation in Community Mental Health* (San
Francisco: Jossey-Bass, 1971, pp. 114-135; H. R. Raush and C. L. Raush, *The
Halfway House Movement: A Search for Sanity* (New York: Appleton-Century-
Crofts, 1968), and R. M. Glasscote, and others, *Halfway Houses for the Mentally
Ill* (Washington, D.C.: Joint Information Service of the American Psychiatric
Association and the National Association for Mental Health, 1971).

23
The names and a few details in the following account have been fictionalized in
order to preserve the anonymity of the players. The essential structure of the
games is in no way distorted, however.

24
Anthony Downs, *Inside Bureaucracy* (Boston: Little, Brown, 1967), Chaps. 8, 9.

25
See Richard E. Neustadt, *Presidential Power* (New York: Wiley, 1960).

26
See Arnold Meltsner, *Policy Analysts and Bureaucrats* (Berkeley: University of
California Press, 1976).

27
See Graham T. Allison, "Conceptual Models and the Cuban Missile Crisis,"
American Political Science Review 63: 3 (September 1969): 708-715. I think this
sketch of the Reputation game is very similar to what Allison refers to as Bureaucratic Politics or "Model III." In speaking of the modern secretary of state, Allison
describes five different institutional roles the secretary typically plays (reminiscent
of Clinton Rossiter's president with ten "hats") and remarks that, "His performance in one affects his credit and power in the others" (p. 709). "Credit and
power" sound to me like Reputation. His description of the play of the bureaucratic politics game sounds very like Odd Man Out—advisers giving advice in such
a way that no one will be able to blame them for being wrong or being soft on the
Russians and especially not both at once. To have been hard on the Russians *and*
wrong would have meant, in the context of the Cuban missile crisis, to have been
dead, along with most of one's countrymen. This rather interesting feature of the
payoff matrices in his more hawkish advisers' several Reputation games apparently
did not completely escape the attention of President Kennedy. He had his own
Reputation game to worry about, which in this case fortunately helped him to
see the problem in a fuller perspective.

28
See Eugene Bardach, "Gathering Data for Policy Research," *Journal of Urban Analysis* 2 (1974), pp. 117-144, esp. pp. 135-138.

29
Pressman and Wildavsky, *Implementation*, p. xi.

30
Neal Gross, Joseph P. Giacquinta, and Marilyn Bernstein, *Implementing Organizational Innovations: A Sociological Analysis of Planned Educational Change* (New York: Basic Books, 1971).

31
Gross, Giacquinta, and Bernstein, *Implementing Organizational Innovations*, p. 151.

32
Gross, Giacquinta, and Bernstein, *Implementing Organizational Innovations*, p. 169.

33
Gross, Giacquinta, and Bernstein, *Implementing Organizational Innovations*, p. 172.

II
Delay in the Game

Implementation takes a long time, much longer than most of the program sponsors had hoped it would take and longer even than the law's hypothetical "reasonable man" might have expected. Pressman and Wildavsky have recorded that it took almost four years for the EDA-Oakland project to begin to get rolling. Derthick has shown that in one city after another, when the New Towns project was not scuttled entirely, it was stalled and thwarted and postponed. If there is one attribute of the implementation process that everyone would agree was symptomatic of "pathology," it would be delay. Unexpectedly high financial costs are not usually considered pathological because we are all aware that policy advocates initially underestimate dollar costs in order to "sell" their idea politically. The perversion of goals and the diminution of performance would not be regarded as pathological either, since most people's notions of how these occur take account of the necessity to compromise idealistic goals in the face of "normal" resistance and obstructionism. But delay is another matter. If certain outcomes are going to be achieved eventually, why not earlier rather than later? ask the policy designers and advocates.

Often enough, delay is a synonym for perpetual procrastination, which is in turn a synonym for effective resistance or obstruction. In such cases delay is not pathological but purposive, in the sense that it serves interests or purposes in the games of at least certain parties. Another type of purposive delay is associated with most of the games described in the preceding chapter. Tenacity, for instance, is a game that deliberately exploits other players' preferences for greater haste as leverage to gain better terms. Odd Man Out in effect does the same. Bureaucrats playing Reputation games might hold up clearances in order to demonstrate their power to command deference.

Yet there are many delays that no one particularly wants or contrives. They seem just to happen. Whether or not they are also "pathological" depends on whether or not they are avoidable. More precisely, it depends on how costly it would be to avoid them. Presumably, no one would want a bridge constructed in half the time if the price were a thousandfold increase in the probability that it would collapse in five years. In this chapter we shall discuss only nonpurposive delays and some plausible (low-cost) means of avoiding them. These delays are associated either with the program-assembly process or with the collective-decision process that overlays some part of the program-assembly process. Although the two processes are inextricably joined at certain points, such as in multiparty negotiating situations, it will be convenient to separate them initially for purposes of analysis. This chapter deals with delays in assembling program elements. The next chapter deals with delays in reaching collective decisions.[1]

Program Assembly

We can construe the contribution of any program element as being effected by a transaction between two parties. One party is a "provider" and the other is a "solicitor." A halfway house operator solicits a permit from the fire marshal, and the fire marshal provides it; or an EDA task force solicits projects from businessmen and public efficials in Oakland, and the port provides several. Clearly, an actor can be involved in many such transactions simultaneously, and his playing the role of provider in some is wholly compatible with his playing the role of solicitor in others. The principal delays in the program-assembly process are associated with (1) the efforts undertaken by solicitors in searching out suitable providers, (2) the time it takes potential providers to decide whether or not to commit program elements under their control and on what terms, and (3) the sheer number of necessary transactions.

Search activities are mundane, but they can be surprisingly time-consuming. It took HUD two months, in consultation with the General Services Administration and the Defense Department, to locate twenty-six parcels of surplus federal land that might be usable for the New Towns program, and almost another two months thereafter to come up with twenty-two more. It took still longer to send teams to survey the forty-eight sites and for the interagency task force eventually to conclude that only twenty-two of these were suitable. These were not necessarily available, however, as they had yet to be declared such by the Defense Department and by the House Armed Services Committee. Nor had the task force ascertained local opposition or support.[2]

Search activity need not involve physical work. It can be purely intellectual, in that a party might undertake a study of several alternative courses of action. Such studies can be "quick and dirty" and consume a few minutes, hours, or days; or they might be relatively intensive and consume weeks or months. Such studies are not ordinarily associated with "implementation" but with the "planning" or the "design" phase of policy development. However, it should not violate our sense of the word "implementation" to say that study and analysis are part of the implementation process as well, though their subject matter is ordinarily more specific and detailed than it would be in the policy-adoption phase. The search for suitable New Towns sites was initially carried on in files, not in the field. The search for airplane designs to satisfy Defense Secretary Robert McNamara's demand for a single-service tactical fighter plane—which led eventually to the TFX, or F-111—went on in the minds of contractors, military brass, and civilian managers. The search took up nearly three years.[3]

When the solicitor party is not an individual but a group, the search process may involve a lot of meeting and talking and memo-writing. As they search for alternative courses of action, the individuals also search out each others' opinions, preferences, and prejudices. In September 1968, several months before L-P-S was to take effect, a task force to plan a "comprehensive mental health program" for San Joaquin County was convened. The group represented nine different interests in the county who were routinely concerned with the delivery of mental health services: the Short-Doyle director, Stockton State Hospital (located in the downtown of the county's largest city), the county mental health advisory board, the county mental health association, the Community Services Division, and a number of private health and welfare agencies. They met weekly for three months to come up with a proposal so vague and abstract that they might never have met at all. They recommended "unanimously" such "principles" as "maintain close liaison with all mental health agencies to assure continuity of appropriate care and treatment." After listing nearly fifteen such principles, their report simply appended statements by each agency representative as to how his agency would "participate in a comprehensive community mental health program for San Joaquin County." Only two parties managed to propose anything different from what they were already doing—although no one thought that the resulting document represented in the aggregate a "comprehensive community mental health program"—and these were the Short-Doyle agency and the state hospital. They proposed to establish a jointly managed "mental health center" located on the grounds of the hospital. This, however, was an idea that had been originated nearly a year earlier—and was destined to take almost another two years to make operational. The task force disbanded after making its report public in May 1969.

That the task force took so long to do so little is not surprising to anyone with the least bit of experience in committee activity. In this particular case, as in so many, delay is the product of such numerous and diverse causes it is hard to represent any particular ones as being very much more, or less, important than others. For the present we may observe simply that the substantive task confronting the group probably played as large a role in their eventual failure as any other cause. The problem of moving from a general conception of an ideal state of affairs to a detailed rendering of its specifics is quite difficult. It is even more difficult if, as part of the plan, one must also specify in some detail how to move from the present into the future. Needless to say, the more difficult the task is, the longer people will take to perform it. Hence, the more delay. That the task might indeed be impossible—as one suspects the San Joaquin planning group's task was—does not necessarily deter people from trying.

The party to whom a solicitation is addressed, the potential provider, ordinarily takes some time in responding—whether positively or negatively. In Chapter 5 we referred to the phenomenon of alternating slack and overload, which makes operating systems appear uncoordinated and inefficient, even though the nature of the world (particularly random processes) guarantees this sort of outcome. The same "queuing problem," as it is called by operations researchers, afflicts organizational units, like a zoning commission or a personnel department, that bear decision-making responsibilities concerning the provision of elements to one or more different programs. It also afflicts parties who in fact are already committed to delivering some resource, whether willingly or unwillingly. More concretely, any organizational unit, even down to the level of the individual, faced by random arrivals of its workload obligations, will develop a backlog unless it has a great deal of slack resources. This latter condition obtains only infrequently, and when it does the unit's strategy in the Easy Life game might lead it to postpone action for a time anyway: it will thus appear to have a backlog and can disguise the existence of slack that might otherwise be taken away. This may have been part of the strategy of the Architect and Engineer's Office of the Port of Oakland, which held up progress on the EDA-financed marine terminal for approximately three months.[4] This is perhaps an extreme case, as the normal lag time for response by an organizational unit is usually measured in weeks rather than in months.

Even when queuing is not significant for any single organizational unit, decision-making processes internal to an organization often consume much time simply because numerous units have to be consulted and the comulative delaying effect of doing so may be large. The routing of a single memorandum through three officials will take fifteen days if each holds it only five days—or if one holds it eleven days, pending his return from a trip out of town, while the other two hold it only two days each. Add to this the time that elapses when one of the three wishes to append a memorandum of comment. After getting it typed and duplicated he then sends it through the other two once again. The progress of such a memorandum will be even further delayed: if any of the parties en route have some political or ideological interest in obstructing its flow; if personal animosities or rivalries between some of the parties preclude direct discussion over its contents when such discussion is genuinely needed; if parties in search of Reputation attempt to demonstrate their power (or their prudence) by delaying the routing for purely symbolic reasons, and so forth. "Standard operating procedures" that multiply the number of hands through which the paper must pass increase delay at least in proportion to the number of prescribed parties. Indeed, the delay will be more than simply proportionate under conditions of bureaucratic organization in which interpersonal rivalry or Reputation games are prevalent: raising the number of checkpoints increases the probability that at least one player will be brought into the circulation who is able and willing to cause disproportionate delay. If a bureaucracy is in the process of being reorganized, as is very often the case, the internal confusion will result in even further delay, especially if the decision concerns a complex or risky matter. HEW and USOE took between six months and a year, depending on how one counts, to develop a set of procedures and guidelines capable of giving school districts any clues as to the likely decisions regarding their Title VI compliance plans.[5]

Once a decision has been made in the affirmative—the potential provider promises that a contribution will be made—more time elapses, often, until the contribution is actually delivered. The time between commitment and delivery may be taken up by a physical production process—for example, a year or two may pass before a promised house or office building is actually built. The time between commitment and delivery may also go simply into waiting for the beginning of some new accounting period or expenditure cycle. The negotiators for Stockton

State Hospital and San Joaquin County Mental Health Services working out the plans for their jointly managed "mental health center" reached essential agreement on the last of the sticking points in March 1971. Yet the program was not to be put into operation until July 1 of that year. Interestingly enough, they were not waiting for *new* money to be committed, so that this was not the barrier between the promise and the delivery. But a number of changes had to be made in contractual arrangements existing between the state hospital and the county, and some additional fine points had to be clarified. From the point of view of the planners, July 1 presented itself as a convenient target date for beginning operations partly because it obviated the need to revise contracts in midyear and partly because it in effect gave all parties a convenient deadline for resolving the remainder of their disagreements. On this analysis, then, dates on the calendar that have special legal and administrative significance, like the end or beginning of the fiscal year, have a constraining effect on implementation processes. In this case the presence of such dates led to extra delay. In other cases it could lead to acceleration. (Actually, the program did not begin until September 1, because it took the state General Services Administration several weeks past July 1 to approve the contracts for the state.)

Another source of delay in program assembly is the necessity to proceed through a number of providers seriatim instead of simultaneously. In the case of bureaucratic memo-routing, which is the clearest example, approval by an official is often contingent on clearance by his or her immediate subordinate or by his or her assistant. Although this "chain of command" procedure is the most obvious case of seriatim provision of requisite elements, there are others. One need think only of the economic concept of the "intermediate product" to understand their nature. An auto fender comes from an intermediate product, rolled sheet steel. Steel itself comes from iron, iron comes from iron ore, etc. The auto fender, in turn, is only an intermedite product between these raw materials and a finished automobile. One of the most common series of intermediate products in implementation processes is political. Consider the mayor of New Bedford, Massachusetts, looking for approval by the city council of a New Towns site and first taking pains to develop support among the business and civic elite. This is a two-step series. No doubt the mayor did not approach this group en masse but one or a few at a time, with the sequence followed being to a certain extent dictated by considering whose support would be valuable as a means of gaining further support down the line. Another common series occurs with respect to setting up a new bureau. Ordinarily, money must be appropriated or promised before the top leaders can be hired. Top leadership must be hired before lower echelons can be hired. The headquarters office must be in a rudimentary operating shape before field offices can be established. In the case of the Area Redevelopment Administration (ARA), private entrepreneurs could not produce jobs and payrolls until the ARA delivered some money. The ARA could not deliver money until guidelines had been adopted and decisions taken about who should get it. The decisions and guidelines could not be developed until a staff was in place, and so on. When program elements need to be assembled in a certain sequence, the process takes more time than if one could proceed on all fronts simultaneously.

Low-Cost Strategies for Avoiding Program-Assembly Delays

1. Assign priority status. Lag time attributable to the "queuing problem" and routing problems more generally may be reduced if the solicitor is given a priority status permitting his request to be processed "out of order" or with unusual dispatch. For a period, at least, the EDA-Oakland did receive such priority treatment by the Washington office. Its priority status did not survive the departure of EDA director Eugene Foley in October 1966, however; and when the Nixon Administration took power the Oakland projects seemed to drop to a very low, almost negative, priority status.

The limits to this strategy are not hard to see. Given our premise that program elements must be assembled from a variety of autonomous actors, it is unlikely that more than a small minority will respect a "high-priority" designation pronounced by any given actor. The port's architect/engineer saw no reason to do so. Another obvious limitation is that some bodies have large backlogs and very little control over priorities in the queue. This is especially true of formal institutions like courts and regulatory agencies. Housing projects, highway projects, large public works projects—more and more frequently, parties who oppose such projects utilize the courts to delay and, they hope, scuttle them. Quite apart from the fact that judicial procedures are inherently very lengthy, affording many opportunities for delay, court calendars are so crowded in many jurisdictions that hearings cannot be scheduled for many months.[6] To get a matter decided by a federal regulatory commission may take years rather than months.

2. "Work around" missing or imperfect program elements. Sayles and Chandler report that NASA personnel at the spacecraft launch site developed "a high degree of skill and an uncanny ability to resolve technical incompatibilities via 'work-around' methods."[7] They could quickly build and install their own generator, for instance, to substitute for the signals of a defective component whatever signals were needed to make the whole system "go."

"Work around" is thus analogous to the strategy "do without" suggested in Chapter 5 for coping with monopolistic obstructionists. Skill, experience, and perhaps a certain bureaucratic bravado are required to make the method work. An example of the method at work in the context of a social program is provided in a study by Byron T. Hipple of the implementation of the 1956 amendments to the Social Security Act. Hipple was deputy commissioner of the New York State Department of Social Welfare for Administrative Finance and Statistics (DSW) during the relevant period and gives us a state administrator's view of implementation problems, the origins of which he locates in the federal

Bureau of Public Assistance (BPA).[8] The BPA was slow in providing a needed bureaucratic clearance, but Hipple worked around this defect.

The 1956 amendments raised a large number of issues, but the one that was to give most trouble to state officials concerned the method of computing federal aid for state expenditures to vendors of medical services furnished recipients of public assistance. Under the formula mandated by the new law, the state could claim reimbursement for some specified proportion of the aggregate of all such expenditures in the welfare case load rather than claiming up to some absolute dollar ceiling for each of the separate individuals. President Eisenhower approved the new law on August 1, 1956, but it was not to take effect until July 1, 1957, in order to provide plenty of lead time to plan the changeover.

Shortly after the president signed the law, the director of the BPA, Jay Roney, convened a meeting in Washington of all state welfare officials to review the legislation and to discuss its implementation. At that meeting it became apparent to Hipple (and others) that the BPA did not know how to proceed. It had to issue regulations suited both to the states with well-developed welfare programs and to the "beginner" states. The BPA asked the more "advanced" states to supply materials that might help the beginner states, but

the Washington officials exhibited a certain diffidence when the experienced states volunteered suggestions that touched on federal policy for administrative fiscal issues in the vendor formulae. The potential magnitude of federal funds committed to the overall program, coupled with uncertainty about actual operating problems in what was for them a new area, seemed to make federal officials uneasy and guarded about giving uncritical acceptance to the practices of the advanced states.[9]

In November 1956, the report of a state task force appointed to plan for the transition, headed by Hipple, was sent to other DSW officials as well as to the state Department of Audit and Control. A month later, Hipple sent the draft proposals to Alice Webber, regional representative of the BPA, with a covering letter stating that if the state department did not hear otherwise within the next month the department would proceed to revise its operating instructions, procedures, and bulletins in accordance with the draft proposals.

By the end of February 1957, Hipple was obviously quite wary of the BPA. Another letter "for the record" was sent to the regional representative stating that "(1) seven months had elapsed since the federal medical vendor payment formulae had been enacted; (2) only four months remained before they became effective; (3) no reply had been made to the proposals submitted by the Department in December; and (4) prompt consideration of these matters was necessary for the Department to give local officials authoritative instructions in time for a smooth transition to the new requirements by July 1." (pp. 17-18.) On March 11, another letter went out requesting replies to the previous letters and urging resolution of the potential issues.

Meanwhile, the department was carrying on protracted negotiations and discussions with other state and local agencies. The New York State Department of Audit and Control was concerned that any moves made by the DSW without explicit federal concurrence might result in a subsequent finding of noncompliance and a loss of federal funds. That Alice Webber of the BPA regional staff had given informal clearance did not satisfy Audit and Control, which wanted "conclusive advice." The DSW was at that point intending to apply to the new medical vendor reimbursement formulae the same policy it had used for many years for a similar type of care with express federal consent. It was unwilling to put to the BPA a direct question about the validity of this policy being extended to the newly covered services, however, lest the BPA, in the "prevailing atmosphere" of tension and disarray, render a negative verdict and require retroactive reimbursement of federal funds. The DSW was also meeting with local officials, trying to give what guidance it could in the absence of cues from Washington.

In late March, the department received from the BPA two "state letters" concerning implementation of the law. Neither, in the judgment of department officials, spoke to the issues concerning New York. Thus, on April 17, the department issued to local welfare districts its draft policies and procedures for calculating medical vendor payments, with the cautionary statement that "we have found it necessary to make certain assumptions regarding such Federal policies and we have proceeded with our plans based on our best judgment of the present situation."

In mid-May, at a meeting held in the BPA regional office in New York City, BPA officials from Washington informed a stunned audience that New York's proposals would not be in conformity with federal regulations then under consideration. In doing so, Washington not only undercut the state DSW, it also undercut Alice Webber, the agency's own regional representative. New York decided to press ahead with its own plans and present the BPA with a fait accompli. Massachusetts and Illinois, however, decided not to take the risk. In those states, and in others, extending the benefits of the new law would simply have to wait. Led by Massachusetts and Illinois, a number of state welfare officials persuaded Congress to pass a law enabling the states to continue operating under the previous provisions of the Social Security Act, if they so wished. On July 17, 1957, Congress went along. It made the provisions of this new law retroactive to July 1, 1957.

New York State and the BPA continued to negotiate throughout the summer and early fall, until by December only one issue remained. This was settled

with a "decision" not to decide. The state's proposal seemed sufficiently equitable to protect federal fiscal interests, and federal officials said they would interpose no objections to the state going ahead for the time being under its new rules. They did warn that circumstances might change, in which case the entire matter would be considered an open question subject to renegotiation. This gave New York enough of a go-ahead to take advantage of the federal amendments of 1956 and to keep its welfare administration wheels turning. It was expected that the administrative difficulties to be resolved before arriving at any alternative solution would be so great that federal officials would not want to reopen the issue.[10]

Thus, Hipple and the New York DSW were able to "work around" the BPA and, indeed, to maneuver the BPA into a position from which it would eventually have to yield. This maneuvering effect of the "work-around" factor is one of its bonus features. Not only does it reduce delay and bolster performance, it also generates—or at least has the potential to generate—political support by closing off the provider's options. Its only problem—and unfortunately it is a large one—is that it leaves the protagonist vulnerable in Odd Man Out games. The federal BPA could quite conceivably have turned up in January 1958 with a wholly negative verdict on the preceding arrangement. Like Piling On, "work around" is best employed when the stakes are small or the risks of losing minimal.

3. Try "project management." Like "work around," this idea comes from the history of large-scale government projects based on an advanced technology. It was the management tool used to build the Polaris submarine fleet and to accomplish most of NASA's space missions. It is now widely used in private industry and has a great many admirers. It is believed to be especially useful for keeping a project on schedule and within certain cost boundaries. It represents an attempt to overcome the limitations of the traditional division of organizational labor along "functional" lines (sales, production, research) when the organization must undertake a large, novel, and costly project requiring specialized and unpredictable inputs from several such departments and possibly from suppliers outside the organization. The project manager ordinarily has the job of overseeing the project from conception to completion. He monitors its costs, charts its status with respect to achieving scheduled subgoals, identifies problems, engages in troubleshooting, negotiates changes in contracts, and so forth. He uses up-to-date techniques of information processing and interpretation—computers, PERT networks, electronic visual displays, and reports directly from "the bench" where the work is being done. He also has power. He can make decisions without going through multiple clearances; he has a separate project budget; and he can, to a certain extent, commandeer resources from the several departments of the organization on a temporary basis. In short, he is savvy and he is boss—so far as the project is concerned.

If this sort of arrangement works so well in the Department of Defense, in NASA, and in private industry, can it not be installed to help implement social programs? If it worked, it would not only reduce delay—the focal problem of this chapter—it would increase program performance and hold down costs by modifying the games described in Chapters 3-6. Sayles and Chandler, in summing up their analysis of NASA's experience with project management, think the prospects are good:

As we noted at the outset [of our book], we are not saying that there are two types of large-scale systems: rational types such as AEC and space programs that brook no political nonsense and political types such as urban development which quickly become a morass of competitive and conflicting interests. All large development organizations constitute *political-business* systems.

With that caveat expressed and understood, we would still insist that these large systems can be understood and managed. And indeed management and organizational skills will be many times more critical in these inherently unwieldy public-private systems than in more traditional organizations.[11]

Lacking more experience with project management techniques in these "political types" of programs, we cannot say conclusively that Sayles and Chandler are wrong. It seems likely, however, that project managers in such circumstances would become just another set of players in the implementation game. They would probably play a more sophisticated Control game than we are used to seeing, but there is little reason to think that they would be able to beat monopolists skilled at Tokenism and protected by political allies, or that they would be able to overcome truly Massive Resistance. Project managers would have to play their own Budget and Territory games and would almost surely have to play Reputation more skillfully than most of the other players in the implementation process. Indeed, Sapolsky's analysis of the Navy Special Projects Office and the building of Polaris suggests that its success was produced by a combination of just such skillful bureaucratic gamesmanship and a climate of opinion highly receptive to the particular Fleet

Ballistic Missile technology the Special Projects Office was trying to sell.[12] The Special Projects Office never succeeded in putting into operation its vaunted PERT/TIME or PERT/COST systems, some of the basic tools of project management and tools that office had in fact invented. They were quite adroit at persuading outsiders that they had this superior managerial capability, however. This was part of a political strategy. The office staff, and particularly its highest echelon, were entrepreneurs first and managers second.

We may in fact have had more experience with project management in the field of social programs than is thought. What else was Amory Bradford, head of the EDA-Oakland task force, if not a project manager? Did not Mayor Edward F. Harrington of New Bedford, Massachusetts, play the role of a project manager in trying to establish a New Town in his city? Neither Bradford nor Harrington succeeded, and neither appears in the case histories by Pressman and Wildavsky and by Derthick to be more than just another player in the implementation game. There is one success story in the EDA-Oakland venture, however, that does suggest the utility of project management. The EDA did provide funds to help start the West Oakland Health Center, a relatively small hors d'oeuvre in the EDA cornucopia. The project was a success by any standard, and Pressman and Wildavsky (following their informants) credit the success largely to George Karras, director of the EDA Office of Public Works. He was "one of the project's most enthusiastic supporters . . . also in charge of much of the machinery for day-to-day implementation. Thus formulation and execution of policy were joined."[13]

Bureaus as well as individuals can function as project managers, the Special Projects Office being the clearest case. Consider also the ARA and its prescribed role as a "lead agency" in effecting interagency coordination in its area redevelopment activities. The ARA was, in theory, supposed to act as a "prime contractor" vis-à-vis "delegate agencies" like the Housing and Home Finance Agency, the Small Business Administration, the Office of Indian Affairs, and various bureaus and agencies in the Department of Labor and in the Department of Health, Education, and Welfare. The system was a failure. "Delegate agencies were inordinately slow in processing applications for ARA financial assistance, but it was the ARA officials who were blamed for the delays."[14] The OEO Community Action agencies were also supposed to play a "lead agency" coordinating role at the local level, as were local Model Cities agencies. Again, the experience has not been such as to warrant great enthusiasm. It is only fair to say, however, that project management techniques have indeed served well in putting men on the moon and that more trial-and-error with such techniques in the field of social programs is certainly warranted.[15]

Notes

1
It should be noted that the "system of games" metaphors used in Part 1 is of slight
use in explaining these nonpurposive delays. Hence, for the remainder of this and
the following two chapters, this metaphor will be placed in temporary storage.

2
Martha Derthick, *New Towns In-Town* (Washington, D.C.: The Urban Institute,
1972), pp. 8-9.

3
Robert J. Art, *The TFX Controversy* (Boston: Little, Brown, 1968); Richard
Austin Smith, *Corporations in Crisis* (New York: Doubleday, 1963), Chaps. 9, 10.

4
Jeffrey L. Pressman and Aaron Wildavsky report that the publicly stated reason
for the delay was that the staff was "busy on other Port projects." *Implementation* (Berkeley: University of California Press, 1973), pp. 38, 99.

5
Gary Orfield, *The Reconstruction of Southern Education: The Schools and the
1964 Civil Rights Act* (New York: Wiley, 1969), pp. 52-113.

6
Martin A. Levin, "Delay in Five Criminal Courts," *Journal of Legal Studies* 4: 1
(January 1975), pp. 83-131.

7
Leonard E. Sayles and Margaret K. Chandler, *Managing Large Systems* (New York:
Harper & Row, 1971), p. 265.

8
Byron T. Hipple, with the assistance of W. Henry Lambright and Thomas Lynch,
"Delay in Washington—A State View of Grant-in-Aid Administration" (Syracuse:
Inter-University Case Program, 1969).

9
Byron T. Hipple, "Delay in Washington," p. 11.

10
Byron T. Hipple, "Delay in Washington," p. 31.

11
Sayles and Chandler, *Managing*, p. 320.

12
See Harvey M. Sapolsky, *The Polaris System Development: Bureaucratic and Programmatic Success in Government* (Cambridge, Mass.: Harvard University Press,
1972), Chaps. 2, 3, 4, 8.

13
Pressman and Wildavsky, *Implementation*, p. 146.

14
Harold Seidman, *Politics, Position, and Power: The Dynamics of Federal Organization* (New York: Oxford University Press, 1970), p. 183. Also Sar A. Levitan, *Federal Aid to Depressed Areas: An Evaluation of the Area Redevelopment Administration* (Baltimore: Johns Hopkins University Press, 1964), pp. 42-45.

15
It is worth noting that there may be high, if not immediately visible, human costs to project management. Project participants suffer more anxieties than those working in functional organizations, according to an empirical study of four companies by Reisner. They feared loss of employment more, were more frustrated by not knowing "their real boss," were more frustrated by "make work" assignments, were more worried about being set back in their careers, felt less loyal to their organization, were more frustrated by conflict with other organizations and with multiple levels of management. Clayton Reisner, "Some Potential Human Problems of the Project Form of Organization," *Academy of Management Journal* 12 (December 1969): 459-467. I am indebted to Wade Brynelson for bringing this article to my attention.

8 | The Collective-Decision Process

In a collective-decision process, as we shall use the phrase, two or more different parties each decide, whether through negotiations or through a sequence of maneuvers and countermaneuvers, to make (or to withhold) certain contributions to (from) a collective enterprise. Such decisions take into account the probability of success or failure of the ultimate enterprise and are therefore sensitive to decision-makers' expectations about each others' intentions and each others' reliability. Very often commitments are offered on a contingent basis: "If B does X or Y, we will then do Z." The structure of contingent commitments that emerges from such a process might be quite fragile. In extreme cases, like that of the V/STOL development cited earlier, the Alphonse-Gaston quality of the process may lead to early collapse. While the collective-decision process is of course subject to all the delays that affect program-assembly activities in general, it also suffers delay from an added handicap, uncertainty.

Unfortunately, there is an almost complete absence of case study material that adequately describes those aspects of collective-decision processes with which we are here most concerned. One can find bits and snatches, hints and intimations, but nowhere a truly adequate record. In the absence of such published material I have had to rely on (1) a small case study of my own connected with the implementation of L-P-S, and (2) the inferential and sometimes quite speculative reconstruction of processes described in existing sources. Even in the case study I conducted myself there are serious inadequacies. First, the collective-decision processes are not as rich in illustrative and anecdotal material as I would like. Second, I did not personally observe or participate in the negotiations, and a lot of the nuances of personal interaction and decision have surely escaped me. I have had to reconstruct the negotiations scenario from the minutes of meetings, from other documentary sources, and from interviews with about a dozen of the participants conducted many months, even years, after the negotiations were over. The reader should regard these efforts, then, as exploratory. I hope they will suggest hypotheses for more careful and systematic investigation by future researchers.

A Case Study

The case study concerns the implementation of a program referred to previously, the intensive-treatment psychiatric ward on the grounds of Stockton State Hospital run jointly by the hospital and San Joaquin County. The negotiations and decisions leading up to this program lasted from the summer of 1968 to the summer of 1971, when the unit started operating. The originally envisaged operation did not begin then in its entirety, however, and negotiations over the remaining portion continued into the winter of 1972, when a drastic modification was made in that portion. What began as a vaguely defined "community mental health center" in the minds of the original planners ended three and a half years later as one hospital ward with fifty-three inpatient beds and a small wing just off the ward with six beds for screening and evaluation. All the participants in the laborious negotiating process regarded this modest outcome as a great success, however. In the October 1972 issue of *ExChange,* the quarterly magazine published by the DMH, the program director of the joint hospital-county operation wrote effusively of its success, with the apparent though implied concurrence in that opinion by the department. The outcome was not as grand as many participants at some point believed it would be; but, then again, the venture signified a breakthrough in state-county relations and in professional relations between hospital-oriented and "community"-oriented mental health workers. The negotiating process had been difficult, the participants agreed in retrospect, but not so bad as it might have been.[1]

In the summer of 1968, Dr. Donald Langsley took up a teaching post in the medical school of the University of California at Davis, and in January 1969, Langsley became director of the Short-Doyle program in neighboring Sacramento County. Prior to his arrival in California he had been doing research at the University of Colorado Medical School in Denver, where he had demonstrated the efficacy of "crisis intervention" in reducing the need for psychiatric hospitalization. His research had gained him a national reputation and he was installed in the Sacramento County Short-Doyle directorship with an implicit mandate to apply his progressive ideas.

Shortly after his arrival at Davis he was approached by the chief of training in the DMH and urged to develop a psychiatric residency program embodying his philosophy of crisis intervention and community psychiatry. Sacramento County Mental Health Services would be an ideal setting. Langsley in his capacity as director would be able to establish appropriate administrative conditions for a training program. Langsley's students from the university would provide a nucleus of residents both in the beginning and on a continuing basis. Patients in the Sacramento Short-Doyle system would furnish the clinical material. It was a perfect arrangement. The medical school psychiatry program would benefit; the patients in Sacramento Short-Doyle would benefit from more progressive and better-supervised care; and the DMH would benefit by sponsoring what might become a nationally recognized program.

The only hitch was that there might not be enough patients coming through the Sacramento Short-Doyle system to sustain a full-fledged training program. And even if there were, it would be useful to have an inpatient setting of the more traditional sort to which the residents could also be exposed. Therefore, it would be highly desirable to have another mental health service linked to the residency program. Stockton State Hospital in nearby San Joaquin County was an obvious choice. In 1968, it was still one of the largest state hospitals for the mentally ill. Dr. Henry Brewster was Chief of Professional Education at the hospital and enthusiastic about the affiliation with a major medical school and a teacher-researcher-administrator as renowned as Langsley. Stockton was only a forty-five-minute drive from Davis. The only drawback from Langsley's viewpoint was that it did not have much of a "community" orientation. It was a traditional state hospital, and he did not see that it would serve the educational functions for his residents that he believed were necessary.

Quite independently of Langsley's and the DMH's quest for a suitable residency site, Stockton State Hospital (SSH) in the summer of 1968 was inching toward a closer connection with the San Joaquin County community mental health program. Beginning July 1, 1969, the state hospital would, it appeared, have to contract with San Joaquin and other counties in its catchment area in order to get reimbursed for services; thus spake the new L-P-S Act. For its part, San Joaquin County was moving toward a more flexible and creative relationship with the hospital. Opened in 1852, the first state hospital for the mentally ill west of the Mississippi, SSH had been handling the county's severely mentally disturbed for as long as anyone could remember. The county had simply taken the hospital for granted. It had never developed much of an inpatient psychiatric service of its own. Since the hospital was so conveniently located, the county never troubled to develop a crisis-intervention or screening capability, either. The state hospital provided these services. Moreover, and best of all, the state hospital provided them free. The county did not have to put up any matching funds under Short-Doyle to buy itself a comprehensive community mental health service. Stockton State Hospital *was* its community mental health service. Of 2,410 patients admitted to Stockton State Hospital in 1968-1969, 49 percent were from San Joaquin County; and 537 of 1,500, or 36 percent, of the resident population was from San Joaquin.

In the late summer of 1968, the county approached the SSH superintendent to negotiate a package of services for the upcoming fiscal year (1970). Essentially, the two parties agreed to do more or less what they had always done with one added wrinkle: the hospital offered to lease the county some space on the grounds, in the Professional Building, "to establish a branch of their clinic where patients could be screened, evaluated, and receive outpatient treatment. Offices of the Short-Doyle staff on the state hospital grounds would provide a more convenient location for many outpatients . . . and would facilitate liaison operations in making arrangements for admission of patients to Stockton State Hospital, for participation of the Short-Doyle staff in release planning, referral, and to insure continuity of treatment." The county had requested more but the superintendent had scaled the request down "to provide . . . services proportionate to [the] size and nature of its plant and the number of its personnel."[2] Roughly during this period, Langsley met with Brewster and with Dr. Andrew Shallenberger, a staff psychiatrist employed by the San Joaquin Short-Doyle program, to discuss the possibility of incorporating a piece of his residency program into what Shallenberger, at least, hoped would become a joint Stockton-San Joaquin mental health evaluation and treatment center located at the state hospital.[3]

Further steps were taken in the winter and spring of 1969. The "Task Force for Planning a Comprehensive Mental Health Program" to which we referred in Chapter 7 was convened on February 26, 1969. Shallenberger was named chairman. At its second meeting, one week later, the basic idea of locating a unit of the Short-Doyle program on the hospital grounds was proposed and met no objection. It was recognized that "details" would have to be worked out:

It is important to negotiate with Stockton State Hospital for contracting; the Department of Mental Hygiene is the final authority here. Stockton State Hospital has been here for many years and have their procedures well established. We will have to set up a working agreement and evaluate as we go along. We have to have the actual pattern of what personnel does and see if this is what we want to buy. If we contracted with Stockton State Hospital with the new standards, this will make approximately 400 beds available. Stockton State Hospital will supply the personnel, physicians, and whatever the house routine is. We should have some supervisory control over this, with accessibility to records, etc. In other words, more or less replace in the scheme of things, the Assistant Superintendent in the particular building designated for our use. This would be worth looking at. In the same sense, we should have some control over the after care of these patients treated at the hospital, referring them to the most appropriate resource in the community.[4] This basic design was what eventually emerged, roughly eighteen months later. It took a long time to work out the details.

No further reference to this notion appears in any of the task force minutes again until those of the group's last meeting, on May 21. At that time, Shallenberger and Brewster reported that a week earlier, on May 13, at a meeting in Sacramento, representatives of the principal parties to the venture "committed themselves to further exploration and planning for a Community Mental Health Center." The DMH "went on record strongly approving the idea and indicated they would do whatever they could to facilitate its implementation at the earliest date." The minutes continue to expatiate: "If such a program and community center becomes a reality, it will be the only such cooperative venture in the State of California, and one of only a few in the entire United States." The Sacramento meeting brought together not a collection of low-level technicians but some of the highest officials from the institutions represented: Dr. Elmer Galioni from the DMH, deputy director in charge of all the state hospitals; Dr. Freeman Adams, superintendent of SSH; and Dr. Louis Barber, director of San Joaquin Short-Doyle and a man of considerable power in the county. Also present were Brewster, Shallenberger, and Langsley.

Yet not much happened. For the next six months, the psychiatric residency program component of the venture was worked out among the DMH, Langsley, the regents of the university, the Sacramento County Board of Supervisors, the Sacramento Medical Center, and the San Joaquin County Board of Supervisors. Among other problems, all parties were concerned about where legal liability would fall in the event of a malpractice suit. Private psychiatrists in San Joaquin County were concerned about the prospect of a university "take-over" of the county's mental health program. And the Stockton State Hospital people were concerned about the loss of autonomy over portions of their real estate and their procedures to San Joaquin Mental Health Services. All but this last issue got resolved by December 1969. It was the most dangerous and the most difficult of all. Informal attempts to resolve it were desultory and unsatisfactory, and the parties in conflict did not take serious measures to come to an agreement until February 1970, when a county-state hospital task force was created, which met weekly until July 24, 1970.

The issues raised by the task force were both technical and substantive. Should the program start small, as a pilot program, or move immediately to full-scale operation? Should patients admitted to the partial hospitalization and screening unit run by the county be given a state hospital identification number? What were the possibilities for enriching the "standard" (SCOPE) hospital staffing pattern on the county-run wards to meet the somewhat higher Short-Doyle standards? Given that the county-run wards would employ "team" staffing, would nonpsychiatrists be given team leadership responsibilities? Given that the teams were to provide round-the-clock coverage, could social workers be given "the responsibility of covering for the team?" Should the teams provide consultation services to community agencies? Which personnel from the hospital would be reassigned to the new county-run units? How might "a team composed of county and state employees . . . float through the county program and state contracted program?" If the new program succeeded in reducing state hospital utilization, as it was supposed it would, what would happen to the hospital employees whose jobs would be threatened by reductions in the hospital population? How could the morale of those hospital employees not assigned to the county units be sustained? And above all, what would be the lines of authority and responsibility controlling operations on the county wards? Would ultimate authority rest with the hospital superintendent or with the county Short-Doyle director?

By July 1, all these issues were clarified sufficiently for the county to begin operating a fifty-three-bed inpatient ward (RT-2) at the hospital.

By July 20, the county was operating a partial hospitalization program on the same ward. Contracts for both services had been approved by the task force participants and had been signed by state officials by the last week in July, when they were returned to the San Joaquin County counsel for the last of the needed signatures.

At this point the entire project collapsed. San Joaquin County ceased to operate RT-2. The Short-Doyle director, the board of supervisors, the mental health advisory board, and the local superior court judge ("Bill" Dozier) accused the state of bad faith, breaking its promises, and, as Judge Dozier put it, double-crossing the county. When asked by the DMH chief deputy director (Dr. Robert Hewitt), "At what point is the San Joaquin County-Stockton State Hospital contract?," Galioni responded in a memo: "In complete chaos!"

What happened? Unfortunately, it is hard to give a definitive answer. The participants' recollections are hazy, their testimony contradictory, and the documentary evidence ambiguous.

My own inference is that the RT-2 venture suddenly became a bargaining counter in a larger Territory game played for higher stakes, with the principal players being the DMH and the entire Conference of Local Mental Health Directors.

In May 1970, as it became clear that the RT-2 unit would actually begin to operate on July 1 as planned, Barber decided to close down the twenty-two-bed psychiatric inpatient unit at the county hospital (Ward 10) and shift the entire county inpatient operation to Stockton State Hospital. In early July, Barber submitted a revised plan for the 1970-1971 fiscal year to the DMH regional office requesting that some $200,000 originally budgeted as "existing program" for Ward 10 be allotted the county for "new and expanded" program, along with $165,000 that the regional office director informed him would be available during the coming year for children's services. The revised plan defined the RT-2 unit as "new and expanded" program.

The DMH turned him down. In November 1969, the department had advised the counties that money for "new and expanded" program would be tied to a reduction in a county's state hospital utilization. In July 1970, the department said that San Joaquin had not reduced its utilization as much as it claimed, that closing Ward 10 would increase state hospital utilization in the coming year anyway, and that the legislature's unanticipated reduction in funding for "new and expanded" local programming in the budget just passed made it impossible to honor the request in any case. In an angry memorandum to the members of the county mental health advisory board, Barber wrote, "We have all been going on the premise that all new programs for the 1970-71 fiscal year would have to be financed out of savings from inpatient services at Stockton State Hospital," and that none of the many new programs the advisory board had approved in the 1970-1971 plan would be financed "due to this change in State Department of Mental Hygiene policy which prohibits the use of savings from the State Hospital program to be used for new and expanded services in the local [Short-Doyle] program."

The larger game had to do with the "change in policy" that Barber alleged. Actually, the department's policy had never been too clear on the question of whether or not a county had the right to reallocate monies from the state hospital side of its budget to the local program side at will. Some Short-Doyle directors assumed that they could not; but others, including Barber, assumed that they could. More precisely, perhaps, the policy question was: Who had the right to decide when a county had reduced its hospital utilization and was therefore entitled to transfer funds to the local programs? And who, furthermore, was to say by how much utilization was reduced over what time span and how many dollars were thereby "saved" in the state hospital side of the budget? Since the department never actually gave these state hospital dollars out to be distributed by the counties, but simply set aside the money in a separate account, the counties did not actually control the funds.

They had to persuade the department to shift the funds from an account they could not use to one they could use.

Clearly, the county had made a technical error in redefining its budget for RT-2 inpatient services as "new and expanded" programming while deleting the money for Ward 10 from the "existing program" side. Instead of simply remedying the technical error, however, and preserving RT-2, the county chose to fight on higher ground. The county insisted on its right to decide how much state hospitalization it had averted and how it would choose to spend the money to which it was, in consequence, morally entitled. Since Barber knew quite well that the DMH was quite eager to have RT-2 in operation as a home for the UC Davis psychiatric residency program, he must have been counting on the threat to back out of the deal as a way of strengthening his hand in the larger game. Thus, RT-2, after only a month in operation, came to its sudden demise.

On August 17, Judge Dozier sent a ferocious letter to Governor Ronald Reagan protesting the state's "double cross," its "chicanery," and the "cheap political gimmick" to shift the cost of programs to the counties "while prating about State economy and savings." Copies were sent to the board of supervisors, to members of the county mental health advisory board, to State Senator Alan Short (coauthor of L-P-S and a representative of San Joaquin County in the legislature) and to Assemblyman Robert Monagan, Speaker of the Assembly and a representative of the Stockton area. On October 5, Barber and others from San Joaquin met with Dr. James Lowry, the DMH director, in the offices of Assemblyman Lanterman. It appears that the DMH held firm. The most that Barber could get was a memorandum expressing support for running a "pilot project" during the then current fiscal year "to demonstrate the potential state hospital savings as a bargaining tool for future allocations."[5] Lowry did not promise additional funding, however, though he did indicate monies were in fact available for such projects.

On December 1, the regional DMH office wrote Barber that no pilot project funds would be given the county.

When negotiations reopened on the design for RT-2, the old agreements had decayed. The question of who would have authority over the program was revived. The older formulation, of May 1970, had given the hospital superintendent continuing supervisory authority over the ward, while the physician appointed by the county would have "programmatic responsibility" and would have to see to it that the unit conformed to general hospital policies. Whatever ambiguity remained in this formulation was evidently acceptable to all the parties—otherwise they would not have gone ahead with the project on July 1, 1970. In a brief encounter with Superintendent Freeman Adams, however, on December 10, Barber reformulated the proposal. He suggested that a county-paid psychiatrist be named project director of the ward and at the same time be given an appointment on the hospital staff so that "he would be directly responsible" to the hospital superintendent. Adams wrote to Galioni in DMH headquarters asking if this arrangement was acceptable. Galioni replied, on January 27, 1971, that it was not: "Only a paid state employee can provide direction to a state hospital operation. I know of no other way that would be administratively feasible or protect the rights of the state in such an operation."

In the meantime, Dr. James Peal, who in April 1970 had joined Shallenberger as virtual codirector of the venture for the county and who had rather more ambitious ideas and a more controversial manner than Shallenberger, drafted another proposal, which departed even more from the one agreed to earlier. In this proposal, dated January 4, 1971, all professional personnel on the ward "would be responsible to the Program Director," who would also

have the responsibility for carrying out this program within the administrative structure that the program requires. He would be responsible for developing or making any procedural changes necessary to implement the program . . . as the need developed. The Program Director would be responsible for the treatment program of each of the San Joaquin County residents, regardless as to which part of the Stockton State Hospital the patient was living [sic]. The Program Director should have the flexibility of securing professional staff for the program both from the Stockton State Hospital Staff and from the professional community of Stockton and San Joaquin County.

Further:

The major effectiveness of the program will lie in the ability to integrate the professional community into the treatment services of the inpatient program, and whatever Administrative and Fiscal mechanisms are needed to provide this, they should be provided so that this is available to the Program Director.

The State Hospital would have to agree to assign the staff that interlocks to this program through the direction of the Program Director, who would have available to him for compilation the services of the various departments of County and State Department Heads as needed. The staff assigned to this program would in fact be detached from their hospital department and assigned to the program, under the direction and supervision of the Program Director.

The proposal was forwarded to DMH headquarters by Superintendent Adams with the comment, "There is very little in the proposal that deals with the current realities or the steps by which such an ambitious program could be accomplished."[6] Galioni concurred and added that the proposal "contains a number of inconsistencies and proposes methods of operation and of administration of the program which are administratively unsound and unwieldy. The proposal raises more than a few issues involving legality, liability, workmen's compensation, etc."[7]

On February 18, a resolution was found. It scarcely differed from certain formulations put forth almost a year earlier by different parties, but this time it had the imprimatur of the second highest official in the DMH. The resolution was that a program director would be appointed suitable to both the state hospital administration and the county administration, and that the state would pay his salary for that portion of time spent in the operation of the twenty-four-hour inpatient program while the county paid for the rest. Thus, the director would be administratively accountable to the superintendent, but it was left as an open question what sort of authority he would have on the ward. In late March, it was agreed that Shallenberger would be the program director and that his time would be paid for 50-50 by the county and the state. The unit was to start operating on July 1. It was also agreed that a county screening, evaluation, and partial hospitalization program would be started at the hospital on September 1, in Ward T-1. The county would at that time vacate its offices in the SSH Professional Building and amalgamate all its noninpatient services on T-1.

Several months later, however, the county was backing away from the large-scale plan for T-1. At a meeting on May 21, 1971, Shallenberger "related that he had reviewed the inpatient admissions to Stockton State Hospital for the past six months and since there has been no inappropriate admissions, he feels that there is no need for the partial hospitalization program." He said Langsley had concurred in this decision. The DMH regional office representative who summarized the meeting indicated that it was long and rather heated, and that the Shallenberger proposal was "at odds with . . . expectations" held by most of the other participants, including Robert Brissenden, the influential business administrator for the mental health program and the county hospital. A week later the group met again, and Shallenberger stuck to his position. Notwithstanding this development, Adams and Barber agreed to send jointly a "letter of understanding" to Lowry in which commitment to a county-operated T-1 unit was reiterated. The regional office representative cautiously noted for the record: "In view of the expressed reservations by Dr. Shallenberger about the program in T-1, even with an agreement between Dr. Barber and Dr. Adams, the screening, crisis intervention, partial hospitalization program may not evolve as an alternative to inpatient care."

The county officially continued its commitment to taking over T-1, even though it became apparent during the summer and fall that Shallenberger was dragging his heels. Finally, on January 2, 1972, the county submitted "revisions and amendments to the 1971-72 mental health budget" that deleted T-1. The screening, crisis-intervention, and partial hospitalization functions would be carried on in T-2, in a special six-bed alcove set aside for the purpose. The average daily census had been running between thirty and thirty-five patients, though the capacity of the ward was fifty. The county also asked that the state not withdraw all the funds originally allocated for the program, as some of the monies were being used to pay for psychiatrists and for psychiatric social workers from the CSD to moonlight and thereby provide twenty-four-hour coverage for the emergency services function.

Future-Testing as a Cause of Delay

We now turn to analyzing certain delay-producing features of the collective-decision process that can be inferred from this small case study and other data sources. In this section on "future-testing" we shall try to show the delaying effects created by actors' uncertain conceptions of the emerging future. First, there is a natural reluctance to commit themselves and resources under their control to some future operation that they can foresee only with difficulty. They are also affected by the uncertainties in the flow of events outside of, or exogenous to, the evolving program and that are beyond their control. Finally, there are uncertainties that they necessarily create for each other in the course of organizing a large-scale collective enterprise. In the following chapter we shall also try to show that the commonly used social mechanism for reducing these uncertainties, bilateral or multilateral negotiation, is relatively inefficient.

Actors who are committed in principle to the development of some new enterprise may hesitate to say so publicly because they are playing some version of Odd Man Out. But they may also be acting defensively out of motives grounded in a general sense of prudence. Aristotle, like many others since, believed that prudence was the political virtue par excellence.[8] The conservative force of prudence does truly make itself felt in all political processes. But its effects seem unusually strong in the implementation process, especially when we contrast its effects in that process with its effects in the policy-adoption process. This contrast is easily sketched. In many respects the policy-adoption process and the policy-implementation process are similar, after all. Both can be conceived as "assembly" processes, the former entailing the aggregation of "support" for a given policy proposal from a large number of semiautonomous actors, and the latter entailing the integration of numerous functional inputs to create an operating program, also obtained from a variety of semiautonomous actors. Both processes are "political," in the sense that persuasion and bargaining, rather than brute force or coercion, are employed to bring about the desired assembly of requisite elements. Both processes are somewhat sensitive to the "timing" of the various assembly activities and to the decision arenas in which persuasion and bargaining take place. Our hypothesis, then, is that actors in the implementation process are relatively more reluctant to commit their resources to a new, operating program than they are to commit their support to a mere verbal proposal.

At the simplest level, it is easy to see why this should be so. The policy adoption process wrests from participants verbal support for a proposal, whereas the policy implementation process demands the contribution of real resources. To put it another way, talk is cheap but actions are dear. The result of a successful policy adoption contest is a policy mandate. The mandate may be fiercely contested, but in the end it is only a mandate.

One can commit oneself to supporting a mandate for a new policy or program with less diffidence than one can commit oneself or the resources within one's jurisdiction to the operating program. In our little Stockton story one could construe the mandate as having been decided upon at the meeting in Sacramento on May 13, 1969 (if not earlier), when representatives of the DMH, Stockton State Hospital, San Joaquin

County, and the UC Davis Medical School "committed themselves to further exploration and planning for a Community Mental Health Center." The parties agreed in principle to a relatively imprecise concept. Reaching that agreement turned out to be much easier than reaching agreement on a concrete operating program that would require real commitments of money, authority, space, personnel, and operating procedures.

Another reason it is relatively easier to secure commitments in the adoption stage than in the implementation stage is that actors in the adoption stage generally know that the slow hard work of the implementation stage is yet to come, at which time they will still be able to revise, amend, augment, and delete. On this interpretation, then, we might even wish to construe the difficulties of the implementation process as "normal" and the relative ease of the policy adoption process as "pathological," not vice versa!

Not all future-testing occurs through direct negotiations, however. Sometimes it involves "watchful waiting," that is, holding tight and waiting for events to unfold that, in their unfolding, might give some clues to the future. This sort of behavior was also evidenced in the San Joaquin-Stockton case—according to my own interpretation, at least—in the period of quiescence on the part of SSH and San Joaquin representatives during the summer and fall of 1969 while details of the residency program were being worked out. It is plausible that the SSH and San Joaquin County administrators were quite sensitive to the difficulties they were likely to experience in settling the SSH-San Joaquin relationship and were unwilling to move forward on the negotiations until they were sure that a residency training component would be part of the new operating program. Reasonable assurance about the availability of the particular input was necessary before either the hospital or San Joaquin County would be willing to commit their own resources to the venture. In particular, the promise of a residency program was necessary to convince the hospital administrators that the resulting operation would provide enough benefits to their institution to make it worth their while to proceed.

Whether direct negotiations with other parties or watchful waiting is the mode of future-testing, the procedure itself takes time and is the cause of much delay. In the SSH-San Joaquin County case one can count roughly twelve months, from May 1969 to May 1970, as the delay entailed by the first phase of future-testing. One can see even longer delays in the Oakland-EDA case. Negotiations over the costs of the World Airways hangar and its minority employment plan lasted nearly five years overall, though a good part of that time was consumed by other delaying factors related to the more mechanical difficulties of processing plans and proposals through intraorganizational decision channels.

Why does future-testing consume so much time? With respect to watchful waiting the answer is simple enough: the events which need to be watched may unfold quite slowly for any of a vast number of reasons. As an instrument of future-testing, negotiations may not so much cause delay as they may exaggerate the delaying effects of deeper causes. They reveal, in a constantly running stream, the problematic features of the future which induce increasing caution and reluctance to approach closure. Although quite often inefficient at controlling the future, they are usually quite efficient at *exposing* as well as delineating and highlighting the most problematic features of the future. In the Stockton case, the more the negotiators talked the more problems they raised, and the more problems they raised the more likely some of them appeared to contain potential complications. It was easy enough for the negotiators to agree that psychiatrists would head the service teams, that the project would be relatively small in scale, that psychiatric social workers would be permitted to act on behalf of the teams even though they would not be entitled to lead them. The more they talked, though, the more they saw that there were sticky questions of power and authority, that the character and style of at least one of the San Joaquin County program directors (Peal) would be an endless source of irritation

to members of the hospital staff, that questions of assigning legal liability would return to plague them if not resolved in advance, and that
the mechanics of assigning patient identification numbers carried strong
implications for the future of the hospital as an institution. This last
problem was not at all obvious at the outset, but it was potentially serious. If the patient did not receive a Stockton State Hospital identification number, it was unlikely he could be counted as an admission or as
a part of the resident patient population. Reducing those particular
statistics would have a direct effect on the hospital's allowed staffing
pattern and hence on the number of employees who would have to be
terminated. On the other hand, if the patient was given a SSH number,
the county would be charged by the state for a relatively highly priced
"state hospital day." Eventually it was agreed that the patient would
initially receive a special "partial hospitalization" number—provided
that the computers in DMH were able to digest such an unfamiliar thing.

In a sense, it should not be at all surprising that the closer one gets to
the details of an operation, the larger they appear; and if they are at all
problematic, the louder they cry out for resolution in advance. The implementation process is the time for such activity. All reasonable people
expect there to be some delay in "ironing out the wrinkles" or in
"working out the specifics." Yet in another sense, it is often surprising
that these activities go so slowly. Amory Bradford seemed to think all
significant problems had been settled once EDA and World Airways had
agreed on the employment plan. In his book chronicling his supposed
success in Oakland, he wrote of his decision to leave the Oakland scene
in November 1966: "Approval of the World Airways Plan, by a Board
that had learned to function well, rounded out all that I had set out to
do when I began in Oakland in January, nine months earlier. It was time
to go."[9] Even in the private sector there is a tendency to underestimate
delay. An engineer with abundant experience in private construction
projects as well as in public programs writes: "Schedules are arrived at
based on imperfect analysis of past experience and unknown future

conditions. Uncertainty seldom prevents expression of confidence in ability to perform at the stage where contracts are sought."[10] The policy adoption stage is normally characterized by a certain euphoric optimism. When goals are not met, it is possible, post hoc, to see that they were "unrealistic," the momentary flash of a political optical illusion. Surely the same illusion distorts people's ability and willingness to estimate delay. We have said above that "the closer one gets to the details of an operation, the larger they appear," but it is equally appropriate, as we try to explain why delays are often so unexpected by policy designers and planners, to say that "the farther one stands back from the details of an operation, the smaller they appear."

Future-testing is a time-consuming activity under the best of circumstances. The best of circumstances would hold the future, once tested, in its foreordained and foreseen shape. Typically, however, circumstances are not so benign. They make of the future an ever-changing thing. Today's circumstances are continually invalidating the results of yesterday's testing of tomorrow's shapes. Hence future-testing must be repeated continually. Every change in circumstances that forces a new probe of the future causes new delays. These delays are conceptually quite independent of the delays entailed in simply adapting to the new circumstances, that is, procuring different program elements or producing new commitments to provide them. These are program assembly delays. The delays involved here are engendered by new rounds of negotiations or by reversion to a posture of watchful waiting. That is, they are collective-decision delays. For the purposes of our argument here, it is irrelevant whether the changed circumstances that inspire new delays for future-testing arise from exogenous variables (outside anyone's control who is party to the prior agreement) or endogenous variables (a party changing its mind).

In the Stockton case we see numerous examples of changing circumstances invalidating earlier estimates of the future and prompting delays to undertake new future-testing. During the summer of 1970 the state legislature decided to trim roughly $3.5 million from the 1971 Short-Doyle budget, making DMH much more chary than it had been about committing itself to fund "new and expanded" programs, including (presumably) the San Joaquin programs. Also during this period, the Department was reevaluating the status of all the state hospitals, including Stockton, to decide which might be phased out, according to what timetable, and what, if anything, should be done with institutions that would not be phased out. Stockton State Hospital's future was particularly uncertain. Relative to official DMH staffing standards, Stockton had an excess of ward nursing staff, a condition that the San Joaquin-SSH arrangement was likely to aggravate.[11] Also, another county, Stanislaus, was negotiating with the DMH concerning the possibility of an arrangement similar to that contemplated by San Joaquin County. DMH planners were obliged to spend several weeks or even months trying to calculate what would be, or should be, the future of the hospital nursing staff (continue with no change, transfer staff to hospitals for the mentally retarded, or establish a unit for the retarded at Stockton); and SSH administrators were meanwhile obliged to reevaluate their own position on the San Joaquin arrangement in the light of any new situation that might be created by the course charted by the Department. San Joaquin County officials were in turn obliged to reconsider their position in the light of what they believed might eventually become of SSH. Of course, San Joaquin's planners were also strongly influenced by what they perceived, during this period, to be the general untrustworthiness of the Department, a perception created by the so-called "double cross" with respect to the county's right to reprogram monies from state hospital utilization to other programs.

San Joaquin's intentions came to be seen in a different light as well. Officials of SSH and the DMH apparently interpreted the intentions of Peal and perhaps Barber and Shallenberger as more threatening than in the spring of 1970. Barber was hinting that the county might abandon SSH even after a joint program was in full operation and had shown its effectiveness. Inadvertent or deliberate statements by Peal reinforced the perception of possible danger arising from such a joint venture. Thus, the mutual distrust of state and county officials, which was in large degree the product of changes over which neither party had much control, itself became a source of uncertainty for each of the parties and hence a reason for further, and more intensive, future-testing.

Unfortunately, there are not many easy answers to the question of how to reduce delays in the collective-decision process in general or those caused by future-testing in particular. The most prominent candidate is bilateral or multilateral negotiations. Yet these, as we shall show in the next chapter, are very often inefficient or positively harmful.

Notes

1

Indeed, in the light of more recent developments, the original agreement can be seen to have been merely the foundation stone for a larger and more elaborate service structure. For 1974-1975, the county had negotiated a contract for 130 beds on at least three wards to serve acute, geriatric, and chronic patients.

2

Minutes of Executive Committee Meeting of Stockton State Hospital, September 16, 1968.

3

Shallenberger had just completed a training program in community psychiatry directed by Portia Bell Hume, grande dame of the community psychiatry movement in California. Although he was approaching retirement age, Shallenberger was eager to apply what he had learned and to help further the cause of community psychiatry.

4

Minutes of the task force, March 5, 1969.

5

There is an interesting indication in the Painter memorandum that Barber was using the RT-2 project as a bargaining tool. This memo summarized a meeting between representatives from the county, Stockton State Hospital, and two staff from the DMH regional office. Painter wrote: "In discussing their project the County made it clear that they favor return to a model similar to that previously undertaken, involving joint County-State Hospital staff on Ward T-2. Dr. Barber indicated that *he would not consider an independent operation at this time based on the cost factors involved.* It was clarified, however, that should the County demonstrate savings and receive additional funding next year to operate the inpatient unit, they would have the option of transferring funds to an independent inpatient operation, assuming they receive approval based on programmatic considerations." (Italics supplied.) If my interpretation of Barber's initial strategy is correct, the threat to go back to an independent inpatient operation was a means of exploiting the DMH's only real vulnerability.

6

Adams to Galioni, January 5, 1971.

7

Galioni to Adams, January 25, 1971.

8

Aristotle's world for it was *phronesis,* generally translated as "prudence" or "practical wisdom." It had a broader meaning than the one intended here, though it included this narrower meaning.

9
Pressman and Wildavky, *Implementation* (Berkeley: University of California Press, 1973), p. 33, quoting Amory Bradford, *Oakland's Not for Burning*, p. 169.
10
Sol Cooper, "On Time and Delay," graduate seminar paper, June 1974, p. 13.
11
These standards had been produced by extensive time-and-motion studies on the wards in 1966.

9 | Negotiations

One of the most obvious of possible solutions to the delays caused by future-testing is for the affected parties to communicate with one another about their intentions and reciprocal expectations. In other words, they should enter into negotiations. Yet negotiations, I believe, are an extraordinarily inefficient means of reducing the delays caused by future-testing. Worse still, they frequently cause as many problems as they solve. In particular, they can, and do, exacerbate delays as well as ameliorate them.

No doubt an entire subspecialty of public administration deserves to be carved out for the study of negotiating processes. At the very least, the subject merits a book-length treatment. Certainly, I shall not do justice to this large and intricate subject, relying for data primarily on only one case, related in the previous chapter, and at that a case studied only after the fact. I shall resist the temptation, moreover, to specify the parameters of this one negotiating process in abstract or theoretical form. Although it seems on the surface that the negotiations described here were between participants in a positive-sum game, that they were multilateral rather than bilateral, that communication among the participants was permitted and indeed encouraged, that the participants played several rounds, that the game was just one of many and but a small game within a larger game, that there was no definite time limit on the negotiations, that prior experience of the participants in a common professional subculture and bureaucratic milieu had created the conditions for what Schelling calls tacit bargaining—although these parametric conditions seem to have held, it is hard to say that they either did or did not make a difference to the nature of the participants' interactions. Indeed, given my own distance from the events and my very imperfect knowledge of how the several participants viewed the negotiations over their full duration, it is hard to say that these parametric conditions actually did obtain or, if they obtained at all, for how much of the time. Suffice it to say here that the negotiating process being analyzed seems to share much with other negotiating processes among organizations in the public sector and that there is much about this one, as there almost certainly is about others like it, that makes them all quite slow, especially when compared to negotiating processes in the policy-adoption phase.

The participants in establishing the SSH-San Joaquin County arrangement regarded it as a triumph, and it is not my intention to strip them of their laurels. What is most interesting about the process analytically, however, is not its ultimate "success," but its long delay in getting there. Naturally, one could argue that had it not been for the superior skill and wisdom of the negotiators the process would have been even more time-consuming. We do not focus on the skill and virtuosity of the negotiators, however—let that be a subject for another researcher—but on the conditions that made negotiations tediously slow. For nearly all practical purposes there was no change in the substance of what came out of the negotiations in the summer of 1971, when RT-2 started, and what had been agreed upon in the winter of 1970—and in a more general sense in the spring of 1969 and even earlier, in the summer and fall of 1968. Why could the negotiating process not produce the final agreement more rapidly?

First, the parties to an explicit negotiating process are not necessarily the right ones. That is, if one of the purposes of negotiations is to help dissipate uncertainty about the future, the purpose might not be achievable simply because the most confounding uncertainties might only be dispelled by parties who cannot be brought to the conference table. Until 1967 or 1968, United States leaders professed to believe that there was little point in negotiating with either the Viet Cong or with the North Vietnamese because the critical elements of the future, which negotiations were to have both tested and stabilized, were in the control of the Chinese. More recently, it appears that the delay in obtaining an Israel-Syria disengagement on the Golan Heights was in part due to both parties'—and especially Israel's—uncertainty about the future activities of the Palestinian terrorist organizations operating out of Syria and the Syrian government's unwillingness or inability to stop them. In domestic political negotiations, the same third-party (or nth-party) problem holds. Some of the uncertainties that plagued the SSH-San Joaquin County negotiations could have been alleviated only by budgetary commitments made well in advance by the governor, the Department of Finance, the legislature, and the Department of Mental Hygiene. Merely to list the n parties is to suggest how unattainable a goal it would be to corral all parties with control over pieces of the relevant future and to extract commitments from them. In the EDA-World Airways negotiations it was not even possible to specify a list of "parties" who could conceivably resolve the uncertainities faced by the two principal participants. As they agreed in their employment plan, approved on November 12, 1966:

World and EDA recognize the extreme complexity of predicting business expansion, designing new training programs which will meet FAA standards, developing instructional and institutional forms which will allow previously unskilled and unemployed Oakland residents to move rapidly into highly skilled positions in a growing industry, and assuming that these persons will be sufficiently trained and qualified to take responsibility for the lives of travelers using World's services.[1]

In contrast to negotiations in the implementation phase, negotiations in the policy-adoption phase are simpler and faster because the participants feel it is less important to resolve uncertainties (they can be taken care of in the implementation phase!) and also because the rules of the game do not really require uncertainties to be resolved. The rules of that game merely require that enough support be brought together to tip the relevant decision-making body in favor of the proposal. The main uncertainties to be resolved at that stage concern the scope and intensity of the opposing coalitions rather than the commitment and capabilities of the collectivity of potential implementers. The typical decision-making forum in the policy-adoption stage—a legislature or a bureaucratic directorate—is relatively sensitive to these general features of scope and intensity and relatively insensitive to the much more specific features of who can produce what operating resources, when, and on what terms.[2] These general features of a coalition's scope and intensity exist in the present and do not need to unfold at some future time. Political decision-makers in the adoption phase may be uncertain about the exact shape of the present, but these are far less troublesome uncertainties than parties to the implementation process confront in trying to assess the shape of their collective future.

A second reason for sluggishness in negotiations is the fact that the parties are often aware that they will find it difficult if not impossible to enforce the terms of any agreement they reach once resources are committed and the program is under way. If one of the parties believes that the other has not fulfilled its part of the bargain, there may not be much they can do about it once they have committed their own resources. When it comes to relationships among public agencies, even the best-drawn contracts are hard to enforce, and in many cases the agreements reached are not even embodied in such formal terms as contracts. The adjudicatory and enforcement machinery that might force a private firm to fulfill its contracts is usually quite primitive in the public sector. Although different units of government do sue each other for breach of contract, the practice is not very common. Characteristically, "higher" levels of government attempt to enforce compliance on "lower" units by threatening to withhold funds or by actually doing so through auditing mechanisms. The "lower" units refrain from attempting to sue the "higher" units—to get more money, say—because their longer-run interests, derived from the Funding game, lie in maintaining cordial political relations with the source of grant-in-aid funds. Agencies at the same level of government are constrained from taking each other to court, even when legally they might do so, because they are in principle supposed to appeal to a higher-level administrator, perhaps to the chief executive himself, to resolve disputes. In practice, agencies are reluctant to push their disagreements up to the higher levels for adjudication, since doing so entails a loss of standing with whomever is called upon to perform the disagreeable adjudicatory task, no matter which way the verdict is rendered. Despite their many disagreements over a period of years with respect to the allocation and control of federal Social and Rehabilitation Service monies, the California State Department of Mental Hygiene and the California State Department of Social Welfare would never have considered taking each other to court. And on only a few occasions did they invite intervention by the director of the Human Relations Agency, their nominal superior, or the governor's office.

Another reason that agreements are difficult to enforce is that our society has not yet developed an array of workable and legitimate sanctions that public agencies could impose on each other in the event of less than full compliance. Disallowing payments following "audit exceptions" is of course one method, but it applies to a relatively small proportion of agreements reached between public agencies. Cutbacks on appropriations through the budget-review process are another method. In addition to the problems with this method already described, there are also problems entailed in reducing an entire agency's budget for a whole year and in having those reductions fall potentially on a whole range of agency activities when the agreements breached are relatively specific. Finally, budget reductions are viable only in cases in which the offended party actually controls budget levels—again a condition applying to a relatively limited number of agreements (between a bureau and its supervising agency or between an agency and a legislative oversight committee). We have as yet developed no system of performance bonds held in escrow by a third party that could be used as penalties for performance failures or noncompliance with prior agreements. We are not likely to do so in the near future, nor are we likely to invent more imaginative alternatives to fulfill the same function.

In the public sector as in the private sector, the principal social mechanism for enforcing agreements is the recognition on the part of participating parties that failure to comply would jeopardize a long-term relationship of value to all those concerned. The resort to formal contracts, courts, arbitrators, performance bonds, and the like is of course common in the private sector but not nearly so common as is reliance upon enlightened long-term self-interest.[3] I suspect that the same is true of public-sector relationships: to the extent that parties can be relied upon to fulfill their agreements—and, more important, to the extent that they are perceived by others as reliable—the reasons exist largely in the mutual desire, or necessity, to perpetuate good relations. To a degree we can see the importance of this motive in the SSH-San Joaquin County case when we compare it to the case of the EDA and World Airways. In the former case, two agencies did manage to reach agreement, and their representatives regarded the product as a success. In the latter, negotiations dragged on almost without end to produce a resolution just barely satisfactory to the EDA and perhaps not much more so to World. The SSH-San Joaquin County bargaining took place between parties who had a continuing relationship of interdependence and who expected to grow closer in the future. The EDA-World negotiations brought together two parties who had had no previous relationship and who could reasonably expect to have none once the project at hand was finished (in whatever fashion).

Conceivably, however, there is a hidden problem here. Public agencies entwined in long-term interdependencies and knowing that they will reach some agreement they will honor (and which they believe the other party will honor) may therefore take more time reaching agreement on specific terms than they might if their time perspectives were foreshortened. If each agreement is valued not only for what it produces in the short run but also for what precedent it sets for the future, the parties may be that much more cautious about what they agree to with respect to any given issue. It seems clear that the Department of Mental Hygiene, speaking through Galioni, was even more cautious about clearing any SSH-San Joaquin County arrangement than were the rather cautious SSH negotiators. The department had a somewhat longer time perspective than did the hospital people. Any agreement reached with San Joaquin County with respect to RT-2 would set a precedent for county-state hospital agreements all over the state, not just in the immediate future but in the five or ten years ahead. The superintendent of Stockton State Hospital was due to retire soon, after more than two decades' service, and would not have to live with the arrangement or its precedent-setting implications for very long in any case. Adams was not of course eager to trade away more of the hospital's domain than was necessary, but the incentives to drive a hard bargain, with all the attendant delays in negotiating it, were not as great for him as they were for officials in headquarters.

The difficulty of adjudicating disputes and enforcing agreements once they have been concluded compounds delays arising from another ubiquitous feature of negotiating situations, mutual distrust and suspicion. What creates such distrust, and what effect it has on negotiations, is not altogether clear. The phenomenon has not been studied very extensively in "real life," though there are a number of reported laboratory studies. We may begin, however, with the observation that rational negotiators have an incentive to conceal their true preferences from each other, especially the minimum conditions they would be willing to accept as the price for ending negotiations and getting on with operations. To have the other side know one's true minimum conditions is to become vulnerable to exploitation, especially if one does not have corresponding knowledge of the other side's minimum acceptable conditions. Hence, negotiators always begin by asking for more than they expect to be offered and much more than the minimum they would be willing to accept. Then the negotiations proceed incrementally and with reciprocal scaling down of demands and scaling up of counteroffers until some mutually acceptable outcome is agreed upon. If all parties to the negotiations are aware that these are the tacit rules of the game, and that such is the likely progression of events, they can proceed through this sequence of moves and countermoves expeditiously and with minimal delay. Because both parties can discount the insistence on the "essential" conditions initially professed by their bargaining partners, the well-understood ritual of joint convergence on an outcome does not necessarily lead to distrust.

Distrust creeps in when one or both parties believe that their partners are going through the ritual only in order to secure information about their own true preferences, particularly the level of their minimally acceptable terms, but intend then to back off and escalate demands once again. Every time the EDA made another concession to World Airways or to the Port of Oakland without exacting a comparable concession in return, it revealed how much it truly wanted *some* project, no matter how unlikely the project was to meet high minority-employment objectives and no matter how much it was likely to cost the federal government. Partly, one suspects, in order to compensate for a whole series of unreciprocated concessions in 1967 and 1968, the EDA began in 1969 to speak to the Port Commission and World Airways in shriller, harsher tones. In response to the port's request to EDA to finance another cost overrun, the head of the EDA wrote:

As EDA has repeatedly stressed, the agency is not in the business of building aircraft hangars or other facilities for port authorities or business firms, particularly firms that have financial resources to build such facilities without government assistance. EDA *is* in the business of creating jobs for the unemployed, the underemployed and the poor. In Oakland, California, this means jobs primarily for Negroes and Mexican-Americans.[4]

On the same day he wrote to the president of World Airways that "Despite EDA's extraordinary efforts to assist both the Port of Oakland and World Airways to come forward with Employment Plans responsive to the needs of Oakland's unemployed and underemployed residents, both the Port and World have failed to meet the minimum assurances that EDA sought."[5] The timing of these moves by the EDA is significant. President Nixon had just assumed office and the EDA could implicitly represent itself as having altered its old style of playing the game. When Ross Davis, President Johnson's last head of the EDA, was replaced by Richard L. Sinnott, the EDA put a freeze on its Oakland projects to give the new administration time to review the record and evaluate the prospects. This freeze lasted for most of the year. While the freeze served many functions, one of them, whether intended or not, was to further redefine the style of play. In effect, the EDA was giving a signal to the other side(s) that it too was going to depart from the ritual of joint convergence. The party change in the executive branch provided the perfect background for making such a signal clear.

The general pattern of the EDA's negotiating tactics over the whole period 1966-1970 was a shift from a reliance on mutual trust and cooperation to a reliance on the threat of mutual destruction (mutual destruction, since it would serve neither the EDA's interest nor the port's nor World's to have the project abandoned altogether). Although neither strategy was particularly effective, one can understand the dynamics of the evolution. It made sense to begin with the first because if it worked it would be to everyone's advantage. If it did not, the recourse to threats was still possible. To have proceeded in the reverse manner would not have left options open: emphatic threats met by counterthreats would have ended the negotiations, and the strategy of presuming cooperativeness and goodwill would not have been available in a climate already poisoned by threats and walkouts. In the absence of effective adjudicatory and enforcement mechanisms it was reasonable for the EDA to rely as heavily on good faith as possible. The EDA officials were painfully aware that "enforcement of plans is difficult" and that the agency was very vulnerable on this account.

If we can generalize from the EDA-Port-World pattern, with the assistance of some laboratory research by social psychologists, we can speculate about how initial vulnerability, especially if one-sided, leads to mutual distrust, which in turn leads to poor communication, which in turn leads to outcomes suboptimal for both parties and to delay—perhaps even increasing delay—in the negotiations process. The more vulnerable party, knowing its own relative weakness, first attempts to invoke norms of mutual trust and cooperation. In some cases, this approach does induce the hoped-for response, but the fairly consistent finding from laboratory research suggests that the much more frequent response is exploitative.[6] Exploitative responses, however, tend to elicit suspicion and possible attempts at retaliation. Once locked into a pattern of threat and counterthreat, escalation follows. Expectations of the best rapidly give way to expectations of the worst, leading to a "self-fulfilling prophecy," the nature of which is best seen in the context of an arms race: once each side begins to fear surprise attack from the other, then each is inspired to launch a preemptive attack; and knowing that the other party must also place a high value on pre-emption, the logical conclusion is that one's own side ought to start the fighting not only first but immediately. In domestic political negotiations the risk of annihilation is usually absent, and the consequences are therefore not as frightening. They may nevertheless be severe. Raven and Kruglanski hypothesize this scenario:

Communication by the other is likely to be distorted and rejected as manipulative. Thus, informational influence is rejected. Expertise will be similarly rejected since even if B attributes superior knowledge to A, he is likely to reject A's recommendations as being merely a use of A's superior knowledge to manipulate or exploit B. The hostility and distrust which accompany competition will undermine legitimate power. Distrust and negative interdependence will further destroy the possibility of referent power. Differences will be emphasized and similarities will be minimized. Reward power may prove effective temporarily but always under suspicion. Reward will be considered as a bribe or as stemming from a desire to maintain dependence and superiority. . . .

Frustration and hostility resulting from being the recipient of coercive power then leads both parties to "move against" in behavior, belief, interaction, and identification. Concern about appearance before third parties and lowered self-esteem increase further the desire to influence the other by means of coercion even where other bases might conceivably prove effective. Thus, the underlying and personal bases of conflict become even greater. The power preferences of the two antagonists then further increase the possibility of further use of coercion by each.[7]

Under such conditions, the outcome eventually reached by the two parties is less likely to be optimal for both jointly than it would have been under conditions of cooperation and trust. Schelling, for instance, describes the problems of distrustful duopolists: if they can agree on a market price and a division of the market that maximizes their combined profits, they will each do better than if they both try to undercut each other, even if the initial division actually favors one duopolist more than the other.[8]

Under these conditions, future-testing is abnormally difficult, and this difficulty will lead to more protracted negotiations in order to give the adversaries additional opportunities to test each others' intentions and capabilities. More iterations are required. Successive iterations might permit the rebuilding of mutual confidence by what Schelling has called "piecemeal bargains," that is, low-risk transactions that might permit the parties to "practice" working in a cooperative mode.[9] All these take time, however, and the unhappy result is implementation further delayed.

Negotiations, we have said, are a form of future-testing; but they are also a form of future-controlling. Through the medium of words uttered in the present, the negotiators attempt to control actions that will take place in the future. Under the best of circumstances this is an unreliable medium. Its reliability is further reduced under the usual circumstances in which negotiations occur: the future is less than perfectly controllable because of uncertainty; there is an absence of adjudicatory and enforcement mechanisms; and there is either a normal or a pathologically derived distrust of relevant other parties. Under these conditions negotiations about the future tend to become bogged down in ritualism. There appears to be much ado about very little. Gross and important features of the future are neglected entirely while negotiations focus on unimportant details, partly because the latter might be easier to control and partly because the illusion of trying to control the future is more comforting than is facing the actuality that many such attempts are bound to be futile. The ritual takes the form of endless quibbling over words and other symbols, proxies seemingly available in the more-or-less controllable present or very near future for dictating conduct in the scarcely controllable very distant future.[10] A detailed, though necessarily tedious, account of such quibbling in the Stockton State Hospital-San Joaquin County negotiations will illustrate this important point. For this purpose I have extracted from documentary materials all significant references to the issue of who would have what sort of supervisory authority over the RT-2 unit and arranged them in chronological order. Most of the extracts come from minutes of the negotiating sessions themselves, though a few are from memoranda and letters.

To the question as to how this program will be administered, there was, as Dr. Gillis [associate superintendent of SSH] put it, no argument that it was the prerogative of San Joaquin County. [February 25, 1970, minutes.]

Dr. Freeman Adams cited the following problems that he saw still unsolved: . . . the function of the dual authority of San Joaquin County and Stockton State Hospital. . . . Dr. Gillis felt that the basics had been set out by Dr. Shallenberger. [April 3, 1970, minutes.]

To the question originally raised by Dr. Freeman Adams concerning the lines of authority in this new unit, Dr. Shallenberger brought the following suggestions: he saw no reason to interrupt the present lines of authority over supervisors; e.g., that of Mr. Warren Webb over his social workers. In regard to San Joaquin County personnel, Dr. Shallenberger would be in charge, his superior being Dr. Barber and his consultant being Dr. Peal. He regarded it as his responsibility to conform with the policies of the hospital. [April 10, 1970, minutes.]

. . . Dr. Shallenberger reports that Dr. Beaghler, in charge of Local Programs [for DMH] in this area, has expressed grave doubt about the aspect of dual control in the program. Dr. Adams acknowledged there were dangers in dual control, as did Dr. Shallenberger, but that this could be coped with by alertness and good will. [April 10, 1970, minutes.]

Close scrutiny was given to the separation of administrative functions and of treatment activities by the personnel on the team. It was the belief of Dr. Gillis that there should be a clear exposition to whom an individual would go when problems arose. [April 17, 1970, minutes.]

From a program prospectus drafted by Peal during the second week in April 1970:

This program is a joint program. . . . The staff from the State Hospital is accountable to the Program Director for their services yet they are responsible to the State Hospital for their scheduling and so on. Wherever possible, the management of incident reports and management of patients and procedures, rules and regulations for managing these administrative problems should be brought as close to the State Hospital's rules and regulations as possible . . .

As modified by Shallenberger, Brewster, and others, the final draft of the prospectus inserts after "scheduling and so on":

The State Hospital is responsible to the local program for the services that it contracts for. What this means to the program operation is that members of the State Hospital staff who do not meet their accountability responsibility would be referred to the State Hospital for action. The State Hospital would be responsible to the program for the services that this person provides, and if this person couldn't provide them, the State Hospital would be responsible to provide someone who could. Department Heads in the State Hospital, through the State Hospital Superintendent, would be responsible for making available to this program the persons called for in the contract. The San Joaquin County program Directors would be responsible to San Joaquin County Mental Health Director for an Inpatient Program, and would be responsible for the direct supervision of San Joaquin County employees assigned to the program. State Hospital employees would be accountable to him for their services and in the event there was some deficiency in his judgment and performance, he would report this deficiency to the State Hospital Superintendent, or his designee, and simultaneously to his Supervisor in the San Joaquin County Mental Health Services. The terms of the contract usually are that the State Hospital will provide these services to the satisfaction of the San Joaquin Mental Health Services, and the San Joaquin Mental Health Services has the responsibility of making known to the State Hospital what satisfaction means.

In a memo to Dr. Robert Hewitt, Deputy Director of DMH, on April 23, Galioni comments on the last quoted sentence:

I informed the staff of the hospital that the agreement as it stands would not be satisfactory since: 1. It does not fulfill the conditions of the agreement with UC at Davis, the county and the Department in that it would be a jointly operated program. 2. This type of agreement abdicates the authority of the Department since it provides no voice for the hospital in the administration of the program while it commits the hospital to full responsibility and liability in the treatment program. In a phone discussion with Dr. Langsley on Tuesday, April 21, he informed me that he is not particularly interested in how the program is operated as long as "the program has the joint commitment and interest from the county and the state hospital." I informed the hospital staff that they are to submit a counter proposal to the county indicating the terms they believe are required to allow the hospital to: . . . Retain the authority for administering the program on a joint basis commensurate with the responsibility that the hospital and the Department maintain.

The following day Galioni attended the weekly SSH-San Joaquin County task force meeting:

Dr. Galioni expressed his disapproval. . . . Dr. Galioni listed three possible approaches to the problem: (1) San Joaquin County could rent a ward in Stockton State Hospital and run it as a distinct entity with their own personnel; (2) San Joaquin County could contract with Stockton State Hospital to provide 24-hour inpatient service with personnel of Stockton State Hospital. He added a third alternative that San Joaquin County could contract with Stockton State Hospital to provide all ten services listed under the Short-Doyle Act. Consideration was given to the administrative lines of authority that would exist under these three different plans. No answer was reached. [April 24, 1970 minutes.]

In a memorandum to Hewitt five days later, Galioni reports another suggestion made at the April 24 meeting:

During the course of discussion the suggestion was made that a half-time director could be appointed to the county program and a half-time or part-time director could be appointed to the state in-patient services which would be contracted for by the county mental health program. I felt this would be a satisfactory arrangement and it would be for the hospital and the county to make an agreement as to who these individuals or individual might be. It was pointed out that this individual could be Dr. Shallenberger and I felt this would be a reasonable arrangement.

At the task force meeting of May 1:

The whole meeting was devoted to a discussion of the nature of the contract for services between San Joaquin County and Stockton State Hospital. The pros and cons of different types of contracts were considered; i.e., a contract by San Joaquin County for in-patient services provided by Stockton State Hospital; a contract by San Joaquin County for ten different services described in the Short-Doyle Act; other variations. Consideration was given to the cost accounting as well as the supervisory function in the different plans. [May 1, 1970 minutes.]

By the following week's meeting it was agreed that San Joaquin County would contract for certain services from SSH under the Short-Doyle Act. "Especial attention was given to the definition of 'the supervisor' of the program and a distinction was made between program supervision and line supervision." (May 8, 1970 minutes.)

At the May 15 meeting there were still ambiguities: "To the question placed by Dr. Adams as to who would be in authority, Dr. Shallenberger saw a reasonable answer. Since the program was to take place in Stockton State Hospital, it would fall under the authority of Dr. Adams and specifically delegated to Dr. Rubinger, who is in charge of Division I. Dr. Peal would be in charge of training the treatment team. Dr. Shallenberger would have the specific duties of supervising the program." (May 15, 1970 minutes.)

Following this discussion, the issue of supervisory authority was apparently resolved. The RT-2 unit began functioning on July 1 and closed several weeks later, as I have already indicated. When the county and SSH resumed discussions concerning RT-2 in the late fall, the issue was open again and earlier agreements were out the window. Barber was proposing to Freeman Adams that the project director from the county have "under his direction all of the treatment personnel. He would have an appointment on the staff of Stockton State Hospital; however, his salary would be paid by San Joaquin County Mental Health Services. As a nonpaid member of the Stockton State Hospital staff, he would be directly responsible to the Office of the Medical Director of the Stockton State Hospital. There will be mutual agreement as to the appointment of the Project Director." Adams indicated his concurrence and his own and Barber's concern that DMH-level clearance be given before the county took further action. (Adams to Galioni, December 11, 1970.)

In a curious letter to Beaghler, the DMH regional mental health director, on January 4, 1971, Barber complained: "The local program and the Stockton State Hospital's top administration have been in dialogue along these lines for well over a year. To date, none of our suggestions for joint utilization of staff have been acceptable to the Stockton State Hospital administration." The attached memo describing the new version of the SSH-San Joaquin County administrative relationship was drafted by Peal and appears to have demanded terms different from those agreed to in May 1970 or proposed by Barber to Adams in December 1970.

This may be the richest collection of data on interagency quibbling ever published. Before turning to an analysis of its ritualistic significance, I should reiterate my judgment that the lengthy debate over the nature of the "authority structure" to be imposed on Ward RT-2 was bound to be irrelevant to program operations once the ward started functioning. It is hard to conceive of a dispute arising in the operating phase that would not be resolved in a manner satisfactory to both the administrative hierarchy of the hospital and the program director appointed by the county. One cannot imagine Shallenberger, or even Barber, using plenary powers—had they been granted—to infringe significantly on the hospital's norms and procedures without Adams's consent. Equally, one cannot imagine Adams or his administrative subordinates interfering in the management of the ward without Shallenberger's consent. Hence my judgment that the debate just chronicled, which was far more engrossing to the participants than even the extracts cited above might suggest, was almost entirely ritualistic. The rituals were not inconsequential, however. On the negative side, they caused delays of many months. They also had several more positive "latent functions."[11]

Perhaps the primary function of these rituals was to relieve anxiety. The symbolism of how many and what kinds of hat(s) would be worn by the ward program director surely invites parody as an incantation in a children's game: "one hat, two hats, whose hat, OUR HAT!" SSH and DMH administrators, clearly worried about the encroachment on "their" territory by county people, were relieved to be able to invoke just such a magical formula. The ward would be jointly owned and operated, and if one didn't believe it one could take comfort in the formula, which clearly stated "OUR HAT" and not "their hat." And it was not only the substance of the formula that helped to relieve anxiety. It was also the process of developing it, which was long, difficult, and involved the other party (San Joaquin County negotiators). Surely a magic formula found in a day, or invented by one side and imparted to the other without the other's exertions, would have had less potency. It would also, on that account, have been less able to relieve anxiety.[12]

A second function of the lengthy negotiating ritual is to symbolize the "essential ambivalence" of all intimate relationships, to quote Lewis Coser.[13] In Coser's formulation, close relationships, in which much positive affect is invested, also cause the participants to suppress hostile feelings. While the SSH-San Joaquin County relationship did not require as much investment of affect as, say, a marital relationship or a close bond of friendship, it did require the display of feelings of mutual trust and regard. Yet it also required the display of defensive and essentially self-regarding feelings as well. The "essential ambivalence" of the relationship could be expressed in the lengthy negotiating ritual. Coser instructively cites in this connection the analysis by the anthropologist A. R. Radcliffe-Brown of the social functions of "joking relationships." According to Radcliffe-Brown, two groups with divergent interests but simultaneously bound in a "fixed," "conjunctive," or "alliance" relationship would use jokes as a "show of hostility" to express "that social disjunction which is an essential part of the whole structural situation, but over which, without destroying or even weakening it, there is provided the conjunction of friendliness and mutual aid."[14] It is not absurd to view quibbling rituals and joking rituals as serving similar functions.

Indeed, to the extent that the negotiating ritual symbolizes growing intimacy as well as "structural" separateness, the ritual itself becomes a force unifying the opposing parties and conducing to the expeditious and mutually agreeable outcome of the negotiating process.

It must be remembered that the spokesmen for SSH and for the DMH were in fact concerned (worried) about a real problem, the actual loss of territory to San Joaquin County and, for the DMH spokesmen, the potential loss of territory in other state hospitals. This was a problem, however, the articulation of which would have been both difficult and illegitimate: difficult because the dimensions of such a loss would be complex, multifarious, and measured often in the subtlest of nuances, and illegitimate because it was bad form to admit that one was concerned with territory at all, when the norm was to act "cooperatively" to promote the well-being of the mentally ill. Given these circumstances, the negotiating talks focused on the "authority structure," which served a dual function for the SSH and DMH negotiators. One was fairly pragmatic in nature, to communicate circumspectly, repeatedly, and in many different forms the nature of their problem. If by the end of a year's discussions of the "authority structure" and the Talmudic disputations over one hat-two hats the San Joaquin people had not figured out what really bothered the SSH and DMH people, they would have been hopeless dullards. Moreover, if they would not react in the short term and in the long term with some sensitivity, then the SSH and DMH people would have certainly been entitled to feel disappointed and betrayed. In this context, then, the negotiating ritual performed a rather direct communications function.

Another function served by the negotiating ritual, and also related to this underlying bothersome issue, was tension release in a socially acceptable manner. There can be little doubt that SSH and DMH administrators were angry and frustrated by the complex constellation of forces threatening to diminish and perhaps even eliminate the state hospital system: the Short-Doyle system, Governor Reagan's fiscal conservatism, Assemblyman Lanterman's ideological libertarianism, the reluctance of the mentally ill to use the hospitals, the mental health professionals' barely concealed contempt for the hospitals, etc. San Joaquin County's proposal was at the same time a boon for SSH and yet another form of assault. It would not have been at all implausible for SSH to have rejected advances by San Joaquin out of hand, all the benefits of the proposed relationship notwithstanding. The scenario drawn by Raven and Kruglanski and cited above suggests how this might have occurred. One could also conceive of the frustration-aggression mechanism leading to a similar result, with the state hospital and DMH officials frustrated by a complex of forces beyond their control displacing their aggression onto San Joaquin County officials. Their frustrations, indeed, were bound to be the greater precisely because they knew they *had to* cooperate with the county if Stockton State Hospital was to survive. Several interviewees volunteered the information that the state hospital administrators did indeed show signs of depression, frustration, and anger. The protracted negotiation ritual quite plausibly, then, served as an emotional "safety valve." Haggling over the form of the "authority structure" was safe, for it did not matter how the question was resolved; but it was also satisfying, since the haggling itself was a way of releasing the underlying tension.[15]

Negotiating rituals can serve latent instrumental as well as expressive functions. We have already mentioned the instrumental function of communicating an illegitimate and hard-to-articulate set of underlying concerns to the county representatives. We may also observe that to a certain extent the negotiations communicated to third parties as well, that is, to "audiences" that watched the process in order to pick up signals about the relative strength of certain forces. There are indications that Fresno regional office officials (like Beaghler) concerned with strengthening the Short-Doyle system, even if at the expense of the hospitals, were watching carefully and were even intervening occasionally to strengthen the hand of the San Joaquin negotiators. Similarly, the progress of the negotiations was being monitored in Sacramento by contending factions within the DMH headquarters to see how far the hospital system, and the hospital division overseers in the headquarters office, might be pushed.

Finally, we may mention the possible instrumental function of such negotiating rituals in creating a sort of legislative history. Subsequent disputes arising in the operating phase would be easier to resolve, or perhaps more amenable to resolution on one's own preferred terms, if one could fill the record with material indicating that one's own terms were part of the initial agreement. (I have found no indications, however, that the history of these negotiations has been referred to subsequently for this purpose.)

In sum, then, trivial as the issue of the "authority structure" was in substance, the negotiations to resolve it almost certainly served a number of useful latent functions. There was a price to be paid for such useful services, however. The negotiations were protracted. The presence of other complicating forces also causing delay makes it difficult to assess just how much delay in starting RT-2 can be attributed to the negotiating ritual itself. One could perhaps count two months in the spring of 1970 and add another two or three months in the late fall of that year and the winter of 1971.

Low-Cost Strategies for Avoiding Collective-Decision Delays

Most of the decisions required to produce elements for the program-assembly process are relatively independent of each other. Party A solicits contributions from parties B and C; B says yes while C says no; B then approaches D, while A approaches E; and so forth. The transactions are numerous but simple. The decisions are also relatively simple. The program-assembly process can be frictional, as we have said, but the friction originates in the sheer number of solicitor-provider transactions.

Delays in the collective-decision process result from compounding the decision problems of one actor by tying them to the decision problems of other actors—for example, A makes his decision contingent on B's decision and vice versa, and both, perhaps, make their joint decision contingent on C's decision. Delays in the collective-decision process arise from (1) the inherent difficulties of "future-testing" under conditions of uncertainty, even when bilateral or multilateral negotiations are employed as a means of attempting to control the future by reducing uncertainty, and (2) the latent functions of protracted negotiations as a ritualistic and instrumental adaptation to residual uncertainties. We are now in a position to consider some possible strategies for reducing or avoiding delays attributable to these causes.

1. Use intermediaries to facilitate negotiations. Third-party interventions have proved most useful in smoothing the negotiating process between labor and management. Mediation in such a context is by now almost a profession, and the function itself has been institutionalized and subsidized by many levels of government, as for example, in the Federal Mediation and Conciliation Service.[16] In the last decade we have seen the spectacular growth of "organization development" (OD) as a field of research, as a body of practical wisdom, as a business, and, some would say, as a profession.[17] OD is, or aspires to be, essentially a form of therapy for organizations in a poor state of mental health. Professional "change agents," that is, OD experts from consulting firms or universities, intervene in the organization so as to encourage more open communications among its members and to facilitate more realistic adaptations to environmental pressures. Can the mediation and/or the OD model of third-party intervention be applied to collective decision-making processes in the implementation of public programs?

In the San Joaquin-Stockton State Hospital case it actually was applied, though implicitly, and with some success. The parties in conflict were the psychiatrists representing the hospital and San Joaquin Short-Doyle, respectively, and the third-party interveners were the respective business managers of the two agencies. As Shallenberger put it, they "on several occasions pointed out that we psychiatrists often demonstrated our professional biases to the detriment of the business at hand." The interesting questions about third-party intervention, though, are not *whether* or *how* it can be effective but *who can* do it and *who is willing* to do it. Apart from the business managers in the Stockton case, I can think of only one other party who could have intervened effectively and would have been willing to do so. Many members of the county mental health association or the county mental health advisory board might have been willing to assist, but they almost surely lacked the necessary stature and the staying power. Judge Dozier might also have been willing, but it is doubtful he would have been perceived as sufficiently impartial. The only other plausible source of successful third-party intervention would have been Assemblyman Lanterman, an author of the L-P-S Act. As we saw in the first chapter, he frequently did intervene in such disputes. But his very plausibility as a candidate for such a role made him highly sought after by a very large number of parties all across the state. Clearly, he could not be every-where at once.

2. Foreclose options by maneuvering. Negotiations are a voluntaristic mode of collective decision-making. This is not the only possible mode. Maneuvering actors into certain inescapable positions by closing off viable alternatives is another mode.[18]

One maneuver of this type is analogous to stimulating a bandwagon movement. Actors join in because they feel they cannot afford to be isolated from what is emerging as a successful enterprise. Sayles and Chandler report some interesting illustrations of this maneuver in two NASA projects:

Initially, some noted astronomers refused to participate in a proposed venture unless the sponsor acceded to their demands regarding the con-duct of the program. Nevertheless, the sponsor went ahead with his plans. After a while, as the astronomers realized that the program pro-vided all sorts of professional opportunities and gave them access to scientific data that they could gain in no other way, they quietly rejoined the project. In another instance, one of four top officers at a sponsor's major operational center refused to cooperate with a new management system for data collection and processing. The officer in question was independent. Since he had his own budget and his own contractors, he saw no need to "waste" his time supplying data to other parts of the system. But he soon found himself out in the cold. He was forced to yield because, as others adopted the new procedures for reporting and analyzing problems, he became unable to communicate in his old manner with men in his own organization or with managers in cooperating contractor organizations. In both cases, instead of expending effort to negotiate the matter, the sponsor let the situation "speak for itself" as it began to generate its own pressures.[19]

A more coercive maneuver of this general type is to remove or vitiate critical sustaining elements of an actor's environment while at the same time arranging for their provision in the setting of the new program. This was the effect, if not exactly the intent, of AB 1640, passed in 1971, which stopped the automatic funding of the Community Services Division by the state and forced the agency into contracts with county Short-Doyle programs (whenever and wherever it could obtain them). Even a threat to execute such a maneuver can be effective, as in the case of San Joaquin County threatening to leave Stockton State Hospital to find its own supply of patients from the general catchment area while the county reestablished its own inpatient unit.

Odd Man Out is a maneuvering for position of the sort described here. In Chapter 6 we have seen some of its adverse effects. It also has positive effects, however, in that certain parties can be coerced into actions that are disadvantageous for themselves but beneficial for the program as a whole. To be sure, this beneficial result can occur only when the maneuvering and countermaneuvering in this game do not lead to players deserting the game and the project. It may be observed that the Community Services Agency halfway house described in Chapter 6 would probably have been delayed for at least another year had the CSA board not been maneuvered into a position of having to pick up the unexpected financial costs.

The limits of such maneuvering strategies as remedies for delay in the collective-decision process are established by the relative infrequency of the conditions necessary to make these strategies work. It is not easy to structure a situation in which all options available to a given actor are made to look less attractive than the single option another actor would wish him to choose. How many actors, moreover, have the political and administrative resources to execute such maneuvers even when other actors are potentially vulnerable to being thus maneuvered? Would it be possible to endow certain actors with such resources, and if so whom? Clearly, these are questions to be posed at the policy-design stage. How to do so is the subject of the concluding two chapters.

Notes

1

Jeffrey L. Pressman and Aaron Wildavsky, *Implementation* (Berkeley: University of California Press, 1973), p. 33.

2

These are not the only features decision-makers look for, of course. Expertise, prerogative, and functional relevance are also considered. See Eugene Bardach, *The Skill Factor in Politics: Repealing the Mental Commitment Laws in California* (Berkeley: University of California Press, 1972), p. 211.

3

I am indebted to my colleague William Niskanen for this observation.

4

Pressman and Wildavsky, *Implementation*, p. 57 (italics in original document). Letter from Ross Davis to Robert Mortensen, February 26, 1969.

5

Pressman and Wildavsky, *Implementation*, p. 58.

6

M. Deutsch, "The Effects of Motivational Orientation upon Trust and Suspicion," *Human Relations* 13 (1960): 123-139; L. B. Lave, "Factors Affecting Cooperation in the Prisoner's Dilemma," *Behavioral Science* 10 (1965): 26-38; V. E. Bixenstine, H. M. Potash, and K. V. Wilson, "Effects of Levels of Cooperative Choice by the Other Player on Choices in a Prisoner's Dilemma Game, Part I," *Journal of Abnormal and Social Psychology* 66 (1963): 308-313; V. E. Bixenstine and K. V. Wilson, "Effects of Levels of Cooperative Choice by the Other Player on Choices in a Prisoner's Dilemma Game," *Journal of Abnormal and Social Psychology* 67 (1963): 139-148. I am indebted to James D. Marver for bringing these articles to my attention.

7

B. H. Raven and A. W. Kruglanski, "Conflict and Power," in P. Swingle, ed., *The Structure of Conflict* (New York: Academic Press, 1970), pp. 103-104.

8

Thomas C. Schelling, *The Strategy of Conflict* (Cambridge, Mass.: Harvard University Press, 1963), pp. 31-32.

9

Schelling, *Strategy*, p. 45.

10

It should be emphasized that the rituals of conflict over words and symbols that are intended to control the far-off future ought not to be confused with a superficially similar conflict over words and symbols that aim at controlling the present or very near future. The distinction is crucial analytically, even though operationally it may be difficult to draw the line. An example of nonritualistic bargaining over words may be found in the recurring controversy during the legislative battle over L-P-S in 1967 and 1968 concerning the definition of "gravely disabled" persons. The civil libertarians who spearheaded the drive for L-P-S wanted a narrow definition; a large number of mental health professionals, particularly the psychiartrists, wanted a broad definition, which would have limited only slightly their customary right to commit persons for treatment "in their own interest" but against their will. Another example of nonritualistic debate over what might appear to be a trivial issue of wording can be found in the origins of the schism between the Bolsheviks and the Mensheviks at the Second Congress of Social Democrats in London in the summer of 1903. Levin and Plekhanov had drafted a platform that restricted party membership to persons who would work actively within the party and accept its discipline. The crucial sentence read, "A member of the Russian Social-Democratic Workers Party is any person who accepts its program, supports the party with material means and *personally participates in one of its organizations.*" The opposing plank, drafted by Martov, substituted for the italicized phrase "personally and regularly co-operates under the guidance of one of its organizations" (Edmund Wilson, *To the Finland Station* [New York: Doubleday, 1953 (orig. 1940)], pp. 396-399; and Lewis A. Coser, *The Functions of Social Conflict* ([London: Collier-Macmillan, 1964 (orig. 1956], p. 97) Lenin's formulation triumphed, the minority faction was forced out of the party, and there is no need to elaborate on the subsequent historical importance of the outcome.

11

These are the consequences that can be attributed to behavior by observers but not by the actors themselves, who are unconscious or unaware of them. The actors are conscious of the "manifest functions" of their behavior, that is, the consequences that they intend; but it remains for the outsider, usually the social or behavioral scientist, to identify the implicit and therefore "latent" consequences. Robert Merton's classic analysis of the latent functions of the political machine illustrates the difference nicely. The political boss intended the machine to work as an instrument of political power: winning elections, controlling officeholders, profiting from government policy and patronage, and the like. Merton points out that in addition to these functions the machine also (1) filled a vacuum in political leadership created by the legally prescribed fragmentation of political power through the system of checks and balances; (2) humanized and personalized the giving of charitable assistance; (3) provided channels of upward social mobility for groups with minimal access to more established and respected channels, and (4) stabilized the business environment for certain entrepreneurs, both legitimate and underworld, by franchises, police protection, and other means. Robert Merton,

On Theoretical Sociology (New York: Free Press, 1967), pp. 126-136. The discussion there is a lot more extended and sometimes uses "functional analysis" in a broader way not intended here.

12
The function of magic in relieving anxiety has been given its classic interpretation by the anthropologist Bronislaw Malinowski. See for instance *The Dynamics of Culture Change* (New Haven: Yale University Press, 1945).

13
Coser, *Functions*, p. 65.

14
Quoted in Coser, *Functions*, p. 64. Original from A. R. Radcliffe-Brown, "On Joking Relationships" and "A Further Note on Joking Relationships," in his *Structure and Function in Primitive Society* (Glencoe, Ill.: Free Press, 1952).

15
Coser, *Functions*, pp. 39-48, has a useful discussion of the "safety valve" functions of certain institutions and rituals in taming otherwise destructive conflict.

16
James E. Anderson, *Politics and the Economy* (Boston: Little, Brown, 1966), pp. 257-258.

17
See Richard Beckhard, *Organization Development: Strategies and Models* (Reading, Mass.: Addison-Wesley, 1969) for a useful review.

18
We exclude from the present discussion collective decisions imposed by edict because of our initial postulate that the relevant actors in the implementation process have considerable autonomy.

19
Leonard E. Sayles and Margaret L. Chandler, *Managing Large Systems* (New York: Harper & Row, 1971), p. 113.

III
Implementation and Policy Design

One of the principal aims of this book is to render practical advice to the analysts, technicians, intellectuals, and officials who are in the business of designing public policies and programs. Certain suggestions have been offered already, albeit in a halfhearted and somewhat skeptical way: six antimonopoly devices; four systems for the few to control the many; three methods for speeding program-assembly processes; and two techniques to smooth and quicken negotiations rituals. At this point we are prepared to integrate these mainly tactical suggestions into a broader, more strategic, view of implementation problems. The essential implementation problem, as we stated in the introduction, is to control and direct the vast profusion of program-related activities carried on by numerous and disparate organizations and individuals so as to achieve program objectives, keep costs down, and reduce delay. It is often said and occasionally written that problems of implementation should somehow be "taken into account" in the policy-design and adoption stage. In the light of our analysis so far, how might this be done?

The Basic Foundation: A Good Theory

First things first. It is impossible to implement well a policy or program that is defective in its basic theoretical conception. Consider the following hypothetical example.

If Congress were to establish an agency charged with squaring the circle with compass and straight edge—a task mathematicians have long ago shown is impossible—we could envision an agency coming into being, hiring a vast number of consultants, commissioning studies, and reporting that progress was being made, while at the same time urging in their appropriations request for the coming year that the Congress augment the agency's budget so that it might undertake the development of a new and more promising sort of compass. After five years, much money would have been spent in vain, congressional sponsors would have dissociated themselves from the whole enterprise, and scholars would gravely cluck over the program's problems of implementation.

Any social program worth having a governmental policy about at all is likely to be a serious and complicated problem and therefore not amenable to easy solution or even amelioration. To state the proposition a little differently, government gets the dregs of our social problems to solve. The easy ones have been dealt with already by individuals looking after their own interests, by families and other social groups looking after their members, and by economic units profitably exchanging labor, goods, and money in the marketplace. Government these days picks up the problems of physically and psychologically dependent persons, of social groups who have historically been stripped of the capacity to protect themselves from other social groups, and of economic units that cannot make it in the competition of the marketplace. To a certain extent these problems have been created as by-products of the successes of governmental solutions to other problems, as in black teenage unemployment being a by-product of minimum-wage legislation. In any case, they are simply "left over" by the nongovernmental (private and customary) and governmental processes that have on the whole done quite well at preventing an even larger incidence of problems. When government today turns to solving the "leftover" problems, it is rapidly discovered that no one knows quite what to do. Overwhelming political pressures often dictate, however, that "something" must be tried. Assertions that the effort is very likely to be futile (or worse) are discounted as weak apologies for the status quo. Clearly, we would all be better off, of course, if government simply stayed away from problems it could not solve. Alas, if only we could know, before trying and failing, what they were!

Any policy or program implies an economic, and probably also a sociological, theory about the way the world works. If this theory is fundamentally incorrect, the policy will probably fail no matter how well it is implemented. Indeed, it is not exactly clear what "good" implementation of a basically misconceived policy would mean. As we have used the term "implementation," it should probably imply that the process of implementing the policy would reveal its defects and that over time they would be removed. The more likely event, however, is that implementation problems will exaggerate rather than ameliorate basic conceptual problems.[1]

Consider the EDA case, for example. The agency was trying to alleviate inner-city unemployment in Oakland by providing capital subsidies to employers who promised to create jobs and fill them with minority-group hard-core unemployed. This capital subsidy strategy was an extrapolation of the agency's previous (and incidentally not very successful) strategy for dealing with the problems of economically depressed regions like Appalachia. Given its "organizational tradition," write Pressman and Wildavsky, "the EDA . . . could hardly be expected to realize that Oakland, though suffering from heavy unemployment, nevertheless lay in the midst of a prosperous region."[2] Furthermore, the agency's "economic theory was faulty because it aimed at the wrong target—subsidizing the capital of business enterprises rather than their wage bill. Instead of taking the direct path of paying the employers a subsidy on wages after they had hired minority personnel, the EDA program expended their capital on the promise that they would later hire the right people."[3] Thus, many of the "implementation problems" Pressman and Wildavsky describe as besetting the EDA's Oakland project were not implementation problems at all. The theory of the program called for capital to precede labor—almost to pave the way for labor. From this theory of program assembly naturally followed the endless delays in which the EDA sought to test the credibility of the prospective employers' promises. Since the will and the ability of the promise-makers to deliver at some distant future date were at best uncertain, and since neither the promise-maker nor the promise-taker could reasonably have been expected to calibrate the degree of uncertainty, how could one expect anything but delay while both parties were negotiating over such nebulous terms? If there were indeed "implementation" problems here, they were the failures of the implementers to see that the theory was faulty and should have been corrected before proceeding any further with implementation activities.

Pick a Strategy for Coping with Social Entropy

As we said in Chapter 5, a Management game is played against the entropic forces of social nature, and there is no permanent solution. Once this fact is recognized, the implication for policy designers is clear: design simple, straightforward programs that require as little management as possible. To put it another way, if the management game is a losing proposition, the best strategy is to avoid playing. Programs predicated on continuing high levels of competence, on expeditious interorganizational coordination, or on sophisticated methods for accommodating diversity and heterogeneity are very vulnerable. They are not necessarily doomed to failure, but they are asking for trouble.

Other things equal, policy designers should prefer to operate through manipulating prices and markets rather than through writing and enforcing regulations, through delivering cash rather than services, through communicating by means of smaller rather than larger units of social organization, and through seeking clearances from fewer rather than more levels of consultation and review. Such maxims are by now virtually the conventional wisdom among policy analysts of almost all shades of political opinion, and there is no need to elaborate on them. The paradigm case of program design that stresses the importance of avoiding the Management game is the attempt to convert administered "welfare" programs into a negative income tax.[4]

Scenario-Writing

Once the basic objectives are screened for feasibility, once the theory behind the policy is deemed to be plausible, and once an entropy-avoiding strategy has been chosen or invented, it is time for the designer to contemplate the system of implementation games—from Easy Money down through Reputation and any others that might be thought of. He or she must think about what types of games should be played, who should be the players, and what should be the stakes. He or she must also consider how to design the rules and to whom to distribute strategic and tactical resources. The object of this exercise is of course to construct a system that will be able to sustain the continued pressure from those implementation games most likely to exert a significant impact on it.

It is no easy task for the designer to predict, and following prediction to readjust, the outcomes of such dynamic and complex processes as are involved in a loose system of implementation games. In fact, the system is so complicated that it thoroughly defies analysis by means of even the most complex models known to any of the social or behavioral sciences. It must be approached through what has come to be known as "scenario-writing." This latter method simply involves an imaginative construction of future sequences of actions→consequent conditions→actions→consequent conditions. It is inventing a plausible story about "what will happen if . . ." or, more precisely, inventing several such stories. Telling these stories to oneself and one's professional peers helps to illuminate some of the implementation paths that the designer does not want taken. He or she is then in a position to redesign some features of the system of implementation games that permit him or her and his or her colleagues to tell stories with happier endings. Trial and error through successive iterations produce better and better endings.

Obviously, scenario-writing is an art. It requires imagination and intuition. One suspects there is not much that can be formalized or codified about how to do it well. This may be one of the reasons why scenario-writing is, in fact, not very common even among the most experienced policy analysts and designers. However, if our own interpretation of the implementation process as a system of games is at all realistic, might it not provide certain insights into how one should go about the difficult business of writing implementation scenarios? I believe the answer is yes, but let us lead up to this conclusion through an examination of two published policy analyses that should be counted among the very rare attempts at scenario-writing.

The first of the two analyses to be discussed is by James Hester, Jr., and Elliot Sussman and is entitled "Medicaid Prepayment: Concept and Implementation Issues."[5] Prepared for the New York City Health Services Administration, it concerns the problems of delivering medical services to Medicaid eligibles by means of "health maintenance organizations" (HMOs). The HMO concept has been and continues to be quite popular in policy-analytic circles and among political leaders of all ideological persuasions. The basic model of an HMO, on which there are many variants, is an organization of health professionals that promises subscribers a full range of medical services in exchange for a lump-sum prepayment. For subscribers the advantages are comprehensive benefits at a cost normally not above the cost of insurance premiums plus coinsurance plus deductibles that they would otherwise pay in the fee-for-service marketplace. For the health professionals associated with the HMO there are the advantages of group practice plus the possibility of reaping some of the rewards of efficient operation through salary bonuses and other forms of incentive payment. Competitive pressures from the fee-for-service sector, and quite possibly from neighboring HMOs, supposedly assure the maintenance of quality care. Competitive pressures also add to the HMO's incentives to keep costs down. While some of these savings accrue to the HMO, others are expected to be passed along to the subscribers in the form of lower rates.

That Medicaid (the government) pays the rates for Medicaid-covered subscribers considerably alters many of this model system's critical parameters. Disenrollment from an HMO by a Medicaid-covered subscriber might occur not because of dissatisfaction with the services but simply because the subscriber had lost his Medicaid (welfare) eligibility. This condition would blunt the cutting edge of pure consumer sovereignty as an instrument of quality control. If such involuntary disenrollments were only a small proportion of total disenrollments this condition would not matter, but Hester and Sussman observe that only 70 percent of the New York City Aid to Families with Dependent Children case load, automatically Medicaid-eligibles by virtue of AFDC status, remain continuously eligible for AFDC, and hence for Medicaid coverage, during one year. In addition, since the Medicaid-covered subscriber cannot *voluntarily* leave the plan without first clearing the decision with the welfare bureaucracy, there is further impairment of consumer sovereignty as a device of quality control.

Second, since the Medicaid enrollee pays neither for his HMO subscription nor for medical services purchased outside the HMO, the government as the third-party payer would be absorbing the costs of out-of-plan use of service by persons whom it had already paid to enroll in the plan.

A further problem is that, because of the casual attachment to the HMO produced by (1) the zero cost of enrollment and the likelihood of subsequent involuntary disenrollment, and (2) the zero cost of out-of-plan use, there would be a tendency of Medicaid-covered subscribers to underutilize the HMO's services. This tendency might arise from other causes as well, which Hester and Sussman are unable to identify, but the empirical findings from pilot projects and from several field studies have documented the tendency beyond dispute.

Calibrating the correct capitation rate also presents difficulties. It might take one or two years' experience (or more) before the government and the HMO could agree on a capitation rate that neither imposed excessive financial risks on the HMO nor milked the public treasury. The difficulties of setting the capitation rate for a nonprofit plan are especially severe, ironically, for it is hard to decide who ought properly to bear the risk of financial loss. Hester and Sussman argue that if the plan ends the year with a deficit, the group most likely to bear the brunt of the poor management is the fee for service registrants who will have to put up with service reduction as the center economizes.

Government, they argue, will not be able to dispense with regulatory methods of controlling the delivery of care either for any single HMO or for the HMO sector in the aggregate. One reason is that the consumer-sovereignty principle does not function well here, and a second is that some Medicaid eligibles might not be able to find an HMO willing to enroll them. Since high-cost or high-risk subscribers decrease the plan's profits, the plan has an incentive to terminate their subscriptions. If the HMOs are not permitted to do this legally, they will certainly seek ways to coax the subscriber to pull out "voluntarily." Hester and Sussman discuss some alternative methods of monitoring plan performance. They also explore some possibilities for designing the contract between the HMO and the responsible government agency so as to make it a more effective instrument of quality control and cost control.

The second study to be reviewed here is by Jack M. Appleman and concerns the implementation of certain provisions of the federal Clean Air Act of 1970.[6] In addition to stipulating rather stringent auto emission standards, the act also requires a manufacturer warranty on all new automobiles that such standards have been met and requires the manufacturer to pay the full cost of repairs on automobiles recalled under such a warranty. Recall could be initiated by the Environmental Protection Agency (EPA) if the agency administrator determines that a "substantial number" of vehicles of a certain class or category do not conform to the emission regulations, despite proper maintenance. An individual owner could also initiate recall, provided that (1) he has maintained the vehicle in accord with manufacturer specifications, and (2) the vehicle's nonconformity with the regulations has resulted in a penalty being imposed on him. In both cases, a showing of nonconformity would have to be established by in-use testing of the vehicle performed by a state-approved inspection facility. The warranty of manufacturer liability would run for the "useful life" of the automobile, defined as five years or 50,000 miles. The law delegates to the states the task of administering the in-use testing procedures and authorizes federal funding for up to two-thirds of the cost of developing and maintaining such testing programs.

Appleman projects several possible scenarios for the implementation of the act, all of which lead to minimal effectiveness and/or to an imposition of quite high costs on the consumer and on government. One possibility is that many states will refuse to provide in-use testing programs due to the high costs. Studies in California by the Northrop Corporation have shown that the capital costs alone for testing the state's twelve million cars would amount to between $10 million and $88 million, depending on the tests selected, and that operating costs would run between $1 and $5 per car. A state-owned and operated program in California would take two years to set up and would cost between $5 and $10 million (for planning, constructing inspection stations, training personnel, and so forth). In some states there might simply not be enough trained labor. The Northrop study indicates that the 400 inspection stations necessary to blanket California would require 400 technicians with at least one year's experience, another 400 inspectors with at least three years' experience, and 100 station managers with at least ten years' experience.

Furthermore, the Northrop projections for California show that because of the natural attrition of older, precontrol vehicles, one can expect a steady drop in tons of pollutants emitted independently of whether vehicles attain the legislated standards. As a consequence, significant delays in implementing a testing program will make it "almost valueless since emission levels a decade from now are projected to be the same with or without testing vehicles." Worst of all, according to Appleman, technical advances might solve the air pollution control problem much sooner than we think, and "this potential for obsolescence presents the danger that a significant capital investment and complex bureaucracy may outlive their usefulness in a relatively short period of time."[7]

Public acceptance of testing will almost surely be low. Since emission test results show extraordinary unreliability (variations in emissions of 50 percent are not uncommon), it will be very difficult to convince someone faced with the choice between, say, a $40 repair job and loss of his registration that he really ought to accept his fate. Given the unreliability of the tests, should he not be entitled to demand a retest? If so, how many subsequent retests? Improving testing techniques would alleviate this problem, but this involves the heaviest capital and labor costs.

To impose on the owner the responsibility of having his car repaired commits him to the fearsome clutches of the auto repair industry. Many owners will conspire with mechanics to dismantle the emission control system or will learn how to do it themselves. The alternative of having state-run emission-system repair shops would mean competing with a well-established private industry and is politically unacceptable.

None of this would be so terrible if the full costs (apart from the owner's inconvenience) could be passed back to the auto manufacturer. In principle, that is, according to the law, they should be. In practice, they are not likely to be. The manufacturers will impose stringent conditions hedging their liability, and "even officials at EPA consider that warranty work is primarily a manufacturer-consumer problem with little likelihood of enforcement."[8] Owners do not read or understand warranty provisions; dealers are reluctant to accept warranty-related work because reimbursement rates for such work are below those for ordinary repairs; and manufacturers do not incorporate quality of service into the criteria by which they judge the "performance competitions" among dealership regions.

Even if the full costs were passed back to the manufacturers, there would still be small likelihood that these would provide sufficiently large incentives for the manufacturers to improve their emission-control technology substantially. Given the internal organizational structure of the major American auto manufacturers, argues Appleman, "the design, manufacturing, and marketing process is so lengthy that the warranty/recall provisions of the Act are likely to have only a remote and unsubstantial effect on the critical production processes."[9] Appleman estimates that six to twelve years may elapse between a faulty design decision and confirmation of its correction. Even rather extreme assumptions about the possible number of recalls and their costs to the manufacturers, for example, 30 percent of new cars recalled in the ten most populous states and a warranty liability of $200 per car, would impose costs lower than either UAW strikes or slumps in demand. Hence, most decision-makers in the auto industry perceive the probable, and even the rather improbable, costs of warranty claims as sufficiently low so that they "do not seem overly perturbed."[10]

What is to be done? Appleman proposes two possible ways "to overcome implementation problems." The EPA might itself undertake a limited but intensive surveillance program in a few states, and on the basis of such sampling call for local or statewide recalls (provided it is willing to invoke its authority and supersede the states), and it might "use funds to wage a campaign of auxiliary programs aimed at training mechanics, public education, public relations, and consultant grants for state agencies. These efforts would aim at reducing the 'acceptability' implementation barriers and bringing internal pressure on some states to adopt inspection." Alternatively, there could be reconsideration of the technological goals of the act—a more fundamental redesign—"in favor of control devices that are less expensive to purchase but more expensive to maintain." This policy would make it more worthwhile for the states to invest in inspection systems and would also localize both the costs and the benefits of air pollution control.[11]

Scenario-Writing: Possibilities and Limits

The principal advantage of such scenario-writing is seemingly trivial but actually quite significant. It forces the designer to think seriously about the "obvious" design problems, particularly the financial costs. Appleman's observations that the inspection provisions of the Clean Air Act would impose enormous financial burdens on the states and that in many states the requisite manpower would simply not be available, are not so much implementation problems as they are problems of the basic policy theory. The "scenario" in which these problems appear is so truncated as to be hardly a scenario at all; they come onstage as soon as the curtain is opened. Both studies also identify certain implementation games, for instance, Easy Money and Easy Life. Auto owners playing Easy Life and auto repairmen playing East Money have a common interest in dismantling the pollution-control devices and no government control strategy projected for the Clean Air Act seems likely to alter the course of these games. In the HMO case, unscrupulous HMOs can play East Money successfully at the expense of both subscribers and the government, and if their costs should rise or their profits fall unexpectedly, the dictates of both Easy Money and Easy Life will impose the most severe short-term burden on the non-Medicaid subscribers to the HMO, who will receive lower-quality service. A third game identified in both studies is Not Our Problem. Hester and Sussman could obviously foresee government agencies trying to dodge the quality-control problem in HMO-supplied services to Medicaid-funded subscribers, and Appleman foresees both dealers and manufacturers saying "Not our problem" to dissatisfied customers.

One conclusion to be drawn from our review of these two studies is that the interplay of at least some forces likely to produce certain adverse effects can plausibly be predicted by an analyst—or a team of analysts—spending time thinking through the moves and countermoves of different players in the games. Easy Money, Easy Life, and Not Our Problem might be somewhat more amenable to such analysis than other games, but my own hunch is that scenario-writing could illuminate other possible games almost as well. A cynic might, of course, argue that both studies described here merely illuminate the commonsensical. Perhaps. In that case, one could conclude that the vast majority of (not unintelligent) commentators on HMOs for Medicaid populations and on the warranty provisions of the Clear Air Act have been less than common-sensical.

A second possible conclusion is that these scenarios might not go far enough. Is there reason to think, for instance, that the United Auto Workers might get involved in the struggle over clean air standards and inspection systems—and, if so, with what effects? Might state and local medical societies affect the performance, or indeed even the survival chances, of HMOs? What, if any, political attacks might be anticipated in conjunction with election-year politicking? It is not asserted, to be sure, that these *are* important questions, only that it would be useful to have a means of raising them.

The following guidelines for writing implementation scenarios are proposed as a means of identifying, while still in the stage of designing a policy mandate, just such questions—what *are* the stresses and strains to which the policy will be subjected during the implementation process? Of course, these guidelines are derived quite directly from the basic theory and analysis of this book, and, in an important sense, the utility of these guidelines in illuminating potential implementation problems is the critical test of the soundness of the basic theory and analysis.[12] I am pleased to report that the proposed guidelines appear to work rather well, judging from the experience of about forty undergraduate and forty graduate student attempts to apply them. A common experience of the better students in essaying this task is that the "same problem" shows up several times but under different "game" rubrics. The guidelines, therefore, embody the virtue of redundancy: if a scenarist inadvertently misses a serious problem at one step, there is a good chance he or she will pick it up at another step. The guidelines also do very well on the main test, which is, of course, to identify problems that the scenarist had not previously seen when thinking in a more ad hoc and improvisational manner.

Writing an Implementation Scenario

I

The Basic Policy Concept

A. State the policy mandate you hope to see implemented.

B. What problem(s) do you hope the policy will "solve" or ameliorate?

C. What do you expect government intervention, as reflected in your preferred policy, to accomplish?

D. What costs—financial and otherwise—do you expect will accompany government intervention?

II

Making an Inventory

List, and describe briefly, the program elements that will need to be assembled. Indicate who controls these elements either directly or indirectly.

III

The Management Strategy

A. How might your policy be designed so as to minimize the need to play the Management game?

B. How will your policy deal with the problems of social entropy:

    1. Incompetency?

    2. Variability in the objects of control?

    3. Coordination?

IV

Dilemmas of Administration

A. Tokenism

    1. Which if any, of the program elements listed above do you regard as *critical* to the success of your policy?

    2. Are any of these controlled by interests (or persons or groups) likely to be resistant or uncooperative?

        a. Will they respond with tokenism, procrastination, or "substitutions of inferior quality"?

        b. Can you think of ways to counteract these problems?

3. Will problems of tokenism, procrastination, and inferior substitutions be aggravated by monopoly conditions?

B. Massive resistance

1. What design features have you (or others) introduced into your policy to deal with the massive resistance? (deterrence, incentives, etc.)

2. How successful do you expect them to be?

V
Diversion of Resources

A. What games will be set in motion that will, in effect, divert important resources? (Easy Money? Budget? Funding? Easy Life? Pork Barrel? Other?)

B. How might you neutralize these adverse effects? Could they be turned to the advantage of the proimplementation party? Would design modifications be in order?

VI
Deflection of Goals

A. What games will be set in motion that will, in effect, threaten to deflect the original goals of the mandate? (Up for Grabs? Piling On? Keeping the Peace? Other?)

B. How might you counteract these games by altering the policy design? Any other strategies?

VII
Dissipation of Energies

A. What games will be set in motion that will, in effect, dissipate people's energies and impede constructive change? (Tenacity? Odd Man Out? Reputation? Territory? Not Our Problem? Other?)

B. How might these games be counteracted or prevented by altering the policy design? Any other strategies?

VIII
Delay

A. Assembling program elements

1. How much delay do you expect from this source?

2. What can you do to reduce such delays?

B. Collective-decision delays

    1. How much delay do you expect from this source?

    2. What sort of negotiations do you expect to take place? Between whom? Over what? How long will they take?

C. Would it help to:

    1. Assign priority status?

    2. Use the project management mode?

    3. "Work around" obstacles?

    4. Enlist intermediaries to help negotiations?

    5. Foreclose options by maneuvering?

IX
Fixing the Game

A. Elite activists

    1. Which officials would you like to play the fixer role? Why? What resources have they?

    2. What incentives have they to play this role?

B. "Eyes and ears"

    1. Whom would you like to furnish the "eyes and ears"? Why? What resources have they?

    2. What incentives have they to play this role?

C. What could be done to bring into being a viable game-fixing coalition?

The relevance of the questions in the first eight sections will be apparent to any reader who has followed the argument of this book so far. It remains for us to elaborate our conception of "fixing the game," referred to in Section IX of the guidelines and the subject of our next, concluding, chapter.

Notes

1

The importance of basic theory is also stressed by Walter Williams, "Implementation Analysis and Assessment," *Policy Analysis* 1: 3 (Summer 1975): 531-566.

2

Jeffrey L. Pressman and Aaron Wildavsky, *Implementation* (Berkeley: University of California Press, 1973), p. 149.

3

Pressman and Wildavsky, *Implementation* p. 147.

4

For an extremely interesting expression of these and similar maxims in the form of concrete program proposals, see the HEW "Mega-Proposal" of 1972 and commentary on it in *Policy Analysis* 1: 2 (Spring 1975).

5

James Hester, Jr., and Elliot Sussman, "Medicaid Prepayment: Concept and Implementation Issues," New York City Health Services Administration, Office of Program Analysis, draft version, April 1974.

6

Jack M. Appleman, "The Clean Air Act: Analyzing the Automobile Inspection, Warranty, and Recall Provisions," *Harvard Journal on Legislation* 10 (June 1973): 537-564.

7

Appleman, "Clean Air Act," p. 547.

8

Appleman, "Clean Air Act," p. 557.

9

Appleman, "Clean Air Act," p. 553.

10

Appleman, "Clean Air Act," p. 556.

11

Appleman, "Clean Air Act," pp. 562-564.

12

The more conventional scientific test for the adequacy of the theory is how well it explains a set of data. This test is impossible to apply in this case because the outcome of interactions in the implementation process are quite sensitive to the *magnitudes* of so-called "stresses and strains," and of resistance to them—and it is quite beyond our present abilities to quantify these magnitudes even roughly.

Scenario-writing is potentially quite useful but is nevertheless severely limited. The future, after all, is inherently unknowable, and one should be especially wary of predictions about the progress of a policy-implementation process. Four types of uncertainties beset any such predictions.

1. How skillfully, vigorously, or cunningly will the relevant actors play their games? Will they recognize all their opportunities? Will they seize them if they are recognized? Will they play cooperatively or exploitatively? What games will merge into larger games—and what larger games will decompose into smaller ones? In the HMO case, for instance, there are many possible scenarios that might be written about the games between the HMOs and the government monitoring agency, an area that Hester and Sussman explored relatively little. The cost-control section of the agency, playing Odd Man Out, might try to impose all the financial risks on the HMOs. Success in doing so would lead to a decrease in services by "cutting corners." The quality-control part of the agency, playing Budget, would attack their fellows in the cost-control section. The two sections would decide to resolve their differences by working up a "model contract." Recognizing the importance of such an instrument, the HMOs would band together to send representatives to the task force working out the contract. The negotiating sessions would become a setting for the Tenacity game. The resultant delays would lead to demands for participation by black and Puerto Rican "consumer" groups, thereby broadening the scope of the conflict and increasing the friction and delay.

Another possible scenario would have the regulatory agency so badly burned by a few atrocity stories connected with certain for-profit HMOs that it would lay down a rule forbidding any for-profit HMO to operate with fewer than half of its subscribers being paid for by Medicaid. The result of this rule (assuming it were effectively enforced) might be to drive a large number of HMOs out of business and the rest into nominal "nonprofit" status. In order to retain their "nonprofit" status, the actual profits of operation would have to be plowed back into the organization or returned to subscribers. The HMOs would prefer the former and would begin to behave like bureaus and other nonprofit institutions playing a Funding game. The regulatory agency would have to police the expenditures of the HMOs, a task they would shortly discover was impossible. The result would be an enforced standardization of subscriber rates across all HMOs in the area, which would be a lot easier for the regulatory agency to police. HMOs with large Medicaid populations might then become more like regulated public utilities than competitive providers of health-care services. In short, they might get to look more and more like the traditional county hospitals.

A source of especially severe uncertainty is the playing out of administrative games. In Chapter 5, we stressed the shortcomings of anti-Monopoly strategies and of systems designed to cope with Massive Resistance partly in order to emphasize the point that these games are highly uncertain in their likely outcomes, matching, as they do, administrators against persons and organizations bent on evading control. Indeed, it is difficult to predict even their tendencies. Will a given amount of deterrence, let us say, lead to (1) a reduction in the incidence of unwanted behavior to acceptable levels—in other words, "success," (2) no effect, or (3) increased efforts on the part of the objects of control to coordinate a strategy of Massive Resistance? Clearly, uncertainty over the possibility of such alternative outcomes was responsible for much of the debate in the USOE and HEW and in the Department of Justice concerning the wisdom of alternative enforcement strategies with regard to Title VI of the 1964 Civil Rights Act. Even in an incentive system there is always some uncertainty about how much and what kind of incentives to offer, as well as about the validity of the accounting data on which the rewards are based. If government started to fine polluters according to the "marginal social cost" of their pollution (a standard recommended by some economists), the government and the polluters would still have to play a bargaining game before they could agree on what that amount was. If a government agency simply tried to impose a schedule of fines on polluters, the latter would fight back through legislative and probably judicial means. What scenario-writer could possibly predict the likely course of such a complicated contest?

2. The scenario writer cannot easily project the behavior parameters of critical population aggregates, particularly clients, consumers, or objects of regulation. If toothbrush manufacturers have a hard time predicting whether or not there is a market "out there" for an electric toothbrush, how is a scenario-writer to predict the level of out-of-plan use of HMO Medicaid subscribers? If there is too high a level of out-of-plan use, as opposed to between-plan switching, the control mechanism predicated on consumer behavior will not work well. But how high is too high? And will there be means to curb or curtail out-of-plan use if it is too high? If there are such means, what problems will be encountered in implementing them? In the auto pollution case, one can easily write a good scenario by assuming all auto owners would rather pay repair bills than fight the dealers and the manufacturers—or by assuming all would choose the opposite course. Such assumptions would be completely unrealistic. But no scenario-writer can meaningfully predict what the true proportion of fighters to payers would be or, more important, what the absolute number of fighters would be.[1]

3. The scenario-writer cannot readily predict who will be playing in the implementation games. Although most of the probable players are identifiable by reason of their having played in previous policy and implementation games in the program area, there may be some new ones. In addition, not all the old ones will actually play.[2] The problem of identifying new players is the more interesting of these, and it has two basic variants. The first variant has new players lured into the game by the prospect of Easy Money, Territory, Pork Barrel, Reputation, or by the sight of some floating program elements that are Up for Grabs.

In retrospect we can see how foolish was the white health and welfare establishment in Philadelphia to have omitted to recruit any black residents of the North Philadelphia target area to the PCCA board. Their omission is indicative, however, of how easy it is to miscalculate who the players in the implementation game are likely to be. And of course the longer the game goes on the greater the probability that the simple turn of events will cast up new players. Six years ago there was no Bay Area Metropolitan Transportation Commission for BARTD to contend with over Territory, but now there is. The longer affirmative action has been around, the more minorities and disadvantaged groups show up to claim a piece of the action in Piling On games, Pork Barrel games, and Reputation games.

Reputation games are quite common in new programs and "settings," to use Sarason's term, for which there is an audience watching for signs of "creativity" or "innovation." The policy planners and designers expect the leader of the new program (whom they have handpicked in many cases) to be bold, innovative, and ambitious for Reputation. Sometimes a leader of this kind will pick associates who are mediocre and hence do not threaten his or her Reputation game. Their favorite games might be Easy Life and Not Our Problem. Just as often, one might guess, such a leader will pick associates who will enhance his or her own capacity to perform well, that is, persons of ability and imagination—and ambition to play their own Reputation games. In either case, the players recruited into the leadership stratum of new programs are not likely to be known in advance, nor are the games they will play. The players and their games are likely to have a large impact on policy implementation and outcomes, however.

The second variant of the new players phenomenon has them attracted to the implementation game out of defensive, even angry, motives. Such players often show up to protect policies or programs with relatively localized, or site-specific, adverse impacts, for example, the establishment of a halfway house for ex-state mental hospital patients or the construction of a new electric power generating plant. Usually it is possible to predict that such "outraged locals" will appear, though it cannot be known in advance of trying to implement a policy just how angry they will be or with what sort of political resources they will come equipped.

Even harder to predict than the identity of "outraged locals" is the identity of "outraged competitors." These players join the implementation game when government gives some subsidy to individuals or firms with whom they must compete in the marketplace. An interesting example of the "outraged competitors" phenomenon comes from the history of the Area Redevelopment Administration. Naturally sensitive to the effects of "unfair competition," Congress, in passing the ARA legislation, attempted to prohibit the ARA from making community facilities loans or business loans that would draw firms (particularly textile manufacturers) away from certain regions (particularly New England) into low-wage-rate regions (particularly the South). Congress did not have the foresight, however, to forbid loans that helped one firm compete against another. Hence, when the ARA tried to boost the failing Delmarva poultry industry by making a twenty-year, 4 percent loan to a local poultry feed producer, it ran into trouble. An outraged competitor who three years earlier had borrowed funds from conventional lenders at 6 percent and for a five-year term blew up. "Why, they could drive me right out of business while I am pinching pennies to pay off my mortgage in five years. . . . We could hardly complain if this were a privately financed operation, but it just isn't fair to use our tax money to build the plant to drive us out of business." The Senate Committee on Banking and Currency admonished the ARA, after its first two years in operation, to "take great care to insure that any new production capacity created will not be obviously excessive to drive other efficient producers in the industry out of business."[3]

4. While it is easy to predict that there will be delays of some sort, it is hard to predict their magnitude or their causes. This is especially so

for those nonpurposive delays analyzed in Chapters 7 through 9. The program-assembly process is vulnerable mainly because it is so complicated and has so many different decision points. While Pressman and Wildavsky are somewhat misleading in emphasizing the sheer number of decisive points, it is surely correct that the larger their number the more opportunities for *something* serious to go wrong. The scenario-writer's problem is that he or she cannot be sure which of the many possible foul-ups will occur. Nor can the scenarist be sure how it will be handled. Will someone like a project manager appear to smooth over the difficulties? Will political forces create a favorable momentum—or lead to demands for "further review" and thus more delay? Delays resulting from collective-decision processes are even harder to predict. Who could have conceived, for instance, that the San Joaquin County-Stockton State Hospital negotiations would drag on for three years?

If scenario writing cannot usefully resolve these uncertainties—Who will play? How will they play? With what effect will they play? How long will they play?—there may be little or no possibility of forestalling all significant implementation problems by means of shrewd analysis and laborious design revisions in the initial policy design and adoption stage. Tinkering with the policy design will inevitably go on during the implementation stage. There will be attempts to modify the basic policy or program so as to improve its chances of successful implementation. These modifications can generally be thought of as *interventions* in the implementation game undertaken by players closely identified with the goals set by the "idealistic" sponsors of the original policy.[4]

Fixing the Game

In Chapter 1 we described the interventions by Assemblyman Frank Lanterman and his staff in the implementation of L-P-S. It is now possible to see how these activities amounted to "fixing the game."

I mean "fixing" in two senses. First, it means "repairing," as when Lanterman carried "cleanup" bills with only technical amendments, or when he recognized that a new substantive policy dimension had to be added to take care of the problem of the mentally disordered offender and the potentially violent individual. Second, and more important, it means adjusting certain elements of the system of games—which in the aggregate can be thought of as a single massive implementation game played against the policy mandate itself—so as to lead to a more preferred outcome. In this latter sense, "fixing" connotes a degree of covertness, as indeed is appropriate, for much of this activity goes on behind the scenes, out of public view. It also connotes a degree of coerciveness. This connotation is sometimes appropriate and sometimes not. Lending a helping hand to the Long Beach Neuropsychiatric Institute entailed no coerciveness except perhaps by indirection. Imposing a new set of priorities on the DMH and the Short-Doyle programs, setting political forces in motion against Brickman in Los Angeles, and trying to rewrite local zoning ordinances did involve a measure of coerciveness. The notion of a "fixer" also connotes impropriety, if not necessarily illegality, for the fixer attempts to rig the game to increase his own winnings. This connotation is also appropriate, but the the idea of "winnings" here must be interpreted to mean policy outcomes in accord with the spirit of the original mandate, rather than purely private gain or profit. No doubt some of the other players would regard the fixer's winnings as their own losses and would insist that the game had been rigged unfairly and unjustly. Of course, the fixer might equally self-righteously say that the others had rigged the game against him, and he was intervening merely to right a prior wrong.

We cannot now know whether an implementation scenario-writer plying his trade in 1966-1968, when L-P-S was in its design phase, would have predicted all the difficulties L-P-S subsequently encountered. Having watched the politics of the early part of the adoption phase myself, I do not believe the designers anticipated most of these difficulties. No doubt implementation would in some respects have been smoother had they tried to do so. Yet, it is also true that they compensated for mistakes of omission made at the design stage by "fixing" problems during the implementation stage. Moreover, they *anticipated* doing so. Given their plans to act subsequently as "fixers," and given also what I believe was their implicit knowledge that the prediction of implementation problems was inherently limited, their "failure" to undertake detailed planning was not unreasonable. Perhaps, on the whole, it was even wise. Policy formation and implementation proceeds by trial and error, after all, not only because it is inevitable, up to a point, but also because it is desirable. Like most successful social learning, good policy development is learning by doing.

In any case, the crucial components of the implementation process *had* been programmed: Lanterman and his people would act as "fixers." If implementation should fail, the reason would be a failure of sustained political will, not an intellectual, or planning, failure. These potential fixers knew they had the right political resources and the willingness to use them.

The "Fixer" as a Coalition

What sort of resources are required to play the role of a fixer? Lanterman clearly had abundant resources, but we can easily imagine someone else with fewer, or with different kinds of, resources who might have played the fixer role almost as well. Imagine, for instance, Lanterman as director of the Department of Mental Hygiene. From that formal position Lanterman might have been able to do even more effective fixing than he did from the legislature. To put the matter somewhat differently, if the DMH would have had a director as dedicated, energetic, and skillful as was Lanterman, there would have been considerably less need for Lanterman and his staff to busy themselves with as much fixing as they did. The fixing could have been left to the director.

Another formal position with the potential resources would have been the governorship. Similarly, the director of the Human Relations Agency, which supervised Mental Hygiene, Social Welfare, and Public Health, could conceivably have played the fixer role.

By way of contrast, however, consider the Citizens Advisory Council for Mental Health. The council was created by the L-P-S statute. Those who conceived it in 1967, when L-P-S was on the drawing boards, thought of it precisely as a game-fixer. The framers did not believe the DMH would do an adequate job implementing their vast new policy mandate, and they wanted the CAC to have the resources to intervene effectively in the implementation process. In the draft legislation, the CAC was given the power to approve or veto county Short-Doyle plans, which implied an extensive power over programming and budgeting. As the draft legislation came under public scrutiny and criticism, however, these powers were stripped away, in deference to the vociferous objections of the DMH. The L-P-S Act, as finally signed into law, stated (in Sec. 5674) that the CAC had the following "powers, duties, and responsibilities":

a. To advise the Director of Mental Hygiene on the development of the state five-year plan.
b. To periodically review all mental health services in California, conducting independent investigations and studies as necessary. . . .
c. To suggest rules, regulations, and standards . . .
d. To encourage, whenever necessary and possible, the coordination on a regional basis of community mental health resources, with the purpose of avoiding duplication and fragmentation of services.
e. To mediate disputes between counties and the state. . . .

The legislature never permitted the CAC a budget for staff, however, nor for anything alse except members' expenses for attending the quarterly meetings of the council.

The CAC's record was one of almost total failure. It is hard to say exactly why. Many members of the CAC believed their failure was due to lack of staff. Perhaps. Even with a staff of three or four, however, it is hard to imagine the council being very effective as a game-fixer by itself. It did not have control over anything of real importance to those who play implementation games. It could not alter or enforce the rules. It could not manipulate the stakes. At best, it could have given a publicity advantage to one or another of the players. With a staff of three or four, it would have been able to deploy its publicity resources better. Whether enhancing that particular capability would have made much of a difference, though, would have depended very largely on who was paying attention and what game-fixing resources *that* actor had! If it was Lanterman paying attention, the CAC's powers of investigation and publicity would have augmented his own game-fixing capability. In effect, the CAC would have extended the reach of Lanterman's staff. Only by allying itself with an actor with quite substantial resources might the CAC have functioned effectively. Indeed, to the extent that the council as a whole (as distinguished from its individual members, many of whom were quite influential in their own bailiwicks) did exercise much power, it did so almost exclusively by working through Lanterman and his staff.[5]

Is all this to say that only "power" counts when it comes to fixing the implementation game? Not at all. Formal authority and formal political resources count for much but not for everything. The fixer must be able to intervene effectively, but he or she must also be able to know where, when, and about what. To know these things, he or she must have access to a great deal of information and have the flow of information summarized, interpreted, and validated so that he or she can make sense of it. Lanterman's staff provided a lot of such information. But a lot flowed in spontaneously. Many people in the state's "attentive public" for mental health policy channeled information to Lanterman because they knew that his office specialized in collecting information and using it for political purposes they shared. Political information is a little like investment capital: the more you have the more you can get for your own purposes, and the more you are likely to be used by others for their own purposes, which they believe coincide with yours. Just as money attracts money, information attracts information.[6] Without information about how implementation games were being played "out there" in the field, Lanterman would have been powerless to do any fixing.

It follows, then, that there was and is an important game-fixing potential for groups like the Citizens Advisory Council or the California Association for Mental Health or the several county mental health advisory boards. Fixers like Lanterman need them almost as much as they need a Lanterman, for they are uniquely equipped to be the fixer's eyes and ears, probing into the numerous small crevices of implementation activity. Fixing the game is a job for *a coalition of political partners with diverse but complementary resources.* It is therefore no different from any other political task. Implementation games, as we have asserted so often throughout this book, are political games.

Implementation Games and Representative Government

Implementation games are also part of the larger game of politics and governance. Just as they draw their characteristic strategies and tactics from the game of politics, so too do they deliver their outcomes back to the larger game. We may well wonder with what implications. One possible implication is that fixing implementation games may lead to unanticipated and undesirable raiding of the public treasury. We have focused in this book mainly on improving performance and reducing delay. Fixing implementation games to achieve these purposes will often entail making side payments to players who would otherwise be obstructionists. Lanterman's efforts to help the hospital employees and the CSD did end up costing the taxpaying public a certain amount of money. The dramatic increases in the total Short-Doyle budget just after L-P-S was passed may also be seen as an expensive distribution of side payments to counties used to getting relatively large allocations that might otherwise have been cut back in order to fund programs in counties where there had been few or no services. Poor performance, resistance, and delay can almost always be alleviated for a price. The price may not be perceived initially as a money price, but eventually the players are likely to find a way to express their dissatisfactions in such a way that a money price can be offered and accepted. On the one hand, the translation of implementation troubles into problems with money as a solution provides us with a very valuable tool. It is valuable for its extraordinary flexibility. But this is precisely the property that makes it dangerous as well, for the treasury vaults yield more readily to such supple instruments than they do to sledgehammer blows.

A second problem with game-fixing is that many of the activities are covert and highly manipulative. It is therefore hard to find out what the fixers are doing and to hold them accountable. Game-fixing is quintessentially government by men rather than laws. It is not necessarily, though, irresponsible government. There are, in the end, certain legal and customary bounds beyond which even the superfixers cannot go with impunity. At this writing a number of once high government officials are in jail or awaiting trial as a result of overstepping the bounds. A United States president has resigned as a result. Government, after all, is full of game-fixers, and our pluralist system comes as close as one might hope to guaranteeing that anyone who tries to get away with a superfix will be brought low by a coalition of all the other, more temperate, fixers.

The real problem, however, is that too few of the would-be fixers know how to do the right thing, are willing to do it if they do know how, and have the political resources to make their will effective. The most problematic role in the fixer coalition, the one that is hardest to come by, is the intervener at the top, the person or persons with powerful political resources. As we indicated in Chapter 1, Lanterman was something of a rarity. There are no scholarly studies, to my knowledge, that describe any political figures playing such a zealous and effective oversight and follow-up role. My inference is that the role is rarely played, principally for the simple reason that those potential fixers with the political resources do not have the incentives. Top career civil servants may often have the resources, but just as often they are part of the problem rather than part of the solution. That is, they are often heavily committed to certain bureaucratic games that are themselves in need of fixing. Top political appointees in the executive branch need a long time to master the details of what is actually happening in implementation games. By the time they have mastered the details, they are almost ready to leave. In any case, it often happens that their incentives are to indulge more in rhetoric and self-display than to pursue the unglamorous tasks of cajoling, pushing, threatening, and so on. Legislators are in a similar position. If they can afford—or wish—to forego self-display and dirty their hands with the detailed aspects of policy and programs, they will attend to the work of crafting new legislation rather than to the work of making the old legislation produce the results intended and desired. Lanterman is the exception that proves this rule: he was nearing the end of his legislative career and he knew that he would receive enormous credit if L-P-S turned out well and equally great blame if it turned out poorly. Very few legislators are in that position.

Where, then, does hope lie? First, let us be clear that pessimism is in order.[7] Still, we may point to two possible institutional locations from which an appropriate game-fixing strategy might be carried on, one in the legislature and one in the bureaucracy. In each case, the strategy relies heavily on staff.

On the bureaucratic side, there is the possibility of setting up policy analysis and evaluation groups under the auspices of the department, or even agency-level, budget office. The group structure is essential to this strategy, since we should expect individual members to stay put no longer than two to three years and any continuity in the pursuit of game-fixing strategies will depend on the recruitment and training of new fixers as a way of compensating for the constant departures of the old ones. The incentives for analysts to involve themselves in political and bureaucratic action at the necessary level of detail are not insignificant. There is, after all, a specialized but fairly large attentive public in any policy area that will appreciate and credit their good works and that can eventually be tapped for career-enhancing jobs and other emoluments. Lanterman's chief of staff for several years, chosen to help him implement L-P-S, had distinguished himself previously working on L-P-S under the auspices of the California State Department of Finance, which contained just such a group as I have been describing.

These analytic groups would have the leverage of the budget process available to them: a bureau head could not completely ignore them if he knew that they made recommendations on budgetary issues. They would also have a certain stability and permanence, provided only that they could offer enough staff service to the political directorate of the organization to make themselves relatively immune to sudden and perhaps capricious destruction.

On the legislative side, my recommendation is for a similar sort of staff group to be attached to an appropriations committee or to a policy committee with a stable membership or at least chairmanship. All the arguments made above in support of such a group in the bureaucracy apply here too: it would have power, a broad viewpoint, semi-independence from political changes, and the ability to develop and continue its own expertise. The same compatibility with career aspirations that was asserted for the bureaucratic staff group would exist for this group as well.

What about the second component of the game-fixing system, the information- and intelligence-gathering apparatus that pokes about in the far-flung crevices of implementation activities? Who can be counted on to perform the "eyes and ears" functions similar to that played by the

California Association for Mental Health and other citizen groups with respect to L-P-S? As a rule, it is best to have the clientele group that benefits from a program play this watchdog role. Programs designed to benefit farmers, for instance, seem to be unusually well implemented, inasmuch as farmers as a whole are vocal, well-organized, and allied with powerful fixers in Congress.

Unfortunately, the general rule is of little use when the clientele population is inarticulate, disorganized, and lacking in political standing. Mental patients are one example. Schoolchildren are another. In such cases, professionals and other service providers, such as psychiatrists and schoolteachers, venture to speak on behalf of the clientele population. Policy designers do not have to worry about stimulating feedback about implementation problems from such groups; it happens automatically. Often, however, such feedback is part of the problem rather than part of the solution, as it is bound to reflect the parochial and selfish interests of professional and provider groups.

There is probably no general solution to this problem. Citizen activists attempted to offset the distortions that were present in the feedback to Lanterman from mental health professionals and bureaucrats. The purpose of the parent participation mechanisms called for in the Elementary and Secondary Education Act of 1965 was to offset the influence of schoolteachers and administrators. From these two examples we may infer that watchdog functions must be custom-tailored for each program- or policy-implementation process: it would have been silly to mandate parent participation, for example, in the implementation of L-P-S. Unhappily, in some cases it may be impossible to design a watchdog institution at all. Who, for instance, would have been an appropriate watchdog for New Towns?

The Implementation Problem in Perspective

When I first began to plan the research for this book, I was convinced that implementation problems were serious, and that I would be rendering a useful service if I could suggest ways to ameliorate them. Now, having completed the work, I am less sure. As I write this concluding paragraph, I am nearing the end of a year-long job in the Office of Policy Analysis in the Department of the Interior in Washington. The longer I watch the evolution of public policies and programs, and the closer I get to the process, the more attached I become to the first two heresies, described in the introduction, which currently threaten the ideology of liberal reform: government *ought* not to do many of the things liberal reform has traditionally asked of it; and even when, in some abstract sense, government does pursue appropriate goals, it is not very well suited to achieving them. Markets and mores are sturdier and more sensible, and government is probably less sensible and less reliable, than liberal reformers have been willing to admit. The most important problems that affect public policy are almost surely not those of implementation but those of basic political, economic, and social theory. In the short run, it is essential to invest a great deal of energy in designing implementable policies and programs. For the longer run, however, it is equally essential to become more modest in our demands on, and expectations of, the institutions of representative government.

Notes

1

Of course, these figures would be expressed as a probability distribution of figures within a range rather than as a single "best guess."

2

For a rather primitive method of mapping the likely players in a policy-adoption game, which method might be adapted to a policy-implementation game, see Eugene Bardach, *The Skill Factor in Politics: Repealing the Mental Commitments Law in California* (Berkeley: University of California Press, 1972), Chap. 1.

3

Sar A. Levitan, *Federal Aid to Depressed Areas: An Evaluation of the Area Redevelopment Administration* (Baltimore: Johns Hopkins University Press, 1964), pp. 125-126.

4

These interventions are independent of policy modifications which result from reevaluating the basic policy concept or model. A useful summary of the methods, the value, and the limitations of policy evaluation research per se may be found in Carol H. Weiss, *Evaluation Research* (Englewood Cliffs, N. J.: Prentice-Hall, 1972). On the meaning of " 'idealistic' sponsors," see Appendix C.

5

A useful overview of the council's first four years is provided in the appendix to the minutes of its September 1973 meeting. Judging from these, much of the council's energies were consumed trying to decide what its role should be, trying to organize itself to play its role effectively once it decided, and attempting to garner funds for independent staff to help it play its investigative role. Those who contributed to the overview in September 1973 credited the council with influencing a number of decisions that almost certainly would have gone the way they did even without the council's contribution. The council arranged for an amicus brief to be filed in the California State Supreme Court test of the constitutionality of L-P-S, for instance, but the court's affirmative decision would have come about without the council's brief.

6

See Eugene Bardach, "Subformal Warning Systems in the Species Homo Politicus," *Policy Sciences* 5 (1974): 415-431.

7

An excellent discussion of the lack of incentives to devote oneself to implementation concerns is in Erwin C. Hargrove, *The Missing Link: The Study of the Implementation of Social Policy* (Washington, D.C.: The Urban Institute, 1975), pp. 110-115. His conclusions on this point are not quite as pessimistic as my own, though in my judgment he is merely unwilling to accept the logic of his own argument.

Appendix A The Impact of the Lanterman-Petris-Short (L-P-S) Act in California

Civil Liberties

L-P-S essentially put an end to the old system of involuntary civil commitment of the mentally ill and persons alleged to be mentally ill. Prior to L-P-S, a person could be indefinitely committed if the court found that the person was "of such mental condition that -he is in need of supervision, treatment, care or restraint" or "dangerous to h--self or to the person or property of others . . ." Under this system, California courts were committing over 1,000 persons per month to state institutions, usually following only the most cursory psychiatric examination and court hearing. For this system, L-P-S substituted another that prohibited involuntary detention for any longer than seventy-two hours unless one of two very stringent conditions were met. If a person were certified as dangerous to himself or others or so "gravely disabled" as to be "unable to provide for his basic personal needs for food, clothing, or shelter," he could be certified for an additional fourteen days of "intensive treatment." After the expiration of the fourteen-day certification period, suicidal persons could be held for up to fourteen additional days, but only if the person had threatened or attempted to take his own life during the period of observation or intensive treatment. For persons adjudged "imminently dangerous" to others, a postcertification procedure for involuntary detention up to ninety days was available. Again, the evidence of dangerousness had to be substantial. The person had to have threatened, attempted, or inflicted physical harm during the period of observation or intensive treatment, or he had to have committed some physically harmful act that resulted in his being taken into custody in the first place. Although certification could be accomplished upon affidavit of professional treatment personnel alone, judicial review through a writ of habeas corpus was available to any detained person who requested it. As for the gravely disabled, upon a recommendation by professional treatment personnel the court could order the appointment of "a conservator of the person, of the estate, or of the person and the estate" to last for up to one year, after which time it was automatically terminated unless a petition to continue the conservatorship was filed by the conservator and granted by the courts. The conservatee had the right to appeal for removal of the conservatorship once each six months. Any person requesting a habeas corpus hearing was entitled to be represented by a public defender. In addition, the L-P-S Act specified a number of patient rights, such as the right to see visitors daily, to refuse shock treatment, and to wear one's own clothes. A list of these rights was to be posted in English and Spanish in any facility used for involuntary detention. In the case of conservatees, there was to be no blanket withdrawal of civil rights like the right to vote or the right to operate a motor vehicle as there had been in the case of the judicially committed prior to L-P-S. For each conservatee the court was to stipulate the particular disabilities it would impose.

The results of the civil liberties provision of L-P-S are suggested in Table 1, which very crudely reflects the decline in relatively long-term involuntary treatment from the period just before L-P-S to a point just three to four years after it had taken effect. Even though there had already been a trend in the early and middle 1960s for mental health professionals to decrease their reliance on involuntary commitments, the impact of L-P-S was to reduce the incidence of involuntary long-term custody by roughly half. Although these data are obtained for only one geographical region in the northern half of the state, the region is quite heavily populated and is probably not unrepresentative of other regions in the state.

Both before and after L-P-S, two mechanisms were used to place a person in custody for initial observation and evaluation for mental illness. One was the "seventy-two-hour hold," whereby a police officer (typically) took into custody a person he had "reasonable cause" to believe fit the criteria for involuntary commitment and treatment as a result of mental disorder. The other mechanism was a court-ordered

Table 1
The Decline in Long-Term Involuntary Custody

County	Involuntary State Hospital Patients Staying More Than 6 Weeks, 1969 (adjusted)[a]	Conservator-ships Granted, 1973	Percent Decline
Alameda	630	231	63
Contra Costa	349	285	18
Marin	191	47	75
Napa	71	44	38
San Francisco	596	269	55
Solano	87	30	66
	1,924	906	53

[a]The adjustment involves an extrapolation from Napa State Hospital, for which data were specially tabulated, to the entire state hospital system. The six counties chosen were the counties in Napa's regional service area in 1967.
Source: Department of Mental Hygiene

evaluation that could be initiated upon approval of a petition filed by a relative, friend, neighbor, or anyone else. The second mechanism was used much less frequently than the first both before and after L-P-S. But in the immediate post-L-P-S period the number of successful petitions dropped dramatically, as is indicated in Table 2. The reasons for this drop were that the criteria concerning who was liable for involuntary treatment were tightened considerably and that more extensive use was made of "prepetition screening" by mental health programs.

The provisions for recertification of persons believed to be suicidal were little used. In eleven counties from which data were obtained by the ENKI Research Institute (including the ones named in Table 2), only eleven persons were recertified during the six-month period beginning January 1, 1970. Comparison of a patient cohort admitted to primary psychiatric screening units in this six-month period in San

Table 2
The Decline in Court-Ordered Evaluations

County	January-June 1969	January-June 1970	Percent Decline
Los Angeles	2,059[a]	171	92
Sacramento	3,216	5	98
San Francisco	592	43	86

[a]Cell entries are numbers of petitions for evaluation filed and approved by the Superior Court in the county.
Source: ENKI Research Institute, *A Study of California's New Mental Health Law* (1969-1971) (Chatsworth, Calif., 1972), p. 86.

Francisco, Los Angeles, and Sacramento counties and a cohort admitted in the six-month period just before L-P-S took effect showed a dramatic decrease in suicides as well. In the former cohort of over 300 persons, no suicides were reported.[1] The postcertification procedures for the "imminently dangerous" were also little used. In the eleven counties reporting data to the ENKI evaluation study, only thirty-six postcertifications were requested, of which the court denied nine.[2]

The L-P-S legislation also stated that by July 1, 1970, a review was to have been made of all current hospital patients and the provisions of L-P-S applied to them. Although the review dragged on until 1971, the result was a rather rapid, and somewhat unexpected, depopulation of the state hospitals for the mentally ill.

Delivery of Services

The L-P-S service-delivery system built upon an infrastructure made up of the state hospitals and the Short-Doyle Community Mental Health Services. Through Short-Doyle the state reimbursed counties in 1969 on a 75-25 ratio for services to voluntary patients from an approved list of five services (inpatient, outpatient, partial hospitalization, emergency services, and consultation and education). The major change wrought by L-P-S in the service-delivery system was to increase county responsibility and resources for the delivery of mental health services. All involuntary patients had to be given an intensive multidisciplinary evaluation by a county evaluation unit before they could be sent to the state hospital.[3] The counties were also given the responsibility of contracting for inpatient services with the state hospital serving their regional catchment area. The reimbursement ratio was raised to 90-10 and the counties were entitled to claim reimbursement for services to both voluntary and involuntary patients. L-P-S made it mandatory for all counties with populations of over 100,000 to participate in Short-Doyle and offered a modest fiscal incentive to smaller counties to come in voluntarily. A fifteen-member Citizens Advisory Council was established "to advise the Director of Mental Hygiene on the development of the state five-year mental health plan" and "to suggest rules, regulations and standards . . ." There was to be "a single state appropriation" for both the state hospital system and the Short-Doyle system, which the DMH was to allocate among the counties annually. The county programs were to be able to shift funds between state hospital services and county-provided services subject to the approval of the DMH. The DMH's control over the system was to be effected by means of reviewing annual county plans containing statements of need and of resources.

As can be seen in Table 3, in the first two years of L-P-S the state hospital resident population declined by 33 percent, even though admissions increased slightly (for reasons no one has been able to ascertain). County outpatient services doubled, county-provided partial hospitalization and rehabilitation services increased by half, and county inpatient services increased by 18 percent. Even under the fiscally conservative administration of Governor Ronald Reagan, the Short-Doyle budget increased dramatically after L-P-S. In fiscal 1969, the last pre-L-P-S budget year, Short-Doyle programs spent $39 million, whereas in fiscal 1972, they spent $96 million.

Table 3
The Large Increase in Local Services Since L-P-S

Service	FY 1969	FY 1971	Percent Change
State Hospital			
Beginning Case Load	18,831	12,671	-33
Admissions	40,358	42,040	4
Total	59,189	54,711	-8
County Outpatient			
Beginning Case Load	36,797	74,211	102
Admissions	106,134	211,661	99
Total	142,931	285,872	100
Partial Hospitalization/ Rehabilitation			
Beginning Case Load	3,738	6,252	67
Admissions	10,512	15,266	45
Total	14,250	21,518	51
County Inpatient			
Beginning Case Load	973	1,115	15
Admissions	36,848	43,532	18
Total	37,821	44,647	18

Source: State of California, Department of Mental Hygiene, *California Mental Health: A Study of Successful Treatment* (Sacramento: Department of Mental Hygiene, March 1972), p. 8.

Whether these substantial increases in services and in expenditures did much to help the mentally ill, their families, and the community at large is subject to much debate. More accurately, the debate concerns how much help and to whom. The Short-Doyle programs have traditionally concentrated on the relatively "easy" cases and permitted the state hospitals to collect the "hard" ones, and there is reason to think that Short-Doyle's target population did not change much after L-P-S.

There is strong evidence that the Short-Doyle programs did relatively little to help the chronically mentally ill, even those who were released from the state hospitals in the great wave of discharges following L-P-S.[4]

It is hard to assess the impact of L-P-S on the families and on the communities that received the released hospital patients or were obliged to keep in their midst persons who might otherwise have been sent to the state hospitals. There is some evidence that families must often absorb considerable inconvenience by having mentally ill members living at home.[5] Whether this proposition holds for California, post-L-P-S, we do not know. No systematic assessment has been attempted (or at any rate published). Nor has there been a systematic assessment of the impact of greatly increased numbers of mentally ill persons in the community at large. Several communities have attempted to exclude residential facilities serving the mentally ill for one reason or another. In some cases, notably the city of San Jose, the sheer numbers of ex-patients pose a threat, real or imagined, to the demographic balance of the neighborhood. In other cases, there is the dark fear of violence. In San Francisco, for instance, one halfway house (a relatively therapeutically oriented type of community residential care facility) was driven out of its residential neighborhood by threats of violence against the residents and the proprietor. The threats by neighbors were prompted by an incident in which one of the halfway house residents clubbed a woman to death with a roller skate.[6] Such accounts of adverse community reaction make the headlines, but we cannot infer from such reports the prevalence across all communities and neighborhoods of reactions of either acceptance or rejection, inasmuch as the instances of acceptance do not make the headlines.[7]

Perhaps the most acute sense of failure about the L-P-S system came from the growing recognition that the residential care (or board-and-care) facilities in the communities that housed the chronically mentally ill who prior to L-P-S had lived in state hospitals were, on the whole, mediocre or worse. The designers of L-P-S had given scant attention to this dimension of the system they were creating. They had assumed that the existing program for posthospital residential care, the Community Services Division's "aftercare" placement program, would handle the problem as well (or as poorly) as it had always done. In this assumption the designers were quite mistaken.

The CSD was a unit of the State Department of Social Welfare (SDSW) between 1966 and 1971. From its founding in 1939 until 1966, it had been located in the Department of Mental Hygiene and was known as the Bureau of Social Work. Its principal responsibility was to place patients discharged (technically, on "leave of absence" status) from the state hospitals in residential facilities in the community, a function it continued when it was removed from the DMH to the SDSW.[8] The CSD also undertook to encourage would-be operators of such facilities to establish an acceptable living environment and in many cases helped them to negotiate the administrative obstacle course on the road to licensure or certification. The CSD had relatively little to offer potential operators of board-and-care facilities, however, except advice and perhaps the promise of a stable complement of clients. It was not equipped to stimulate rapid growth in the board-and-care sector or effectively to regulate its performance. L-P-S triggered a massive, if largely unanticipated, shift of responsibility for the welfare of the chronically mentally ill from the public sector (state hospitals) to the private sector (board-and-care facilities). Both state and county government were ill equipped, and largely unwilling, to recognize the shift of responsibility and to develop programs and administrative techniques to deal with its implications. Neither state nor county government wished to share any of the financial risks of board-and-care operation with the private sector. The designers of L-P-S did not contemplate the issues involved in extending the licensure and certification policies of the era prior to L-P-S to the community residential-care system that inevitably was to emerge from L-P-S. Hence, a large number of mentally ill persons were placed in homes or large facilities that many observers deemed substandard or worse. This failure, if indeed it was a failure, must be counted as the principal blemish in both the design and the implementation of L-P-S.

Whether or not these observers' standards were realistic or appropriate is an interesting question. I think they were not. I also think facilities licensing was and is a useless instrument, and perhaps a very harmful one. See Appendix B for an elaboration of these views.

Notes

1

ENKI Research Institute, *A Study of California's New Mental Health Law (1969-1971)* (Chatsworth, Calif., 1972), p. 152.

2

ENKI, "Study," p. 154.

3

In some cases, the counties contracted with a nearby state hospital to provide these evaluation services, but the basic responsibility was still the county's.

4

See Introduction.

5

David Mechanic, *Mental Health and Social Policy* (Englewood Cliffs, N.J.: Prentice-Hall, 1969), pp. 82-87.

6

San Francisco Chronicle, November 12, 1973.

7

Larry Sosowsky, "Putting State Mental Hospitals Out of Business—The Community Approach to Treating Mental Illness in San Mateo County," Master's thesis (Graduate School of Public Policy, University of California, Berkeley, June 1974), argues convincingly that former state hospital patients do show a higher propensity to engage in acts of violence than does the general population. He does not, however, show how much *additional* burden the mentally ill have placed on the community relative to the existing burden of violent crimes. By my rough calculations from his data, it would probably be in the range of 5 to 10 percent.

8

During its life within the DMH it was almost always something of a stepchild, a relatively small organization of professional social workers attached to a large organization headed by psychiatrists and physicians. It was shifted from the DMH to the DSW partly in order to protect it from imminent destruction at the hands of the DMH directorate. (See Eugene Bardach, *The Skill Factor in Politics: Repealing the Mental Commitment Laws in California* [Berkeley: University of California Press, 1972], Chaps. 7, 8.) As it turned out, it fared little better in the DSW. Called at first the Division of Adult Protective Services, it was subsequently downgraded symbolically to the Community Services Division and then to the Community Services Branch. In 1973, it was returned to the newly formed State Department of Health, where it was called first the Alternate Care Services Unit and then the Community Services Section. For convenience we shall refer to it as the Community Services Division or CSD.

Appendix B Upgrading the Quality of Residential Care for the Long-Term Mentally Ill in the Community: An Alternative to Licensing[1]

The first injunction to physicians in their canon of professional ethics is to do no harm. This should be the first injunction to policy-makers as well, especially those who set out with good, even noble, intentions. We have seen a good deal of legislation enacted and executed by persons with the highest motives that has probably done more harm than good. When government intervenes in complex social arrangements, the results are often quite unexpected. That is the nature of complex systems, to behave in counterintuitive ways. They are like silly putty; push it into one shape and it wraps itself into something different. Government regulation of the railroads crippled the railroads over the years, and distorted the economic structure of the national transportation system so as to cost the American public about a half-billion dollars a year in shipping costs that might otherwise have been saved. Government subsidies to industries and municipalities for sewage treatment have discouraged the introduction of much cheaper and ecologically more sound recycling technologies and raw materials inputs. When law enforcement cracks down on heroin pushers, the street price goes up and so might the incidence of addict-committed crime.

How fortunate we should count ourselves, then, that the adoption and implementation of L-P-S has not made the plight of the mentally ill worse than it was. Indeed, one even suspects—at least I do—that the mentally ill are vastly better off than before L-P-S. For one thing, they have their freedom. The actuality and the threat of involuntary and prolonged incarceration have greatly diminished. It is probably even true, though admittedly hard to assess, that more services, and more effective services, are reaching a larger proportion of the population in need. Even with respect to the residential care of the mentally ill in the community—which is the Achilles' heel of the new system, and about which I will speak principally—the patients are almost certainly better off than they used to be. Unfortunately, this fact, if it is a fact, is scarcely recognized because almost no one has taken the trouble to ask the patients themselves what they think about their residence in the community as compared to the state hospitals. The attitude of almost all mental health professionals and concerned lay activists on this question has been and continues to be inappropriately paternalistic: they look at former Agnews State Hospital patients living in board-and-care facilities clustered in downtown San Jose and say, "Tut-tut, isn't that a shameful ghetto . . . poor mental patients living in these converted rooming houses in a semicommercial district . . . ," and so forth. Now, a lot of solid citizens in San Jose don't like the idea of so many ex-hospital patients having moved into that area, but my hunch is that the patients like it quite a lot. Colleagues of mine at the School of Social Welfare at Berkeley have interviewed a large number of board-and-care residents in that area as well as in many other areas around the state. Their overwhelming impression is that the patients prefer their present situation to their situation in the state hospital. One middle-aged gentleman released a year ago from Agnews and living in the so-called ghetto in San Jose told me, in a conversation I had with him in a laundromat, "Sure, it's better here. At Agnews you always had to do what they told you. Here I can do what I like, like come wash my clothes in this place." Ms. Dorothy Moses, a past chairman of the California Citizens' Advisory Council on Mental Health and a professor of nursing at California State University, San Diego, had her students interview a hundred mentally ill residents in facilities in San Diego, and only one alleged that she would prefer to be back in the hospital. The California State Employees' Association, for quite obviously self-serving reasons, has accumulated atrocity stories about roaches and filth in particular residential facilities. But atrocity stories alone are not a good basis for public policy redirection—as my grandmother used to say, "For instance is not a proof."

Reformers Fallen on Hard Times

If life is better for the mentally ill patients, though, could it be worse for the mental health reformers?—that is, for most of us here today.

The answer is yes, for three reasons. First, once the immediate goals of any reform are accomplished, there is less momentum to continue on the very important follow-up that is almost always needed—a job, incidentally, that Assemblyman Lanterman and his staff have done superlatively—as well as less tolerance for further reform by those who were only barely acquiescent all along. Second, the problems of reform now are much more difficult than they were in 1966-1967 when L-P-S was conceived: that is, it is not at all clear what ought to be done or how and at what cost, etc. Finally, and in a sense related to the first two reasons, the generation of mental health reformers that came of age fighting the state hospital system has lost its traditional enemy but is unable to shake off the old and relatively successful doctrines of the past to engage with the new and quite different enemy. The new enemy seems to be the board-and-care system, but it is a curious enemy in that reformers need to tame and domesticate it rather than destroy it.

Consider for a moment the great convenience of the old state hospital system as a target of reform compared to the very great inconvenience of the board-and-care system.

Accountability
The state hospitals were only fourteen in number, but there must be at least 1,200 private residential facilities caring for the mentally ill and mentally retarded.

In the state hospital system there are clear lines of hierarchical accountability reaching from the ward attendant all the way up to the director of the Department of Health. In principle there is always somebody to pin the blame on and point a finger at. But the board-and-care operator is a private agent, responsible to no hierarchical superior.

In the state hospital system there are clear standards of professional competence against which to measure performance. When professional care is poor, reformers can always complain that the professionals are incompetent or derelict by their own standards. But since board-and-care operators are not a profession, when they behave badly one can only say that they behave badly. (Similarly with the business side: you could reasonably complain about bad business management in the hospitals, but nobody really expects board-and-care operators to be great business managers.)

Stability
The state hospitals have been sitting ducks. Bureaucratic conservatism in the Department of Mental Hygiene and economic significance to localized population centers made it likely in the past that the hospitals would stay put while reformers took aim and fired round after round. But relatively small privately run facilities don't necessarily stay put under fire. They may go out of business. No bureaucracy has a vested interest in keeping any particular facility around, and the economic significance to the local community is more likely to be on the negative than the positive side.

Improvability
For the state hospitals reformers have had an easy remedy: more money and more staff. For the board-and-care system reformers have a less plausible, if equally simplistic, remedy: stiffer regulation through licensing. At best, reformers seem ambivalent about improving the board-and-care system by giving operators more money.

For the state hospitals there is a clear-cut if not necessarily reliable or valid measure of success: the rate of discharge. The patients when discharged went out to reside in the board-and-care system, which was in the mid-1960s hardly noticed by anyone much less criticized with any ferocity. For the most part, moving out of the board-and-care system meant failure: moving down the ladder again, back to the state hospitals. Now people seem to think that moving out of the board-and-care system is a mark of success. The residents are supposed to move not downward to the hospital but upward to something else, though it is not clear what.

The state hospitals in the mid-1960s were regarded as not very good but "moving toward" better care. They were institutions constantly in a state of slow but progressive transition. Their very scale and stability made it possible for at least some of them, at least some of the time, and in some way, to experiment with new approaches, to take the risks of innovation without fearing that adverse results would put them out of business. Also, as the patient population declined over the years, staffing ratios improved. But in the private sector, an experimental approach that fails (on the part of a halfway house, for instance) or a 30 percent reduction in a facility's resident population might be enough to drive a facility out of business—or discourage new facilities from entering. People who ran the state hospital system were not known for being innovators and risk-takers, but at least there were no serious economic obstacles in the way, and hence reformers could feel free to demand more innovation and faster progress. They cannot so readily demand innovation and progress from private facilities that face greater risks.

In sum, then, it appears that we have slain the dragon only in order to battle the hydra. Where once there was a single enemy, imposingly large but of a species well understood, now there is a multitude of smaller and less menacing creatures belonging to diverse species of whose habits we know little. In a quandary as to what to do, reformers, several years ago, reached for the only weapon they have found in their arsenal, licensing, an instrument of public supervision of private facilities for the mentally ill that dates back to the statutes of King George III. Schools of social work have long taught facilities licensing as a special course in the curriculum. In all the standard scholarly work on facilities licensing that I have read there is an implicit assumption that it does in practice what it is supposed to do in theory, which is, of course, to protect the public from unscrupulous or incompetent providers of service that members of the public, for one reason or another, are not in a position to evaluate for themselves. I have not seen a single study, however, that put this proposition to the test, much less one that showed that it was in fact true. My own hunch is that licensing not only does no good but is an instrument of positive mischief. In the name of doing good, government is doing what it lamentably seems so often to do, causing harm, and thereby violating what I have said earlier should be its first ethical prescription. Let me state my reasons.

The Illusory Benefits of Licensing

First, everyone agrees that facilities licensing cannot do much if anything to upgrade facilities, that is, to improve quality. It can at best set a minimum floor of decency.

Second, everyone also agrees that it cannot set a floor under any quality of the facility that cannot be easily described in words and in a sense measured by "objective" indicators. Hence the common and correct complaint that most licensing takes a "bricks and mortar" approach.

Third, denial or revocation of licenses is very difficult if not absolutely impossible. Licensing workers often believe that people have a right to try and operate a facility if they wish without arbitrary and possibly prejudicial restriction by government bureaucrats. And if they take the view that denial is legitimate whenever it is believed that the applicant will not run a *good* facility, it is hard for them to know on what to base this belief or how to justify it to the applicant or to others. Revocation is even more difficult, since the legal requirements of the administrative code put the burden of proof entirely on the agent who would wish to revoke the license.

Fourth, even if one could *threaten* naïve operators with the revocation of a license, and thereby use licensing for its deterrent effect, such threats could—or perhaps should—only be made for the most serious violations and abuses. The threat of license revocation would be downright silly as a method of encouraging an operator to serve better food or give residents access to the backyard patio.

Finally, when the vacancy rate in a community is low—that is, when there is a shortage of supply relative to demand—it is usually better for the patients to have *some* facility, even if it is not up to standard, than *no* facility.

These are the reasons why licensing does not, or cannot, do much to improve the quality of residential facilities. The reason it is a positive harm is that licensing restricts the entry of potentially beneficent private facilities. Licensing, you may recall, is technically defined as "the administrative lifting of a legislative prohibition." When licensing laws are in effect, one may not operate unless specifically exempted by the licensing agency. Now, licensing regulations are invariably very complex and the method of their application Byzantine. Administrative regulations or legislative statutes are constantly changing the licensing standards and procedures, and the very uncertainty and complexity of the licensing process thus discourages operators from entering the market. This problem is especially severe for halfway houses, which typically operate on a shoestring budget with no capital reserves, with uncertain occupancy factors, and hence without even the prospect of modest financial reward that induces some brave souls to battle the licensing process and occasionally even triumph over it. All these, incidentally, are objections to licensing in principle rather than to the way it is presently practiced by the State Department of Social Welfare or the Department of Health. The licensing people in these agencies are surely able to do a better job than they have been doing—like all the rest of us. But their main problem is that they are obliged to go through the motions of developing a rational policy around the licensing principle when in fact that principle is simply not capable of being rationally applied in the present circumstances.

What To Do

Hold Placement Workers Accountable

Licensing is useless and harmful and, thankfully, not really necessary. There are alternative instruments to accomplish the same ends of public protection that are more effective and more efficient. For many years, the California State Department of Mental Hygiene used one, namely, the certification program of the Bureau of Social Work for board-and-care facilities. Under this program, social workers in a county or region developed a list of facilities that they thought could do reasonably well as residences for ex-hospital patients. If the social workers did not like a place they did not necessarily decertify it but they stopped sending patients there, and they might have tried to move patients who were already there. If placement workers took their jobs seriously, and if there was some slack on the supply side of the market, the natural effects of competition among providers worked to the benefit of the resident, or ex-patient, population. In theory, the long-term effects of this provider competition should have been to upgrade gradually the quality of care and residential amenities being offered by facilities operators. Notice, by the way, that the real responsibility for making this market-type system work well lay on the placement workers and their supervisors. Although licensing is ostensibly a way of regulating facilities operators, it is actually a way of regulating placement workers' conduct. If we could trust placement workers not to place people in low-quality facilities but to place them only in high-quality facilities, there would be no need to forbid the low-quality facilities from operating. They would get no business anyway.

Create Slack in Supply

Please take note of the second condition I mentioned that is necessary to making this market work to the advantage of the consumer, "some slack on the supply side." There is no reason to think that this slack will occur automatically in the optimal amount. Indeed, since licensing discourages entry, governmental policy actually works against the existence of slack. And this brings me to a crucial point about our deficiency in thinking about how to deal with the new set of problems arising under L-P-S: there is no viable policy doctrine at hand that suggests the appropriate relationship between public agencies and private caretakers and residents. Halfway houses provide a very good example of the results of this deficiency. There are too few of them. Almost everybody thinks so. But nobody wants the state or the counties actually to own and operate them, for they would surely succumb to all the problems besetting other public "charity" institutions. On the other hand, the private sector is sparsely populated by the breed of visionaries and philanthropists prepared to launch such enterprises themselves. Until the state and the counties come around to understanding that they cannot expect the private sector to assume all the risks and uncertainties of starting such ventures, and that public agencies will have to share them to some extent, there will continue to be a dearth of halfway houses. To a degree, the same can be said of long-term (or "L") facilities. As to the garden-variety board-and-care facilities, if one believes as I do that creating and maintaining a little slack on the supply side will, in conjunction with placement worker effort, go a long way toward upgrading the quality of residential facilities, then public agencies should figure out a way to share the costs and risks of preserving modest vacancy rates with the operators in the private sector. It is hard to say how much it would cost the state to implement such a policy, but I doubt that the cost would be very great. My impression is that supply *almost* tends to keep up with demand in most counties. If supply stands at 95 percent of demand, there are shortages and no room at all for market forces and placement agencies to work to elevate the quality of residential care and services being offered. On the other hand, if the state can convert a 5 percent shortage into a 5 percent excess, let us say, we will then have a handle on the quality-control problem we could not have had before with relatively little added cost. I would like to take this opportunity to recommend that the state attempt to do this on a limited scale, in two or three counties where there appears to be a problem at the moment. Such an experiment could conceivably produce much useful knowledge not only about the impact of a sheer increase in supply by itself but about some of the other features of the residential-care market that we know too little about.

Improve Information to Consumers

In particular, we know too little about the effects of information on those who act as consumers in this marketplace, whether the patients themselves or the placement workers. Assemblyman Lanterman's AB 2262 certainly has the right idea in calling for a rating system to be applied to residential-care facilities. Licensing, of course, is an implicit rating system. It is very crude, however, having only two categories: acceptable and not acceptable. In principle, it would be better to have three or four gradations. Indeed, it would be desirable, in my view, to have two separate ratings, one made by professional mental health workers and fire and safety inspectors that focused particularly on the rehabilitative potential and structural safety of various facilities; a second made by mental patients themselves, with some assistance, I would guess, that evaluated the purely residential amenities of a facility that are probably quite important to the patients and that are certainly better understood by them than they are by people who do not actually have to live in those circumstances. Written agreements analogous to leases between landlords and tenants might be tried. It might prove interesting to encourage operators to advertise for residents, as they did in nineteenth-century England. For instance, we find a printed handbill from 1816 advertising one of the largest English provincial asylums that reads as follows:

1st. Separate apartments, four guineas per week—those who pay this price have the best apartments; each male is allowed a man, and each female a woman servant, and every proper indulgence suitable to their disorder. Three guineas per week—the treatment in all respects the same, except having a separate servant.

2nd. Associated apartments, two guineas per week, having convenient rooms allotted them. The above classes dine with the family, when their cases will admit of it.

3rd. The Lodges. These are detached buildings, with wards for each sex and courts for air and exercise; of this department there are three classes: 1st. One guinea and a half per week, are more nicely dieted and lodged than the undermentioned. 2nd. Pay 25 shillings per week. 3rd. class, one guinea per week; not allowed tea.

There are two detached squares for pauper lunatics of both sexes, who pay fourteen shillings per week, and one guinea entrance. . . . No patient is taken for less than a quarter of a year, but should one be removed for any cause whatever before that time, the quarter must be paid for. The same rule observed in case of death. Curable patients, after the first quarter, are charged only for the number of weeks; but a week entered upon, the whole is reckoned.

All patients find for their own use two pair of sheets, and four towels, pay the sum charged for one week as entrance, and five shillings per quarter for servants. . . . No patient can be admitted until Mr. Ricketts had visited them, that it may be ascertained if it is proper to receive them, for which visit a reasonable fee is expected.[2]

Give Operators a Status within the System

An important lesson can also be learned from the history of the state hospitals. It is widely believed that the professionalization of the ward nursing staff over the years was most beneficial. "Ward attendants" became "psychiatric technicians," and over the years more attention was given to training and to the use of probationary employment periods. In the mid-1960s, before L-P-S, there was a definite move to expand the career opportunities, or elongate the potential career ladder, of these employees. In general, it can be said that there was a slow but steady movement toward giving the ward nursing staff a *status* in the system of care delivery that was more commensurate with their real operational significance in the system, which one could realistically say was larger than that of any other providers of care. There is every reason to try to repeat this with the board-and-care operators, who are now the functional equivalent of the hospital-based ward nursing staff. There are all sorts of things one could do for them or with them, ranging from simple training and consultation to granting them degrees of accreditation to contracting with them so that the good ones might receive a small monetary premium or bonus in addition to the revenues from charging for board and care. There is an unreasonable and unrealistic attitude on the part of many mental health reformers that operators are invariably tainted with the desire to make profits. I should hope so. If they were not I should be sorry, because then my proposal to upgrade quality by inducing operators to bid for placements could not work. In addition, if they hadn't the desire to make a little money—at least to cover costs—in return for the extraordinary amount of work many of them do and the financial risks many incur, they would be pathologically abnormal and not fit to care for the mentally ill. How many doctors or social workers or hospital administrators or legislators or professors do you know who are willing to do *their* good works for a pittance?

More Sophisticated Reimbursement Methods

As my last suggestion, let me propose that a more sophisticated way be found of reimbursing operators for unusual expenses incurred in the course of caring for their residents—a principle that again I think is acknowledged in AB 2262. At present, the reimbursement scheme is an extreme version of a prepaid care plan. Physical health services are moving toward prepaid care and away from fee-for-service, and this direction is regarded as progressive. In the case of board-and-care facilities, however, it might be desirable to move a little in the opposite direction. Anyone who has to drive a resident two or three times a week to a physical therapy appointment or to a day treatment center should not be expected to pay out of his own pocket for the costs of transportation. It will not be simple to accomplish these reimbursement schemes administratively. There is bound to be some mismanagement and some deliberate fraud. But I think ways can be found if the will is there. At any rate, the development of more sophisticated reimbursement schemes can also proceed by way of social experimentation on a limited scale. There is no need to rush into anything statewide before pretesting it in one or two counties.

Conclusion

In conclusion, let me harken back to the point I tried to make at the outset. Is L-P-S good? Is it working? The answer depends on your frame of reference. There are still faults, especially in the residential-care system in the community, but the overall situation of the chronic mentally ill is probably *considerably* better than it was when they were shut up in state mental hospitals. For all its faults, I find it difficult to conclude that the emerging system of private residential facilities is worse than the older system of public institutions. In replying to charges that private asylum operators were mercilessly exploiting their patients and their families for the sake of what was called "the prospect of certain profit" and an excessive desire of "gain," the editor of the English *Journal of Psychological Medicine* wrote in 1852:

The self-same charge, may . . . be brought against the managers of public asylums [i.e. county asylums]; they have an exchequer to maintain; they have an interest in keeping up the full complement of patients in the house; they must keep their revenue up at par; and to satisfy the grumbling rate-payers, they must have their contracts cut down to the most transparent shaving; they also must exhibit a satisfactory amount of receipts upon their balance-sheet. They, therefore, have a "personal interests," as the learned baron calls it, in taking charge and keeping pauper lunatics, quite as strong as might be supposed to actuate any unworthy proprietor of a private lunatic asylum.[3]

History does seem to be repeating itself, at least in rhetoric. But let us seize our present opportunities to make future historians acknowledge that we have been able to learn from history rather than unwillingly continuing to mutter its stale rhetoric and stumbling into its well-marked pitfalls.

Notes

.

1
Address delivered at the January 1974 King's View Foundation Symposium on Community Mental Health and Developmental Disabilities, Fresno, California.

2
L. Parry-Jones, *The Trade in Lunacy* (London: Routledge & Kegan Paul, 1972), p. 123.

3
Parry-Jones, *Trade*, p. 85.

Appendix C Methods in Studying the Implementation of L-P-S

In an appendix to *Implementation*, Pressman and Wildavsky assure their readers that there is scarcely any "significant analytical work dealing with implementation."[1] My own search has turned up relatively little that they did not already find. Nor have I found much in the way of simple empirical materials—"case studies" if you will—that could be used to illustrate the hypotheses advanced in the preceding eleven chapters. Notice, I say "illustrate," not "test" or "prove." The systematic study of implementation processes, problems, and remedies, is in its infancy. My objective in this book has been to suggest, describe, and illuminate certain problematic tendencies of the implementation process and to offer a preliminary assessment of strategies that might offset them. I hope other researchers will find the suggestions sufficiently interesting to examine them more systematically.

I have not restricted myself to a secondary analysis of existing studies, however. I undertook to gather material of my own with regard to the implementation of the Lanterman-Petris-Short (L-P-S) mental health reform law enacted by California in 1967. Since I had studied the politics surrounding the passage of the legislation in 1966-1967, I knew much of the background and many of the relevant actors in the implementation process. From 1967 to 1970, I resided outside of California, but after my return in 1970 I maintained and extended contacts with individuals and groups concerned with the implementation of L-P-S. From the fall of 1971, when I decided to undertake a study of policy implementation and to use L-P-S as primary case material, I intensified my efforts to keep abreast of developments.

During the course of my research, I gradually discovered that the single biggest problem in gathering data on the "implementation process," no matter how the process is conceived, is that there is too much. When one sets out to study the policy-adoption process, one has at least a starting point: the authoritative body, like a legislature, that has made (or will make) the ultimate decision on the issue. From there one can trace the various influences that led up to the decision. The nature of the phenomenon thus restricts the scope of the relevant data (provided, of course, that one is not so foolish as to become mired in the infinite regress of cause-and-effect relations). The nature of the implementation process is exactly the opposite: instead of becoming concentrated in one place, it gets dispersed to every place. In the case of L-P-S, for example, a bit of the implementation process is going on in every clinic where a psychiatrist sees a patient; in every county board of supervisors meeting where the mental health budget is discussed; in every agency office where a social worker picks up the telephone to attempt a client referral.

How is the researcher to cope with all this? First, he must define his objectives. If he wants to study certain narrow aspects of the implementation process and if he has certain relatively well-formed ideas about what he must look for, it is possible to collect data systematically. If, on the other hand, the objective is to gain an overview of the whole process, then rigorous and systematic methods are simply not feasible. A respectable sort of impressionism is all that can be achieved. Even if one were to employ the most sophisticated sampling procedures to select one hundred informants across the state, and even if one were to conduct lengthy and maximally productive interviews with each of the hundred about their views of the implementation process, one would still end up with merely a collage of impressions. My own collage of impressions about L-P-S seems to me sufficient to warrant drawing on them to illustrate hypotheses about the implementation process. It is usually not sufficient to warrant assignments of praise or blame to the many individuals who have actually been engaged in the implementation of L-P-S; and I hope no unjust inferences of this sort will be either drawn or suspected.

My research assistants and I attended numerous conferences of mental health administrators, treatment professionals, and lay activists like the California Association for Mental Health. We conducted many interviews and executed a number of small-scale exploratory studies. Our research was aided during this period by the appearance of studies by other researchers attempting an overview of the L-P-S system. In February 1972, the ENKI Research Institute published *A Study of California's New Mental Health Law (1969-1971),* the product of a large-scale research effort funded by the National Institute of Mental Health. In March 1972, the California State Department of Mental Hygiene (DMH) published *California Mental Health: A Study of Successful Treatment,* which contained much useful statistical material. In December 1972, the California State Department of Finance released a two-volume, two-hundred-page "management audit" of the L-P-S system. In late 1973, two very useful analyses by graduate students were made available to me. One was the draft of a doctoral dissertation by Ron Luke that was to be submitted to the Harvard public policy school. It covered mental health efforts in four states, of which California was one. The other work was by Barbara Barkovich, a student in the public policy program at the State University of New York, Stony Brook. It was prepared for the New York State Department of Mental Hygiene, which was planning to revise its mental health system along lines similar to those of California. Some studies of specialized topics in the implementation of L-P-S also appeared.[2]

The "Point of View" Problem

As we said in the introductory chapter, the "implementation problem" is a control problem. It must now be said, however, that one person's problem asserting control may be another person's problem escaping it. All parties in the implementation process are involved, in some degree, both in trying to control others and in trying to avoid being controlled by them. That is to say, all parties in the implementation process have implementation problems, and what some of them perceive as "solutions" others will see merely as aggravations, or worse.

As analysts, we would like to be not only objective but neutral as well. Unfortunately, it is not possible to be strictly neutral. We must decide, for analytical if not necessarily political reasons, just whose implementation problem we would like to solve. In the case of L-P-S, I side with the originators of the legislation, the initial policy mandate. Indeed, throughout this book I tend to adopt the point of view of the sponsors of the mandate. One reason is political: ordinarily, a mandate means change, change ordinarily means "reform" and "progress," and ordinarily—though with many exceptions, and often reluctantly—I sympathize with progressives and reformers. A second, and equally important, reason for adopting the perspective of the mandate sponsors is intellectual: it is easy to think of ways to subvert implementation, but it is quite challenging to reckon means of making the implementation process succeed.

To say that we will take the view of the mandate sponsors, however, does not solve all our methodological problems. The sponsors of any policy mandate are typically a coalition of persons and groups with somewhat diverse and possibly even incongruent goals. Which sponsors —and which goals—ought we to have in mind?

For convenience we may divide the sponsoring coalition into two subgroups, a group that is program-oriented or "idealistic," and a group that is interested in "selfish," nonprogrammatic benefits like bureaucratic expansion or the opportunities to secure governmental contracts or other forms of subsidies. The coalition behind ESEA Title I, for instance, included both antipoverty reformers and teacher groups interested in the prospect of raising teacher salaries. The food stamp program was sponsored by a coalition of liberals concerned with feeding the hungry and conservative agricultural interests more attuned to what they (mistakenly, it seems) believed were the prospects of expanding the market for agricultural products.[3] When we speak of sponsor goals we have in mind the goals of the more "idealistic" members of the sponsoring coalition. It is readily conceded that the distinctions be-

tween idealism and self-interest are not always clear. Idealism is sometimes a mask for self-interest. Sometimes the two are not only
compatible but mutually reinforcing. However, the alternative to defining standards of success by what at least some of the sponsors meant by
it is simply to substitute our own standards. In the case of L-P-S, at
least, it was quite clear that Assemblyman Frank Lanterman, the leading member of the sponsoring coalition, was in the more "idealistic"
subgroup.

Another methodological problem that deserves passing mention is in
knowing what the sponsors' idealistic goals actually are. Typically, one
expects that the goals as stated during the policy-adoption phase, that
is, during the struggle over the mandate, are excessively ambitious,
perhaps even utopian. One expects that the implementation phase will
induce realistic revisions in the level of aspiration and in the means
prescribed to attain it. Of all these successive revisions, which can we
say represent acceptable refinements in the basic programmatic goals
and strategies and which unacceptable perversions of the program or
policy?

There is perhaps only one sure way to know whether successive modifications are acceptable to the original (idealistic) sponsors: the sponsors must be participants in the process of program or policy modification, and the scholarly observer must be able to note their actions and
reactions. It is likely that this first condition is not often met, particularly in the case of legislative sponsors. There are, to my knowledge, no
published studies in the literature of public administration or political
science that describe the follow-up, or oversight, activities of those
legislators who initially sponsored a major piece of reform legislation.
Almost certainly this lacuna is more an indication that such follow-up
rarely takes place than that scholars have chosen to ignore the phenomenon. Most sponsors are content to receive credit for getting a measure
enacted and to leave the dirty work of following up the implementation
to others. A small literature does exist on the subject of congressional

oversight of administration, but it is devoted to the very general theme of executive-branch accountability to the legislature.[4] There is also some attention paid to this subject in certain works on the budgetary process, since the appropriations committees and subcommittees of each house, and especially those of the lower house, scrutinize agency practices in the course of the annual budget cycle.[5] Oversight activities by individual legislators have simply not been documented. Fortunately for my researches, Assemblyman Lanterman and his staff were indefatigable interveners in the implementation processes flowing from the L-P-S Act; and they kindly made their written records and their memories available to me.

Notes

1
Jeffrey L. Pressman and Aaron Wildavsky, *Implementation* (Berkeley: University of California Press, 1973), p. 166.

2
Uri Aviram, "Mental Health Reform and the After Care State Service Agency: A Study of the Process of Change in the Mental Health Field," Ph.D. dissertation (School of Social Welfare, University of California, Berkeley, 1972); Uri Aviram and Steven P. Segal, "Exclusion of the Mentally Ill: Reflection on an Old Problem in a New Context," *Archives of General Psychiatry* 29 (1973): 126-131; H. R. Lamb and V. Goertzel, "Discharged Mental Patients: Are They Really in the Community?" *Archives of General Psychiatry* 24 (1971): 29-34; Julian Wolpert and Eileen R. Wolpert, "The Relocation of Released Mental Hospital Patients into Residential Communities," draft manuscript (April 1974); Wendy Pfeffer, "The Use of Operator Training Programs to Improve the Quality of Care in the Mental Health Residential Aftercare Sector," Master's thesis (Graduate School of Public Policy, University of California, Berkeley 1974); Larry Sosowsky, "Putting State Mental Hospitals Out of Business—The Community Approach to Treating Mental Illness in San Mateo County," Master's thesis (Graduate School of Public Policy, University of California, Berkeley, 1974).

3
Gilbert Y. Steiner, *The State of Welfare* (Washington, D.C.: The Brookings Institution, 1971), pp. 191-236.

4
Arthur McMahon's classic essay, "Congressional Oversight of Administration," *Political Science Quarterly* 58 (June-September, 1943): 161-190, 380-414, deserves special mention. See also Morris S. Ogul, "Legislative Oversight of Bureaucracy: Explanation, Incentives, Structure," paper delivered at the 1975 meeting of the American Political Science Association.

5
See Aaron Wildavsky, *The Politics of the Budgetary Process* (Boston: Little, Brown, 1964); and Richard F. Fenno, Jr., *The Power of the Purse: Appropriations Politics in Congress* (Boston: Little, Brown, 1966).

Index

Abel, Elie, 127

Adams, Freeman, 203, 208-210, 227, 232, 235-236

Agnews State Hospital, 296

Aid to Families with Dependent Children, 44, 256

Allison, Graham T., 43

Allott, Gordon, 87

Alquist, Alfred, 28

American Association for the Advancement of Science, 40

American Farm Bureau Federation (AFBF), 99-100

American Medical Association, 88-89

AMSOC (American Miscellaneous Society), 86, 87

Appleman, Jack M. 257, 261

Area Redevelopment Administration (ARA), 72, 77-79, 187, 194-195, 272

Bakal, Yitzhak, 103

Banfield, Edward, 75

Barkovich, Barbara, 312

BART. *See* San Francisco Bay Area Rapid Transit District

Barber, Louis, 203, 205-208, 210, 217, 232, 235-236

Barnard, Chester, 110-111

Bascom, Willard, 86, 88, 89

Beach, William, 161

Beaghler, Dr., 232, 236, 239

Berkeley (California) Police Department, 98

Bernstein, Marilyn, 171-172

Board and care homes, 12-13, 25-26, 28-29, 123-127, 161, 291-293, 297-308

Bolton, Arthur, 14, 16

Bradford, Amory, 170, 194, 215

Bradley, Valerie, 14, 16

Brewster, Henry, 200, 202-203, 233

Brickman, 23-25, 274

Brissenden, Robert, 210

Brown and Root, 86-88

"Budget," 70-76, 77, 169, 193, 265, 268

Bunker, Douglas R., 40-42

Bureau of Social Work. *See* Community Services Division

Burton, John, 28

California Assembly Office of Research, 14

California Assembly Ways and Means Committee, 13, 14, 16, 24, 31

California Association for Mental Health (CAMH), 14, 108, 278, 282, 311

California Citizens Advisory Council for Mental Health (CAC) 14, 107, 276, 278, 289, 296

California legislature, 9-13, 223; 13, 28

California Medical Association, 100

California State Department of Finance, 14, 223, 312

California State Department of Health (formerly Public Health), 13, 19, 161, 276, 297, 301

California State Department of Mental Hygiene (DMH), 11-30 passim, 74, 107, 109, 121, 123, 132, 152, 160-162, 167, 199-240 passim, 274-276, 287, 289-290, 298, 302, 312

California State Department of Social Welfare (SDSW), 17, 19, 20, 21, 152, 161, 225, 276, 292, 301

California State Employees Association (CSEA), 27, 28, 296

California State Human Relations Agency, 17, 19, 225, 276

318
Index